CONTINENTAL COMPLEXITIES

A MULTIDISCIPLINARY INTRODUCTION TO AFRICA

Revised Edition

Edited by Ibigbolade Aderibigbe and Akinloye Ojo

University of Georgia

cognella™
San Diego, CA

Bassim Hamadeh, CEO and Publisher
Christopher Foster, General Vice President
Michael Simpson, Vice President of Acquisitions
Jessica Knott, Managing Editor
Kevin Fahey, Cognella Marketing Manager
Jess Busch, Senior Graphic Designer
Zina Craft, Acquisitions Editor
Jamie Giganti, Project Editor
Brian Fahey, Licensing Associate

First published in the United States of America in 2013 by Cognella, Inc.

Printed in the United States of America

ISBN: 978-1-62131-133-1 (pbk)

www.cognella.com 800.200.3908

Contents

Chapter One

The Study of Africa: An Introduction

Ibigbolade S. Aderibigbe and Akinloye Ojo

The expansiveness and diversity of the African continent are vividly captured by the maxim, "Almost everything said about Africa is true and almost everything said about Africa is false." In tandem with this paradox, Africa has always been a fascinating "dilemma" for the rest of the world. Its progressive and compelling history of a "journey" through facets of ancient kingdoms and civilizations, trans-Saharan trade, transpacific trade, transatlantic trade, colonialism, independent states, and neocolonialism, has made the African continent constantly a "fertile land" for exploration in all areas of natural and human concerns. Unfortunately, in spite of the prominence guaranteed by these landmark experiences, the misconceptions about Africa and Africans are most stunning. Gordon and Gordon (2007) express this so well in the following observation concerning some Americans' perspectives of Africa and its peoples:

> It is not uncommon to hear a college student refer to "country of Africa" or for people to think about Africa as inhabited only by "tribes" of "savage" people living in "jungles." (p. 1)

While it cannot be denied that Africa has had its shares of civil wars, famine and drought, economic and political challenges, it is most uncharitable to construct the African story solely on these negative conceptualities. Consequently, the interest of the West, particularly the American population, in the various sociopolitical and economic issues unfolding in Africa, should avail itself of the accurate and authentic situations and happenings on the continent. In providing meaningful and objective "resources" to achieve this goal, it becomes imperative that engaging in the study of Africa must involve dynamics of telling the African story credibly and authentically. These dynamics are invariably set firmly in place from the outset, providing credible information pertaining to the African story. Such information should entail intelligible generalizations capturing the diversity of the continent and its peoples, especially in areas of cultures, languages, histories, societies, religions, and politics.

Second, the story should be contextualized. This primarily entails finding appropriate descriptions of the African condition. With such a disposition, the balancing of extreme negative and positive positions on the African story, for example, celebration versus prejudice, romanticism versus narrow-mindedness and good-news Africa versus bad-news Africa, can be achieved. Third, there should be the "right" education about the African story. Such an engagement would definitely provide the opportunity to examine in detail issues associated with Africa and compare them to those in other parts of the world. Potential issues of interest necessarily include social, political, educational, economic, religious, and cultural sensibilities. Fourth, a combination of the three dynamics above would certainly enhance vivid and effective clarification and illustration of the African story. Through clarification, a deeper understanding of the African past, as well as the implication of this understanding for the present and the future, is secured. The "worlds" of traditional and contemporary Africa are sustainably linked. Illustratively, the accurate African story is objectively narrated, and the common and convenient misconceptions, misinformation, and half-truths about Africa are significantly eliminated. Such misconceptions include, but are not limited to assertions such as Africa is mostly jungle with wild animals; Africa is nothing but poor rural dwellings; life is perpetually dangerous in Africa; cannibalism is practiced in parts of the continent; Africa is a country; Africans are tribalistic and primitive; Africans are not capable of religion; Africans eat strange things, such as bugs and pets; Africans are under the control of witch doctors and sorcerers.

When the "clouds" of misconceptions, misinformation, and half-truths about Africa are cleared, there are some notable facts and figures that are instructive of the physical and human prominence and influence of the continent in world history. For example, Africa is generally designated as the "mother" continent. Many scholars have noted that Africa was the central part of a single continent, until about 100 million years ago, when there occurred the drifting away of other continents, through continental drifts or plate tectonics. The theory of Africa as the "cradle of humanity" has also been evidenced by different human fields of study such as anthropology, geology, archaeology, history, and linguistics. Indeed, it has been argued that the geographical shape of Africa attests to this claim. This is demonstrated when the following three features are considered:

(1) the Great Escarpments (steep edges) in the eastern part of the continent
(2) deep rift valleys in East Africa, which are proof of continuous drifting
(3) remapping of all plates by geologists showing the seven major plates merging well.

The African continent is very sizable. Indeed, it is the second largest of Earth's seven continents, Asia being the largest. Africa covers about 23 percent of the world's total land area, which translates to nearly 11.7 million square miles. The distance from north to south (Cairo to Cape Town) is 4,500 miles; from east to west (Dakar to Mogadishu) is 4,400 miles. Often divided in popular discourse into North Africa and sub-Saharan Africa, the continent has fifty-five different countries (with the creation of South Sudan in July 2011) including forty-nine mainland nations and six surrounding island nations. Actually, in terms of landmass, the United States, Argentina, India, Europe, New Zealand, and China all will fit well into the landmass that makes up the African continent.

In addition, Africa has a population of over 900 million. This means that about 13 percent of the world's people reside in Africa. Some scholars predict that, based on the current rate of growth, the population of the African continent might soon hit one billion. The four most populous countries and their estimated populations (in millions) are Nigeria (≥140m), Ethiopia (≥84m), Egypt (≥83m), and the Democratic Republic of the Congo (≥68m). Meanwhile, the four least populated countries and their estimated populations (in thousands) are Equatorial Guinea (≥600K), Sahrawi Arab DR (≥200K), Sao Tome and Principe (≥160K), and Seychelles (≥81K).

Africa is indisputably a wealthy continent. Its wealth lies in its abundance of natural resources. Despite the perception of Africa as being poverty-stricken, the links between global economics and African natural resources are quite interesting, both historically and currently. Historically, the continent's wealth in human and natural resources was the reason for the "immoralities" of the transatlantic slave trade and colonialism. The transatlantic slave trade was part of an international economic system in which Africans were taken as slaves to the Americas for the production of sugar, cotton, and rum. Slaves were transported to Europe and exchanged for manufactured goods and guns that were then transported back to Africa. This vicious circle is what came to be known as the "triangle trade." In the colonial era, too, Africa's natural resources and raw materials (ivory, rubber, gold, cocoa, palm oil, and so on) were used

Table 1: Regions and countries of Africa

Region	No. of Countries	Countries
North Africa	Six	Algeria, Egypt, Libya, Morocco, Tunisia and Western Sahara (SADR).
East Africa	Fifteen	Kenya, Tanzania, Somalia, Djibouti, Eritrea, Ethiopia, Uganda, Rwanda, Burundi, Sudan, South Sudan, Madagascar (island nation), Comoros (island nation), Mauritius (island nation), Seychelles (island nation).
Southern Africa	Ten	Angola, Zambia, Namibia, Botswana, Zimbabwe, Malawi, Mozambique, South Africa, Lesotho, Swaziland.
Central Africa	Eight	Cameroon, Central African Republic, Chad, Congo, Democratic Republic of Congo (formerly Zaire), Equatorial Guinea, Gabon, São Tomé and Príncipe (island nation).
West Africa	Sixteen	Senegal, the Gambia, Guinea-Bissau, Mauritania, Mali, Niger, Burkina Faso, Guinea, Sierra Leone, Liberia, Ivory Coast, Ghana, Togo, Benin, Nigeria, Cape Verde (island nation).

Table 2: Regions and sampling of peoples

Region	Examples of peoples in the region
North Africa	Egyptian Copts, Arabs, Berbers or Amazigh, and Nubians
East Africa	Amhara, Swahili, Hutu, Kikuyu, and Somali
Southern Africa	Shona, Ndebele, Zulu, Chewa, and Xhosa
Central Africa	Bakongo, Lunda, Bamileke, Fang, and Gbaya
West Africa	Akan, Wolof, Fulani, Yoruba, and Mende

to fuel the Industrial Revolution in Europe and build several Western economies. Currently, Africa continues to produce and export crude oil (major exporters: Angola, Libya, Nigeria), precious gems and metals (diamonds, gold, copper, and coltan from such countries as South Africa, Sierra Leone, Congo, and Angola), and labor to all parts of the world.

Africa is a continent with variations of vegetation and landforms found in different areas. North Africa is dominated by the Sahara Desert, the world's largest desert. The Sahel (a mixture of semiarid grasslands to thorny Savannah) cuts across the continent right below the Sahara from west to east, through the countries of Senegal, Mauritania, Mali, Burkina Faso, Niger, Nigeria, Chad, Sudan, and Eritrea. Below this are the savanna and the savanna woodland, spreading across West Africa and inland into southern Africa as well as across the water to Madagascar. Interestingly, the rainforest for which Africa is renowned is mostly limited to parts of West and Central Africa (in countries such as Nigeria, Cameroon, and the two Congo Republics) and some of the African islands. The geographic landmass that is Africa with its fifty-five countries can be divided into five regions as shown in Table 1.

Apart from its diversity in variations of vegetation and landforms, Africa is also clearly diverse in languages and peoples. More than two thousand languages are spoken on the continent, some with multiple distinct dialects. In addition, many non-native languages, such as English, Arabic, French, Portuguese, German, Italian, Dutch, and Spanish, are commonly spoken. This variation has led to the evolution of many pidgins and creoles. In terms of ethnicity, Africa's many different peoples can be found all over the five regions of the continent. A representation of some of the different peoples in the different regions is presented in Table 2.

About two-thirds or 63 percent of Africa's population reside in rural areas. Thus, Africa is the least urbanized continent. However, it must be noted that though an estimated 37 percent of the population is currently in urban areas, Africa is rapidly becoming an urbanized continent. This is because urban growth is resulting from rapid movement into cities and abandonment of agriculture. For instance, the Cairo metropolitan area has about 12 million inhabitants, and Lagos and its surrounding suburbs are home to close to 17 million people. By 2015, the population of the Lagos metropolitan area is expected to be more than 23 million, and it probably will be one of the most populated metro areas in the world.

In recognition and response to issues highlighted and discussed above, this volume, *Continental Complexities: A Multidisciplinary Introduction to Africa*, is written with the intention of providing deep insight and understanding of the selected topics on Africa and its people as well as complementing existing literature in the field of African studies. The book is unique because all the contributors are either professors who have years of personal, physical contact with Africa and have actually taught these topics in the Introduction to Africa classes at the University of Georgia or scholars currently teaching their respective topics in universities in Africa. The topics examined in the book are deliberately selected with the intention of giving priority to issues currently relevant to the African discourse and which should constitute popular items of presentations in Introduction to Africa classes.

In realization of this objective and focus, this chapter is essentially introductory, providing the basic background of the required dynamics essential for studying the "African story" free of the usual and rampant misconceptions, misinformation, and half-truths. We also briefly highlight and discuss the physical and human factors about Africa, which project the authentic and current status of the African continent. In the rest of the chapter, we present summaries of the contents of the other chapters in the book. In chapter 2, Sandra Whitney examines the importance of geology and geomorphology in the study of the African continent. She premises this submission on the argument that both geology and geomorphology of an area have fundamental significance and influence on its physical, economic, and human sectors. In the specific case of Africa, she identifies and discusses some of these as the influences on travel and habitation and colonization zones; the influences on the development and composition of soils, which are critical determinants of soil fertility; potentiality of warning people about possible risks of flooding and earthquakes and volcanic hazards; the location and accessibility of minerals, petroleum, and water resources; and the economic benefits of identifying and providing potential sources of income both for local populations that supply food, lodging, and guides as well as for governments through fees paid by tourists.

Akin Alao and Benjamin Akobi in chapter 3 provide a historical survey of the significant developments on the African continent from the earliest times to the present century. In their survey, they focus on the several historical changes that have altered the fortunes of Africa and have added to the complexities of the multiethnic and multicultural continent. Some of their focused changes include the incursion of aliens such as Arabs and Europeans as well as the colonization and decolonization of Africa. Following up on the historical contextualization done in chapter 3, Akinloye Ojo and Willie Udo Willie present some important insights into language and language-related issues on the African continent in chapter 4. Their generalized introduction to language in Africa includes the impact and classification of the multitude of languages and their variants existing on the continent. They also examine the roles of language and the influence of the continent's linguistic diversity in the cultural, social, and ethnic identities of the many people on the continent. Finally, with special focus on the work of African linguist Ayo Bamgbose, they consider the critical sociolinguistic and politically significant issue of language planning in the multilingual African environment, with emphasis on the two elements of status planning and corpus planning.

Religion has always been a dominant part of the African continent, beginning from its traditional settings. Today, in spite of diverse influences and outside contact, Africa and its peoples remain still largely religious. However, religious affiliations and practices have assumed dramatic changes and influences over the decades. Ibigbolade Aderibigbe, in chapter 5, examines the African religious space, focusing on three major religions—African Traditional Religion, Christianity, and Islam—being practiced on the continent today. African Traditional Religion, which was the only and dominant religion of Africa in the past, has suffered significant setbacks from the onslaught of converting strategies of Christianity and Islam. On the other hand, both Christianity and Islam, once considered "foreign" religions in Africa, are today the two main religions, nearly splitting the continent into two equal halves in membership. Both religions now exert significant social, economic, and political influences in Africa.

In chapter 6, Akinloye Ojo focuses on some of the social institutions found across the continent. Based on most African societies being oral or oral dominated, the chapter first provides a discussion of six of the many practical sources of information needed to comprehend African oral societies and then a succinct reflection on the indigenous systems of instruction. The chapter also provides a detailed discussion of the rites of passage across Africa with illustrations from across the continent. Finally, Ojo endeavors to outline some of the possible generalities about kinship systems and marriage across the continent.

Gender issues, particularly the status of women in Africa, have always been interesting and controversial. Felisters Kripono and Janet Musimbi M'mbaha join the debate in chapter 7. They examine the social, economic, and political implications associated with the issues, in precolonial, colonial, and postcolonial Africa. While identifying colonialism and capitalism as the "game changers" in introducing inequality and subjugation of African women, they recognize the potential power and the importance of the African women through change and development. This status, they claim, can be attained if the society changes its attitude toward women and views them as partners in development rather than as competitors in the society.

In chapter 8, Maria Navarro examines the implications of Millennium Development Goals on agriculture in rural Africa. She highlights the multidimensional and global commitments located in the development goals in the endeavor to eradicate poverty and hunger; achieve universal primary education; promote gender equality and empower women; reduce child mortality; improve maternal health; combat HIV/AIDS, malaria, and other diseases; and develop a global partnership for development, among others. She argues that a path to achieving these goals is being created through focus on improving agriculture as a means to better the lives of the small and poor farmers of Africa, particularly in sub-Saharan Africa. She concludes that the success of the programs depends largely on program personnel's constant engagement in comprehensive needs assessment and strategic planning together with the stakeholders and intended beneficiaries of the program, the farmers themselves. This, she believes, can be achieved by engaging in in-depth analysis of three very important components of the needs assessments:

the characteristics of small-scale agriculture in the target area; the factors that affect the lives of project stakeholders; and the role of agricultural development in achieving the Millennium Development Goals.

Mwita Chacha focuses on the quest for development in relation to integration in Africa in chapter 9. He examines Africa's attempts at promoting economic development through the use of regional integration arrangements. He begins by noting the puzzle that although many African states had similar economic development profiles with Asian states such as South Korea in the 1960s, they have not yet attained growth levels comparable to the Asian tigers fifty years later. To address this puzzle, the chapter explains that the mismanagement of regional integration has contributed to Africa's underdevelopment. Specifically, overlapping memberships, institutional weaknesses, and lack of regional leadership have adversely affected the management and performance of regional integration arrangements as conduits toward sustainable economic development.

Perhaps the greatest challenge to the African continent today, particularly its health sector, is the dreadful disease HIV/AIDS. Its pandemic nature has practically defied all efforts thrown at it by governments of various African countries, their agents, nongovernmental agencies, and many international organizations. In examining the unfolding ravaging impact of HIV/ADS on Africa, Ibigbolade Aderibigbe and Simon Mutembo, in chapter 10, revisit the status of the health care system in Africa. They explore the characteristics of the African traditional health care system and its holistic physiological-cum-spiritual nature. Also, the history of transition to the Western health system with its attendant challenges is discussed. The chapter then discusses the prevalence and the socioeconomic impact of HIV/AIDS on Africa and its population, arguing for complementary efforts of both the traditional and Western health care system as the panacea in combating the disease in Africa.

In chapter 11, Tayo Ogunlewe provides an introduction to African literature. He focuses on what African literature is. He submits that it cannot be explained in a monolithic term. Rather, it should be seen as referring to works of imaginative literature written by Africans, depicting an African worldview. He further argues that no serious introduction to African literature can afford to ignore Africa's oral literary traditions because, as a "body," it constitutes one of the forces that influenced the growth and development of modern African literature. To him, the ignoring of this fundamental and important part of African literature is the direct consequence of the damage done to the African psyche by the influence of colonization and Western hegemony. Ogunlewe thereafter explores modern-day African literature of both the Anglophone and Francophone schools with citations of prominent Africans in the field of African literature from both schools. The totality of their works, in his opinion, succinctly captures African literature's unique "unity in diversity."

In chapter 12, Freda Scott-Giles presents some useful notes on African drama and theatre. As she notes, the culture of community is the basis for most, if not all, African performing traditions. This means that the expectation in any African performance is that everyone, including the audience, will be part of the performance. And, in her consideration of the African performing traditions, she discusses the disparate notions of mimesis and methexis. The discussion allows her to define some of the technical notions in African performance traditions. Finally, in response to the understandable limitation of any effort to provide, in one chapter, an in-depth discussion of drama and theatre in the expansive and diverse African continent, the chapter focuses primarily on sub-Saharan Africa and representative African writers from Anglophone countries. And, as Scott-Giles noted, these focused writers have their plays more readily available in texts in the United States.

Adeluwa Okunade's chapter 13 introduces readers to the basics of African music from its concept, through characteristics, foreign legacies, instruments, recruitment and training in its holistic feature. He argues that in traditional African society, the performance arts discipline of music is a combination of other arts that culminate in creative thinking and performance practice that exhibit the societal ethos, values, and norms. Even today, with his highlighting and discussion of various types of music and musical instruments with complementary influence from outside cultures, Okunade submits that music in Africa is a community art, and not a "separatist" style of stage presentation.

In the final chapter of the book, Jepkorir Rose Chepyator-Thomson and Kipchumba Chelimo Byron discuss sport in the context of indigenous, colonial, and postindependent Africa. They argue that prior to the arrival of the Europeans in Africa, indigenous Africa was rich in sporting culture. The culture of sports was interwoven into the fabric of life and was complexly influenced by geography, history, religion and economics, as well as by social-class dynamics and variations in ethnicity. Sports inculcated cultural and social skills that allowed children and youth to adequately prepare for adulthood. The colonial period promoted de-indigenization of African sports and games, revealed a marriage between indigenous and European sports and games, and eradication or devaluation of physical activities that were wholly African. The postcolonial period has seen sports players and sports themselves attain a new identity, including political as well as social identity spanning local, national, and international levels. The period saw sport serving as a vehicle for social change at many levels: individual, social, and political. African people have tried to revive indigenous sports and games, a trend under way at present in some countries.

Review Questions

1. Identify two of the various African peoples found in each of the five regions of Africa.

2. Despite the various challenges facing the African continent, the chapter warns against constructing the African story solely on these negatives. What are the ways outlined in the chapter that are best to tell the African story?

3. What are some of the most common erroneous opinions or stereotypes about Africa and Africans? What do you think are some of the reasons for these common misconceptions?

4. What are some of the reasons why it is important to study Africa?

5. What is the estimated population of Africa? How soon is this population expected to reach about one billion?

Bibliography

Davidson, Basil. 1994. *Modern Africa: A Social and Political History*. New York: Longman.

Gordon, A. April, and L. Donald Gordon, eds. 2007. *Understanding Contemporary Afric*a. Boulder, CO: Lynne Riernner Publishers.

Harris, E. Joseph. 1987. *Africans and Their History*. New York: Penguin Books.

Khapoya, B. Vincent. 2010. *The African Experience: An Introduction*. New York: Longman.

Ojo, Akinloye, and Robert Shanefelt, 2007. *Introduction to African* Online course. Athens, Georgia: Georgia University System African Studies Certificate (CIASP) project.

Wiley, D., and M. Crofts. 1984. *The Third World: Africa*. Guilford, CT: Dushkin Publishing Groups.

Chapter Two

Geology and Geomorphology of Africa

By Sandra Whitney

Introduction: Why Study the Geology and Geomorphology of Africa?

Why are the geology and geomorphology of Africa important? The geology of an area influences travel, habitation, and colonization zones through its influence on the geomorphology and topography of an area. The geology and geologic history of an area influence the development and composition of soils, which are critical determinants of soil fertility. Geological awareness can provide necessary information to those knowledgeable of its significance to recognize potential risks of flooding and earthquakes and volcanic hazards. Warnings of dangers can then be issued and preparedness measures taken. The study of geology explains the location and accessibility of minerals, petroleum, and water resources. Geologic prospecting can find mineral and fossil fuel resources to provide employment and to fund governments and development. Geotourism is a potential source of income both for local populations that supply food, lodging, and guides as well as for governments through fees paid by tourists (e.g., Mt. Kilimanjaro, Lake Victoria).

Africa makes up approximately 20 percent of the land surface of the earth. Containing some of the oldest rocks in the world, it formed the core of several "super continents" during the first four billion years of Earth's history. It also contains some of the youngest rocks on Earth at volcanoes such as Ol Doinyo Lengai in Tanzania and Nyiragongo in the Democratic Republic of the Congo, which have been active in the twenty-first century. Africa contains several major mountain ranges, from the Atlas Mountains (with peaks over 13,000 feet high) in the northwest to the Drakensberg Range (rising to over 11,000 feet) in the south. The Ethiopian Highlands (over 15,000 feet high in some areas) and the snow-capped Ruwenzori Mountains (more than 16,000 feet high) between Uganda and the Democratic Republic of the Congo are the result of the uplift of old Precambrian (>550 million years) basement rocks by the mantle forces lifting up the East African Rift. These mountains are often capped by volcanic rocks related to the opening of the rift. The Atlas Mountains are the result of folding and faulting caused by the collision of Africa with Europe and North America 300 million years ago. There are numerous smaller mountain ranges across Africa, which are remnants of ancient uplifts of the granites and gneisses that formed the ancient core of the continent. Some of the tallest mountains in Africa are volcanoes related to the East African Rift.

Background: Plate Tectonics and the Development of the Foundation of the Continent

Plate tectonics is the geological theory that explains the physical development of the continent through time. It explains the type of rocks and mineral resources and their locations across the continent. This scientific theory can predict both the location of valuable resources and potential natural hazards. The continent of Africa has some of the oldest rocks on Earth in three areas known as "cratons." These areas are made up mostly of granites and metamorphic rocks (such as gneiss and greenstones, which were originally older sedimentary and volcanic rocks). These three cratons—the West African, the Congo, and the Kalahari/Kaapvaal—crashed together to form "Africa" over a billion years ago. The major features of the African continent have been in place since that time. However, eons of erosion and geologically recent tectonic uplift have shaped the landscape that we see today.

Some of the oldest evidence of life on Earth, bacterial mats preserved in fine-grained chert that dates to 3.6 billion years ago, is found in the rocks of the Kaapvaal craton. Approximately 2 billion years ago photosynthesizing organisms began to produce free oxygen molecules, changing the earth's atmosphere drastically. In Africa there are extensive deposits of iron oxide that resulted when the iron in solution in the oceans was oxidized and settled to the bottom of the ocean in what is known as the "Banded Iron Formations." These formations are an excellent potential source of iron ore. Around the same time as early plants were filling the air and the ocean with oxygen, a huge volume of lava was intruded into the Kaapvaal craton. This two-billion-year old group of igneous rocks, known as the Bushveld Igneous Complex, is one of the world's major sources of platinum-group ores, gold, chrome, and many other economically significant minerals.

Africa has been the center of the movement of the continents as they have coalesced and split up repeatedly over the eons. Africa formed the core of the great southern continent, Gondwanaland, during the late Precambrian time (over 550 million years ago) when what is now South America crashed into the west side of Africa, what is now Antarctica (together with what is now Australia) attached itself to the southeast, and what is now Madagascar and India were wedged against the east.

As the continental crust drifted across the globe, pushed by convection currents in the underlying mantle, Africa has shifted latitude significantly. The megacontinent of Gondwanaland was located over the southern polar region of the earth during most of the Paleozoic (from 540 to 250 million years ago). Starting approximately 375 million years ago, the northern continental blocks (including parts of what are now North America, Europe, and Asia) collided with Gondwanaland to form the Pangea Supercontinent. This placed Africa in an even more interior location, in which position it remained until about 200 million years ago, when Pangaea began to break apart. This breakup left small parts of the old West African craton attached to what is now the coastal plain of Georgia and Florida, where rocks identical to those in northwestern Africa can be found under more recent coastal plain sediments.

Evidence for the theory of continental drift/plate tectonics also comes from many other observations of the geological and biological history of Africa. Some of the earliest scientific support for this theory came from the correlation of rock units between continents, specifically between rocks in Brazil and Gabon, Brazil and West Africa (Ivory Coast to Nigeria), and Argentina and South Africa. Geophysical research has discovered magnetic signatures in rocks on land and on the seafloor that line up with the locations of the magnetic poles of the earth, shifting as the continent moved through geologic time.

Fossil evidence is found in the rocks of Africa, South America, and Antarctica, suggesting that they were once part of a single landmass. Examples are fossils of the land reptile Lystrosaurus from locations on those same three continents, while fossils of Mesosaurus (a freshwater reptile rather like a small crocodile) are found both in Brazil and South Africa. There are even similarities among unusual living species descended from common Gondwanaland ancestors, including large flightless birds (ratites) such as the African ostrich, the South American rhea, and the Australian emu. During the Late Paleozoic (from approximately 300 to 250 million years ago) Gondwanaland suffered extensive glaciation. The evidence for this glaciation is found in deep grooves (striations) in bedrock and the accumulation of sediments characteristic of glacial deposits from this time period. The Karoo Supergroup of rocks in southern Africa is the most well-known of these deposits. Similar rock units are known from Argentina and parts of Australia and India.

Long after the breakup of the supercontinent of Pangaea, Gondwanaland also began to break apart as India, Antarctica, and Australia started to split off about 180 million years ago. South America was finally separated from Africa about 120 million years ago, as rifting opened up the South Atlantic Ocean like a zipper. Madagascar was separated from Africa about 65 million years ago (which allowed prosimians like lemurs to evolve without the competition of the higher primates). What we now know as the continent of Africa then attained most of its current size and shape.

The most recent evidence of plate tectonic movements affecting the African continent is found in the East African Rift (starting approximately 31 million years ago). There are actually three parts to the rifting currently occurring in Africa. The rifting forms a "triple junction" in the region of the Afar Triangle. Two of the branches of this triple junction form what are now the Red Sea and Gulf of Aden. These rifts are pushing Arabia toward the northeast. The third branch of the rift continues south across Africa, bifurcating around Lake Victoria. The continental crust in this area is stretched and thinned over material rising in the mantle between the earth's crust and its core. Huge blocks of bedrock are thrust up, while other blocks drop down between the uplifted sections forming valleys. These rift valleys are often filled with lakes (e.g., Turkana, Manyara, Albert, Tanganyika, Nyasa). This tectonic activity is often accompanied by volcanism as lava rises along fractures created by the rifting. The African continent and the East African Rift are caught between other major oceanic rifts (in the Atlantic and Indian Oceans) with no subduction zones on the east or west side (subduction is occurring only on the north, where the African plate is being forced under the European plate). This may restrict or prevent spreading, which may result in increased uplift relative to the rate of spreading. Consequently, these rift valleys fill with lakes and continental sediments rather than with ocean and marine sediments. So far, only along the northern and eastern branches of this rift system have the valleys been opened up to the ocean.

Evidence for the active rifting apart of the continent came in dramatic fashion in the Afar region in September 2005 when a 60-kilometer-long crack opened up in just three weeks. Basaltic lava was injected into a crack that was dozens of yards wide in some places. At the same time, satellite and GPS measurements show that the entire African continent is moving about 5 cm/year toward the northwest, toward Europe, closing the Mediterranean. This movement is responsible for many of the earthquakes occurring in southern Europe. Fortunately for Africa, the earthquakes that are generated along rift zones tend to be relatively small (<magnitude 6 on the Richter scale). In contrast, the most destructive quakes occur along subduction zones (e.g., off the coast of Japan) and along major transform faults (e.g., the San Andreas fault in California).

Formation of the Modern Geologic Surface of Africa

The formation of many of the rocks we see on the surface across Africa took place within the last 300 million years. After eons of cratons crashing together and mountain ranges being thrust up, erosion carved down the high mountains and deposited the sediment across the surface of the continent. The old basement rocks have been warped into a wavy surface, with erosion of the higher points and deposition in the low areas. Among the largest group of sediments deposited during this process is the Karoo Supergroup, a sequence of sediments laid down from South Africa and Botswana northeastward to Tanzania between 300 million and 150 million years ago. The first sediments laid down in this group are vast thicknesses of glacial till, the result of that great Ice Age (300–250 million years ago) that covered so much of Gondwanaland. This Ice Age was followed by a warm period of extensive swamps that resulted in the formation of thick layers of coal across most of this area. Today these coal beds are a significant potential source of power for industry and transportation in Africa. Above the coal layers are sediments laid down as deltas in rivers and lakes. Some of these sediments contain alluvial (placer) deposits of economic minerals such as gold or uranium. As the climate changed yet again, windblown sand dunes covered the land. By this time, the megacontinent of Gondwanaland was beginning to break up, and extensive lava flows covered the older sediments.

In northern Africa, the remaining high points in the basement rocks stand out as isolated mountain ranges (e.g., Tibesti and Ahaggar) across the Sahara Desert. Between these ranges, thick sequences of both terrestrial and shallow marine sediments were deposited. Some of the oldest of these sediments (225–135 million years old) have yielded fantastic dinosaur fossils as exploration has been able to penetrate the harsh desert environment. Within the younger sediments (6–7 million years old) hominid fossils have been found. These sediments are also important as aquifers and as oil reservoirs from Morocco and Algeria to Egypt. The freshwater springs that originate in these aquifers have supported human settlements for millennia, and now provide a source of water for irrigation in some areas. The oil reserves are currently providing energy resources for North Africa and Europe.

Over enormous periods of time the erosion of Precambrian basement rocks reduced the old mountain ranges to a rolling peneplain over much of the surface of the African continent. However, remnants of these older rocks can still be seen sticking up above the plains as "inselbergs" or "kopjes." Excellent examples of these remnants can be seen in areas such as the Serengeti, where erosion and later deposition of volcanic ash has created a large, relatively level plain surrounding the old granites and gneisses of the kopjes (e.g., Naabi Gate, the entrance to the Serengeti National Park).

Soils across Africa reflect the underlying geology and influence the agricultural production in each region of the continent. The soils that have developed over millions of years have been leached of many nutrients necessary for plant growth. Tropical soils over these old terrains can only maintain their fertility if the vegetative matter remains intact and nutrients can cycle quickly from the plant to leaf litter and decaying plant material in the shallow soil and back to the roots of the living plants. Clearing land interrupts this cycle and can reduce the fertility and productivity of the soil. The result of overclearing and farming in these areas is often a creeping desertification. On the other hand, younger, usually volcanic, soils still have many of the nutrients needed for agriculture. This is why so many people live and farm in areas of recent volcanism such as the highlands along the East African Rift, and even on the slopes of dangerous volcanoes like Nyiragongo in the Democratic Republic of the Congo. Indirectly, it also explains the fertility of old river valleys such as the Nile, as the annual river flood brought down nutrient-rich sediment from the Ethiopian highlands.

Geomorphology: Landforms and Their Influence on People

Highland areas that have been uplifted (during the last 30 million years) in southern and eastern Africa include the East African Rift valleys with associated faulting followed by volcanism and sedimentation into valleys (e.g., the area now occupied by Oldupai Gorge). The highland areas within the tropical zone were prime locations for European colonization because the elevation moderated the tropical climate. Rainfall was adequate for farming and ranching, and the cooler weather meant fewer malarial mosquito problems. The edges of this highland region often form escarpments, relatively steep slopes down to the coastal plains.

These narrow coastal plains, backed by steep escarpments, result in relatively few rivers that are navigable into the interior of the southern portion of the continent. The limitations on travel due to rapids and waterfalls delayed European exploration and colonization in many parts of southern Africa. Many of the colonies existed primarily along the coast for this reason. In contrast, major river valleys that drain tectonic basins, such as the Congo and the Nile (as well as the Niger, Zambezi, Orange, Senegal, and Limpopo), supported the explorations of early travelers and settlement by Europeans in the late nineteenth century. In this way, the Europeans were just following in the footsteps of earlier African civilizations, taking advantage of the relative ease of water travel.

The "Great Lakes" district of east Africa also supports large populations around Lake Victoria (in a basin between the rift valleys) and along the shores of the Great Rift Valley lakes (Turkana, Albert, Tanganyika, Malawi/Nyasa). Soils in this area are young and fertile, allowing productive agriculture to support significant populations. Although Lake Victoria is in the middle of the East African Rift, it is different than its neighboring lakes. It occupies a basin between two branches of the rift. Whereas the lakes that fill rift valleys are long and narrow and can be very deep (Lake Tanganyika is the second deepest in the world at nearly 5000 feet at its deepest section), Lake Victoria is broad and shallow (maximum depth less than 300 feet). At times in the geologic past, Lake Victoria has completely dried up.

Africa also has several major internal drainage basins. The Okavanga Delta in southern Africa supports a unique ecosystem and wildlife preserves. The Niger basin, with its narrow outlet to the Atlantic Ocean, has been the center of major African civilizations for centuries (e.g., the city of Timbuktu). The Chad basin (Lake Chad) has, during wetter centuries, supported large fishing-based populations. These basins tend to have old soils and low fertility. They also are at latitudes with minimal rainfall.

The two major areas of African deserts are the Sahara and the Namib. These deserts are largely latitude dependent because the prevailing winds keep moisture from the oceans away from the land. There is evidence that as the climate has changed, these areas, and others across the continent, have fluctuated between wet and dry conditions. Radar images that "see" below the sands of the Sahara indicate large river systems below the modern sand-covered surface. In contrast, there are sand beds below the Congo Rainforest that suggest times of desertification in the geologic past of this area.

The semiarid areas of East Africa have resulted from the formation of a rain shadow, as the East African Rift rose up high enough to block rain from the Atlantic, which now falls on the west side of the rift and flows down the Congo River drainage to the Atlantic Ocean. East Africa is dependent on the monsoonal rains from the Indian Ocean, and suffers from extended dry seasons each year. This change in local climate over the last 6 to 7 million years is seen in the fossil record of changing species. Forest-dwelling monkey and pig species changed to open-grassland dwelling grazers like baboons and hominids as well as gazelles and wildebeest and zebras.

Geohazards

Geologic hazards in Africa can be grouped into floods, earthquakes, and volcanoes. Flooding is possible along major rivers and in flat lying basins and coastal plains. Flash floods occur in semiarid regions with minimal vegetation cover to absorb sudden rains. These floods often are due to weather conditions far upstream, so that those in the flood zone may have little or no warning. The classic annual flood of the Nile is now controlled by the Aswan High Dam which created Lake Nasser. This prevents disastrous floods, but has stopped the recharge of nutrient rich sediments onto the farm fields of the river valley. The construction of hydroelectric dams now controls flooding along many African rivers. Along rivers that do not have dams, citizens who live down on the flood plain are at risk of inundation. Earthquakes present a relatively minor

Table 1: List of African countries in which some major mineral resources can be found

Mineral Resource	African countries with deposits
Gold	Angola (alluvial); Benin; Botswana; Burkina Faso; Burundi; Cameroon; Central African Republic; DRC; Ethiopia; Gabon (alluvial); Ghana; Ivory Coast; Kenya; Liberia; Mali; Namibia; Niger; Nigeria; Rwanda; Sierra Leone; South Africa; Sudan; Swaziland; Tanzania; Uganda; and Zimbabwe.
Diamonds	Angola (Cretaceous kimberlites and placer deposits); Botswana (kimberlites); Burkina Faso (alluvial); Cameroon; Central African Republic (alluvial); DRC; Gabon; Ghana; Ivory Coast; Lesotho (kimberlites and alluvial); Namibia (alluvial offshore); Sierra Leone; South Africa; Swaziland; Tanzania; and Togo.
Petroleum	Algeria (Paleozoic marine sediments); Angola (offshore); Benin (?); Cameroon; Chad; Republic of Congo (offshore); Egypt; Equatorial Guinea; Gabon (offshore); Libya; Nigeria; and Sudan.
Iron	Algeria; Angola (Banded Iron Formation); Cameroon (BIF); Egypt; Gabon; Ivory Coast; Liberia (BIF); Mauritania (BIF); Senegal; South Africa; Swaziland; and Uganda.
Limestone For cement and lime	Benin; Kenya; Rwanda; Sudan; Tanzania; and Togo

Note #1: Many other precious metals and industrial stone resources are exploited in Africa. See the Geological Atlas of Africa for detailed country-by-country descriptions of these natural resources.

hazard along the East African Rift. There are no subduction zones or active transform faults to create major earthquake hazards. However, since there are few construction standards that take possible earthquake hazards into consideration, many structures are vulnerable to collapse even in minor earthquakes.

Nyiragongo and Nyamuragira in the Democratic Republic of the Congo are two very dangerous volcanoes. They lie along a failed rift left over from the opening of the Atlantic Ocean when Gondwanaland split apart. Nyiragongo has an active lava lake and has had lava flows extend down into the city of Goma. Its lava is very fluid, and its slopes are very steep, resulting in very fast flowing lava (up to 60 mph), which makes it highly dangerous when the lava lake overflows. There are three water-filled lakes in this area that present unique geohazards. Because there are still reserves of lava below this area, large quantities of carbon dioxide are still escaping from deep underground. Lake Kivu, on the border of the Democratic Republic of the Congo and Rwanda, has large quantities of methane and carbon dioxide dissolved in its water and trapped in the sediment on the bottom of the lake. If a lava flow from the neighboring Nyiragongo volcano entered the lake, large quantities of these toxic gases could be released. Several times in recorded history (and an unknown number of times in prehistory), Lake Nyos in Cameroon (a volcanic crater lake) released large quantities of carbon dioxide, including the terrible tragedy in 1986, killing over 1,700 people. Carbon dioxide, heavier than air, displaces the oxygen as it rolls downhill, resulting in the asphyxiation of all animal life. As the carbon dioxide naturally dissipates, it leaves little trace of the cause of death for the people and animals caught in its path. There is now a monitoring system in place to try to warn residents if another eruption of carbon dioxide gas occurs so that they may have time to move out of the way of the dangerous gas. The third lake in this group is Lake Monoun, which erupted carbon dioxide gas in 1984, killing thirty-seven people.

Mineral Resources—types and distribution

Africa has major reserves of bauxite (aluminum ore), chromite, cobalt, coltan (columbite-tantalite, used in modern electronics such as cell phones and computers), diamonds, gold, manganese, phosphate, platinum-group metals, titanium minerals (rutile and ilmenite), vanadium, vermiculite, zirconium (Geological Atlas of Africa). Mineral resources can provide economic benefits, but also fueled colonialism and still are the source of conflict. Most recently the sale of diamonds has been used to fund wars in countries such as Sierra Leone and the Democratic Republic of the Congo.

Petroleum production has the potential to fund major development in African countries. However, even when oil companies pay significant royalties to governments, very little of that money has been spent on improving infrastructure or encouraging other business ventures in the nations involved. This has led to conflict in countries such as Nigeria, and may fuel popular uprisings in other countries if the resources are not applied to the public good rather than to just the enrichment of select officials.

Major mineral resources, although widespread, are not evenly distributed. Their distribution is controlled by the underlying geology and by the tectonic and erosional processes that created and redistributed them across the continent. Some minerals are found in the original rocks in which they formed, such as diamonds in volcanic deposits known as "kimberlites" or gold in veins in metamorphic rocks such as gneisses and greenstones. Others have been concentrated by alluvial action (erosion and deposition in river beds, lake sediments, or along beaches creating "placer deposits"). Geologic prospecting uses the knowledge gained by mapping the various rock types to determine where to look for these mineral resources. Table 1 above presents a brief listing of the countries in which some of these major mineral resources can be found:

In spite of the potential wealth that could be gained by tapping into the natural mineral resources of Africa, not all countries are able to take advantage of that potential. Relatively mineral-poor countries and countries with limited exploration include: Guinea Bissau; the Gambia; Eritrea; Equatorial Guinea; Djibouti; Malawi; Morocco; Mozambique; Somalia; Tunisia; Western Sahara. Some of these countries simply may not have the geologic foundation to provide them with mineral assets. Others may have potential mineral riches within their borders, but political problems and internal conflicts prevent exploration and/or development of those resources (e.g., Somalia).

Geotourism

Many nations in the world take advantage of unique geologic features to generate income from tourism. In the United States, the world's first National Park, Yellowstone, is a geologic wonder that brings jobs and income to a remote part of the country. Similarly, the Grand Canyon and Yosemite are economic engines for their regions. Unfortunately, relatively few places in Africa have tapped into this potential. One area that is taking advantage of potential geotourism is northern Tanzania. Each year this country hosts thousands of tourists who come to climb Mt. Kilimanjaro. Zambia and Zimbabwe have tapped into the potential for geotourism to Victoria Falls, but political instability has hurt their ability to attract tourists to that area. North African countries like Tunisia and Morocco have traditionally capitalized on both their proximity to Europe and their beautiful beaches to attract tourists, and Egypt adds the Nile and its Red Sea beaches to its cultural heritage as attractions for tourists. Countries like Kenya, Tanzania, and South Africa have marketed their wildlife viewing more than their geologic sites in attracting tourists. However, many tourists include geologic sites like Mt. Kenya, Mt. Kilimanjaro, Ngorongoro Crater, and Table Mountain among their destinations. The countries of Egypt, Morocco, Algeria, Tunisia, Tanzania, Kenya, and Botswana each earn more than half a billion dollars each year from tourism.

Geology and Hominid Evolution

The evolution of human beings had its beginnings in Africa. This is where the earliest fossils of hominids (a.k.a. hominines) have been found. Hominids are bipedal apes, including modern humans, our evolutionary ancestors, and similar species that went extinct, leaving no descendants. The preservation of fossils, and their subsequent discovery, depends in large part on the tectonic and geologic conditions. It is also dependent on political stability allowing researchers to safely operate in an area.

East Africa provides ideal conditions for the preservation and discovery of fossils because the rifting produces depressions that relatively rapidly accumulate sediments that can bury bones before they can be destroyed. The continuing uplift of this area later causes rapid erosion that now exposes those fossiliferous sediments, allowing paleontologists and paleoanthropologists to find the fossils on or near the surface. East Africa has the added advantage that frequent volcanism has deposited widespread ash layers between the sediment layers. These ash layers can be dated using radiometric techniques so that we can organize the fossils according to their geologic age. Southern Africa also has many excellent sites for fossil preservation and discovery. However, many of these sites are in cave deposits, and the lack of volcanic ash layers makes determining the age of the fossils more difficult.

Paleoanthropologists work with geologists to determine the location of sediments of the right composition and age in order to decide where to look for fossil hominids. Most of the fossil hominids have been found along the East African Rift from the Afar Triangle in Ethiopia (including the Australopithecus afarensis fossil known as "Lucy" and the Ardipithecus ramidus fossil known as "Ardi") south through Kenya into Tanzania (where the Oldupai Gorge has yielded numerous fossils and stone tools, and the Laetoli site with its hominid tracks that look very much like modern human footprints). Ar. ramidus fossils have been dated to approximately 4.4 million years ago, and Au. afarensis fossils have been dated to between 2.9 and 3.8 million years ago. However, many hominids have also been located in South Africa, including the first hominid described from Africa—the "Taung" child (Australopithecus africanus, dating to approximately 2.5 million years ago) described in 1924. Interestingly, recent excavations in Chad have turned up what are (so far) the oldest hominid fossils, dating to between 6 and 7 million years ago. There have not been any hominid fossils dating to earlier than 2 million years old found outside of the African continent. Therefore, Africa is seen as the birthplace of humankind. (See From Lucy to Language for more detailed information and many life-sized photographs of the fossils.)

Review Questions

1. Why are the geology and geomorphology of Africa important?

2. What are the major mountain ranges of Africa, and how were they formed?

3. What are the major "cratons" of Africa, and why are they important?

4. What "supercontinents" was Africa part of in the geologic past?

    What is the evidence for the existence of these landmasses?

5. What is the "East African Rift" and why is it important?

6. What is the evidence that the East African Rift is splitting apart?

7. How is Lake Victoria different from the other rift valley lakes (e.g., Turkana or Tanganyika)?

8. When did southern Africa undergo a period of glaciations? What is the evidence?

9. What is the Karoo Supergroup? Why is it important?

10. What are the ages of the sediments covering the Sahara? Why are they important?

11. How does the underlying geology affect the soils of Africa?

12. How does the development of the East African Rift affect the climate of East Africa?

    What is the evidence?

13. Why are the Nyiragongo volcano and Lake Nyos dangerous?

14. What economic minerals are found in significant quantities in Africa?

15. What areas of Africa are known for hominid fossils?

    What geologic conditions influence the occurrence and discovery of these fossils?

Bibliography

Burke, Kevin, and Yanni Gunnell. 2008 "The African Erosion Surface: A Continental-Scale Synthesis of Geomorphology, Tectonics, and Environmental Change over the Past 180 Million Years." *Geological Society of America Memoir* 201.

Carlson, D. H., C. C. Plummer, and D. McGeary, D., eds. 2008. *Physical Geology: Earth Revealed*, 8th ed. McGraw-Hill.

Johanson, D., and B. Edgar. 1996. *From Lucy to Language*. Simon & Schuster.

Lutgens, Frederick, and Edward Tarbuck. 1999. *Foundations of Earth Science.* 2nd ed. Prentice Hall.

Petters, Sunday, and Springer-Verlag. 1991 "Regional Geology of Africa." W. M. Adams, A. S. Goudie, and A. R. Orme. eds. *The Physical Geography of Africa*. Oxford University Press.

Schluter, Thomas. 2006. *Geological Atlas of Africa: With Notes on Stratigraphy, Tectonics, Economic Geology, Geohazards, Geosites and Geoscientific Education of Each Country.* Springer.

Tarbuck, E. J., F. K. Lutgens, and D. Tasa. 2010. *Earth: An Introduction to Physical Geology.* 10th ed. Prentice-Hall.

Chapter Three

A Historical Survey Of Africa From Earliest Times To The Twenty-First Century

By Akin Alao and Benjamin Akobi

Introduction

Africa has a long history spanning several centuries filled with fortunes and reversals. Several changes occurred that have rapidly altered and added to the complexities of the multiethnic and multicultural continent of Africa. These include the incursion of foreigners especially Arabs and Europeans, the introduction of Islam and Christianity, and the colonization and decolonization of Africa. Several works have been written on diverse themes and periods of the history of Africa. Long before the discovery of the New World and the founding of America and Australia, early historians such as Herodotus and Polybius had produced written works on Africa's past about five centuries before the birth of Christ.[1] In recent times, the history of Africa is reconstructed from Egyptian, Arabic, Amharic and Western records, evidence from various fields including archaeology, anthropology, linguistics and oral traditions. This chapter is a historical survey of significant developments in Africa from the prehistoric period to the present twenty-first century.

Precolonial Africa

The Early Ages

Africa is reputed to be the oldest continent, the home of the earliest man, and the main center where the physical and technological development of man began. Evidence of earliest hominids dated to about two million years ago have been found by researchers such as the famous archaeologist, Louis Leakey in Olduvai Gorge in Tanzania, East Africa. It is believed that from East Africa early hominids spread to other parts of the world.[2] The prehistoric period of Africa has been classified into the Early Stone Age, the Middle Stone Age, the Late Stone Age, and the Iron Age. The Early Stone Age was characterized by three cultures: the Oldowan, the Acheulian, and the Sangoan. The earliest culture in the world, known as the Oldowan, has been dated to about two million years ago when man started making stone tools. It is named after a site in Tanzania where the tools were first discovered. Later Stone Ages reflect improvement in toolmaking and in the techniques of hunting and food gathering.[3]

The era of sedentary living and domestication of crops and animals referred to as the Neolithic Age started at the close of the Late Stone Age. The origin of the knowledge of domestication of plants and animals is a subject of dispute between the Diffusionist and Evolutionist schools. The Diffusionist school claims that domestication of plants and animals began in Anatolia, spread first into Lower Egypt, then into the Sahara region from where it diffused into various parts of Africa following the emigration of people from the Sahara when dessication started about 2000 BC. The Evolutionists assert that the knowledge of food production was indigenous to Africa and claim that wheat and barley grown in temperate southwestern Asia cannot be cultivated in tropical Africa.[4]

The domestication of food plants and stock-raising had significant consequences. Sedentary living became established, changes occurred in the family structure, division of labor and social stratification began, and the human population began to increase. The Neolithic revolution with the exception of the Industrial Revolution has been acknowledged as causing the greatest change ever experienced in the history of human society and culture.[5] Further advancement in culture and human mastery of the environment was facilitated during the Neolithic period when iron-working technology was introduced about 1500 BC in eastern Anatolia. Knowledge of iron-working spread to North Africa through the Phoenicians; the diffusion southward from the seventh century BC was facilitated by the iron-using Assyrians who, after conquering Egypt, introduced the technique of iron working to Nubia. The presence of large deposits of iron ore transformed Nubia to a reputable center for iron working. Carthage and Cerne have been identified as other centers from where iron-working technology diffused to other parts of Africa. Availability of iron tools allowed improvement in agriculture and greater dominance of the environment by man. In time, kingdoms and empires started to emerge, especially in areas where iron-working technology was first acquired.[6]

Kingdoms and States in Precolonial Africa

Numerous civilizations, states, and empires existed in various parts of Africa in the past. Several factors accounted for their emergence and decline. Before the features of some of these civilizations and states are highlighted, a clarification of the concept of civilization would be appropriate. Ehret provides an objective description of what constitutes a civilization:

> "Civilization" refers to a grouping of societies and their individual cultures, conjoined by their sharing of deep common historical roots … The societies in question share a range of fundamental social and cultural ideas … stemming either from many centuries of close cultural interaction and the mutual diffusion of ideas or from a still more

ancient common historical descent of the societies involved from some much earlier society or grouping of related societies.[7]

Ehret classified historically linked societies of Africa as the Afrasan, Niger-Congo, Sudanic and Khoisan civilizations.[8] The Nile valley in northeast Africa was the first center of civilization in Africa. The Egyptian civilization, believed to have emerged as early as 3100 BC, was not only one of the two oldest civilizations in the world, but also its remarkable achievements cannot be overlooked. In the fifth century BC, the ancient historian Herodotus described Ancient Egypt as the "gift of the Nile" because of the centrality of the Nile River in the sustenance of Egypt and the facilitation of many of its numerous achievements. Before Western Europe emerged from its relative backwardness, Egypt had become an important center of human civilization. The wealth of Egypt was well recognized in ancient times to the extent that it was branded by many as "the cradle of Civilization." Some of the achievements of early Egyptian civilization include the beginnings of urban culture, the building of pyramids, the introduction and practice of the monarchical and centralized system of administration, the art of writing, the making of the calendar, and the practice of medicine. The invasion of Egypt by the Assyrians in 666 BC and the sacking and raiding of its capital marked the decline of Egyptian civilization from which it never recovered.[9]

The Kushitic kingdom of Nubia, situated to the south of Egypt, became the successor state to Egypt; it covered areas of the present-day Republic of Sudan and parts of areas to its south. The Nubian territory was endowed with abundant mineral resources, especially gold called *nub* by the Egyptians, from which the name of the territory was derived. Nubia was under Egyptian control from about 2000 BC to 700 BC. During this period, aspects of Egyptian culture were embraced by the Kushites. The Kushites capitalized on the decline of the power of Egypt from about 1100 BC to invade and conquer Egypt around 700 BC. The Kushites were driven out of Egypt by the Assyrians around 666 BC, and their capital, Napata, was captured by Amasis and Potasimto during an Egyptian attack in 593 BC. A new capital was established by the Kushites at Meroe, which had assured sources of water supply from rainfall and annual floods of the Nile and Atbara rivers. In addition, Meroe had abundant deposits of iron ore and timber, which facilitated the development of Meroe as a reputable center of iron mining, leading to its description by archaeologists as "the Birmingham" of Africa.[10]

Meroitic culture flourished for a number of centuries before its eventual decline around AD 350 when Meroe was sacked by an invading army from Aksum that had been a rival of Meroe for centuries. Aksum emerged from the intermarriage and intermingling of migrant Sabean-speaking people of southeastern Arabia and the indigenous people then inhabiting the territory later known as Ethiopia. A new language with its alphabets known as Ge'ez developed, the use of Ge'ez in addition to the Greek and Sabean languages, and the strategic location of Aksum, enabled the emergence of the kingdom as the major center of commerce between the Mediterranean Sea and the Indian Ocean. Aksum thrived on trade and was able to extend its territory and influence as far as Saba (Yemen) in south Arabia. Aksum became the first African state to mint its own coin and a major center of Christianity from the fourth century AD. A number of factors, including the disruption and diversion of trade with India and Eastern Mediterranean, contributed to the decline of Aksum around AD 800.[11]

Several states and kingdoms of varying sizes and cultural complexities existed in other parts of Africa. The Swahili Civilization emerged from a synthesis of the cultures of the Azanians indigenous to the East African coast and the immigrant Arabs. The process of the intermingling of the Azanians and the Arabs began around AD 100 and became intensified after the introduction of Islam. The trade in ivory, gold, slaves, cotton, ambergris, oriental pottery, Indian silk and other goods engendered the increasing settlement and intermarriage of the Arabs and the indigenous Bantu peoples, and the development of the Swahili language and culture between the tenth and the fourteenth centuries. Islam became widespread on the East African coast leading to the emergence of small states ruled by local Muslim dynasties. The typical Swahili town contained a few coral stone houses, a mosque(s), and a Muslim ruling family. The Swahili civilization suffered reversals and eventual decline from repeated attacks of the Zimba, decline of agriculture and maritime trade, and finally Portuguese invasions in the seventeenth century.[12]

A state that has been regarded as the most impressive memorial tribute of African cultural development in sub-Saharan Africa was the Shona state of Great Zimbabwe located near the modern town of Fort Victoria in Zimbabwe. Great Zimbabwe started developing from about AD 100 and grew from production and trade in gold and iron with the Swahili on the East African coast. Massive stone buildings and enclosures erected by the Shona people of Great Zimbabwe have been proved to have been accomplished independently of external influence. The depletion of available resources, coupled with increasing population, and diversion of trade from Great Zimbabwe, possibly caused the abandonment of the site around AD 1450 and the later formation of the Monomotapa Empire by some of the migrants around the Zambezi River.[13]

West Africa was home to several states of repute including the Sudanese states of Ghana (AD 700–1240), Mali (AD 1050–1500), Songhai (AD 1350–1600) and Kanem Borno (AD 800–1900). Some others are the Hausa States (AD 1000–1800), Ife and Oyo States (AD 1400–1850), Benin (AD 1400–1800), Dahomey (AD 1700–1900) and Asante (AD 1700–1900).[14] These states emerged in the forest and savannah regions of West Africa independently of external influence and succeeded in building remarkable and dynamic political and economic systems. For instance, Kanem Borno had one of the longest lasting dynasties in the whole world. A few of these states grew into empires with vast territories and influence before colonization, and virtually all of the states had leaders of prowess who brought their skills and capability to bear on the development of their societies. For example, the name of Mansa Kanka Musa is associated with the greatness of the Mali Empire, and Askia Mohammed with the Songhai Empire.[15]

Migrations and Invasions

The complexities and diversity of societies and cultures in modern Africa are traceable in part to a series of incursion of aliens and their impacts on African societies. Centuries before the birth of Christ, Africa had attracted migrants and invaders from places close to and far from the Mediterranean. The Phoenicians from Palestine had between 1000 BC and 800 BC established trading colonies along the shores of North Africa and Spain. Carthage emerged as the principal colony and later grew into an empire that became a rival of the Roman Empire until its destruction by the latter around 146 BC. The relations and intermarriage of the Phoenicians with the indigenous Berbers of the Maghreb brought about the rise of the Carthaginians whose economic activities were believed to have stimulated the development of the trans-Saharan trade.[16]

Prior to the rise of Carthage, Egypt had been invaded by the little-known people referred to as the "C Group" about 2160 BC, but their conquest of Egypt was short-lived. Egypt came under the suzerainty of the Hyksos invaders from Asia who ruled Egypt from about 1780 to 1580 BC before they were expelled by Thutmosis III. Egypt, in subsequent centuries, came under the dominance of the Assyrians, the Persians, and the Greeks. The Roman conquest of Egypt in 31 BC granted the Romans wider control of the territories of North Africa, which became known as Roman Africa. The Greeks and the Romans had significant impacts on the societies of North Africa. New cultural elements, such as Greek and Roman languages, architecture, social and economic institutions and religion, were introduced during the Greek and Roman control of North Africa successively. During the period of Roman control, North Africa became the hub of Christianity and home of some of the most famous early Church Fathers and prolific theologians, including Origen, Tertullian, and St. Augustine.[17]

The Romans ruled North Africa until the invasion of the Muslim forces in the seventh century. The successful conquest of Egypt, which began in AD 640, opened the gateway for the penetration and gradual takeover of North Africa. The Byzantines were finally expelled from Egypt in AD 646, but the conquest of the Maghreb was not accomplished effectively until about a hundred years later. The conquest of North Africa by the Muslim armies and subsequent waves of migrations of Arabs into various parts of the region had significant lasting consequences primary of which was the Arabization and Islamization of North Africa. Furthermore, a number of Muslim states and empires emerged in North Africa; the Almoravid (AD 1042–1145) and the Almohad (AD 1121–1269) were the greatest to exist before the imposition of Ottoman rule.[18]

The Arabization of North Africa was not accomplished solely by conquest. Migrations of nomadic Arabs into various parts of the region, along with social relations with the indigenous inhabitants, enabled the penetration of Arabic culture and religion into the interior regions. These parts, because of their poor economic prospects, had often been neglected by previous invaders. Islam and Arabic culture remained urban phenomena in North Africa until the eleventh century when the migration of the Bedouin Arabs, the Banu Hilal and Banu Sulaym, started. With the migration of the Bedouin Arabs, North Africa became increasingly nomadic and rurally organized.[19]

The incursion of the Ottomans into North Africa occurred during the period when the Almohad Empire was consolidating its grip on the Maghreb. The founder of the Ayyubid dynasty, Salah al-Din, recruited Mamluk slave soldiers from Turkey and wrested the control of Egypt from the Fatimids in AD 1171. The Mamluks succeeded in uprooting the Ayyubid dynasty in

1250 and established two successive dynasties that ruled Egypt until 1517 when the Ottomans regained control of Egypt. The Ottomans turned Egypt to a springboard for the extension of their empire to other parts of Africa. Southward expansion brought them into conflict with the Funj Sultanate with some gains including partial control of the commerce on the Red Sea. The Spanish and the Portuguese, who were struggling to establish their power in North Africa, became stumbling blocks to the westward expansion of the Ottoman Empire. The Spanish and the Portuguese were expelled from North Africa with the aid of the Ra'is or corsairs, the two most famous of whom were Khayruddin and Arrudj known as the "Barbarossa" brothers. The Ottomans maintained a loose control of North Africa until the nineteenth century when its power began to wane and the European conquest of Africa had commenced.[20] Two other significant migrations in African history would be briefly considered before the elucidation of European penetration and conquest of Africa by the Europeans.

The Bantu migrations and expansion from the Benue-Cameroon border area into East, Central, and southern Africa has been regarded as one of the greatest migrations in the history of man. The Bantu migrations account for the multiplicity but linguistic affinity of over six hundred languages spoken over the greater part of Central, eastern, and southern Africa. The spread of new ideas such as iron-working technology and pottery making and the development of more organized and advanced societies in the greater part of sub-Saharan African had also been attributed to the migrations of the Bantu.[21] Another migration of historical significance in Africa was the movement of the Fulani people from their homeland in Futa Jallon to various parts of West Africa. The Fulani were responsible for the revival of Islam and three successful jihads in the nineteenth century.[22]

The European Penetration and Partition of Africa

The penetration of Africa by the Europeans started with the Portuguese voyages of discovery in the fifteenth century. The Portuguese enterprise in Africa was the longest in duration compared to other European nations. As noted by scholars, the Portuguese were the first to settle in Africa and the last to leave—and most reluctantly.[23] The Portuguese reached the island of Arguin in 1443, arrived at the River Senegal and Cape Verde in 1445, and twelve years later reached the mouth of the Gambia. By 1497, three Portuguese vessels had reached the Cape of Good Hope and from there sailed into the Indian Ocean. The explorations of the Portuguese opened up the coastal areas of southern, West, and East Africa to the commercial and missionary activities of the Europeans. The European contacts with Africa were at the early period restricted to the coastal areas because of lack of knowledge of the terrain of the interior, the fear of contact of diseases debilitating to Europeans, especially malaria, and other challenges such a venture demanded. The quest to trade in exotic African items such as gold, ivory, rhinoceros horns and pepper, and the desire to evangelize Africa and spread European civilization, characterized the nature and tempo of early European-African relations.[24]

The discovery of the New World, subsequent establishment of mines and plantations, and the need for labor contributed to the development of the trade in African slaves across the Atlantic. The Atlantic slave trade, also known as the triangular slave trade, connected the New World, Europe, and Africa. Slave trade was not new to Africa; slaves were sold in the markets of the Western Sudan and in the slave markets of the trans-Saharan trade routes connecting Tripoli, Fez, and Cairo. The island of Zanzibar on the East African coast was a major center and the entrepot of the Arab slave trade from where slaves were exported to the Middle East and ivory to Europe and America. However, the Atlantic slave trade has been adjudged by some scholars as a destructive phenomenon in the history of Africa. The trade in African slaves across the Atlantic eclipsed other trades in Africa during the period between the sixteenth and the nineteenth centuries. The volume and impact of the trade on Africa remains a controversial subject among scholars of African history.[25]

The nineteenth century marked a turning point in the history of Africa. It was a century of significant developments with far-reaching impacts on Africa. The slave trade was abolished in the early decades of the century, while the European partition and conquest of Africa was largely accomplished in the closing decades of the century. Several factors accounted for the abolition of the slave trade in the nineteenth century, but the economic dictates of the period appear to be more prominent. The commencement of the Industrial Revolution in Britain in the last half of the eighteenth century had rendered obsolete the demand for slave labor; what was required instead were raw materials to feed the industries and expanded markets for the products of the European industries. The experience of Europeans in Africa in earlier centuries, coupled with some other favorable developments, turned Africa once again to the prime target of Europeans for the attainment of their economic objectives.

The penetration of the African interior came to be facilitated by the acquisition of better knowledge of the interior based on information supplied by European explorers, missionaries, and traders, and the production of quinine and cinchonine drugs in the early nineteenth century. Imperialist interests influenced the development of legitimate trade between Europe, Africa, and Asia; in the course of the nineteenth century, competitions and rivalries between the European merchants and trading companies almost snowballed into outbreak of hostilities between them and their parent countries. Political and socioeconomic developments in Europe had created tensions between the European nations. In 1876, an international conference was convened at Brussels by King Leopold II of Belgium to map out strategies for the exploration of the interior of Africa for commercial purposes. The outcome of the conference was the formation of the International African Association with committees in member-countries. To forestall the possible descent of European nations into war over Africa, the Berlin Conference of November 1884 to February 1885 was summoned by Bismarck the German Chancellor where the terms of the partition of Africa were agreed upon by the competing European nations.[26]

Conquest and Colonization of Africa

The scramble of European nations for the establishment of ownership rights over the territory and resources of Africa was kick-started by the 1869 discovery of gold and diamonds in South Africa and the opening of the Suez Canal, as well as Leopold II's acquisition of the territory he called Congo Free State.[27] The Partition of Africa, started in 1830, was largely accomplished by 1914. The Partition was executed through the process of a series of treaty signing and military conquest. In many parts of Africa, resistance to European incursion was strong, but the superior weapons and strategies of the Europeans facilitated the victory of Europeans. The Maxim machine-gun patented in 1884 was used to massively devastate the African armies who relied on muzzle-loading muskets.[28]

By 1914, Germany had become the master of Tangayika, Togoland, and Cameroun; Spanish Morocco had become the possession of Spain; Belgium had earlier taken possession of the Congo while Angola and Mozambique fell to Portugal. Italy possessed Somaliland, Eritrea and Libya. Britain and France were the largest beneficiaries of the Partition of Africa. Britain gained control of West Africa while France dominated most of North Africa. The countries of Nigeria, Gold Coast, Sierra-Leone, Gambia, Kenya, Uganda, Rhodesia, and Zanzibar came under the rule of the British. France succeeded in securing control of Senegal, Mali, Upper Volta, Mauritania, Ivory Coast, Dahomey, Niger, Chad, Gabon, Madagascar, and parts of the Congo. In North Africa, the French became masters of Algeria, Tunisia, and Morocco.[29]

Colonial Administration of Africa

The political and economic philosophies adopted by the European colonizers of Africa, although divergent according to the objectives of the colonizers, were essentially similar. The colonies were conceived as dependencies that served the major purposes of supply of raw materials for European industries and markets for the manufactured goods of Europe. The colonial administrative policies devised by the colonial powers reflected the prevailing ideologies in the metropolises. In addition, colonial policies were dictated by the exigencies of the situation met in each conquered country, the nature of administration prior colonization, the availability of European personnel, and the disposition of the principal colonial officer on ground at a particular time. [30]

The colonial experience of Britain in India proved handy in the application of the Indirect Rule system of administration to her African territories. The Indirect System was undergirded by the perception that the colonized peoples are better ruled through their traditional institutions; thus, it was in the best interest of the colonial administration that the indigenous cultures and traditions were left undisrupted. Nevertheless, the British hoped not only to preserve the positive aspects of indigenous cultures but also to introduce modern ideas, albeit in a gradual manner for their improvement.

In contradistinction to the British administrative policy, the policy of Assimilation, which the French adopted, was influenced by the French idea of centralization of administration. Thus, the French-administered colonies were perceived and treated not as colonies but as France's "Overseas Territories." The policy of Assimilation was predicated on the assumption of the superiority of French culture to which the French then sought to assimilate the people of her colonies. The failure of the French to make French men of the African peoples necessitated the adoption of a new policy referred to as policy of Association that exemplifies ideas similar to that of the British Indirect Rule.

The Portuguese adopted a colonial policy of administration similar to that of the French referred to as *Assimilado*. The Belgian colonial policy, described as Paternalism, was similar to that of the French, but the policy excluded the colonies from participating in the administration; colonialism was envisioned by the Belgians to last for a very long time. Thus, the Belgians were not in a hurry to educate and train the colonized peoples for self-government. The administrative disposition of the Belgians was later to have dire consequences for the Belgian Congo after independence.[31]

Colonialism has been described as basically exploitative; it was a relationship designed to subvert the colonies politically and economically with the sole aim of facilitating the development of the metropolises. Thus, the socioeconomic development of the states under alien control became impeded and subject to the intrigues of the colonizers.[32] Africa was integrated into the periphery of the international economic system as the supplier of raw materials such as cocoa, cotton, and rubber. Thus, the economy of Africa was propelled by the demands and dictates of the industrialists of Europe and their agents in Africa. The demands of the European industrialists stimulated the expansion of economic activities in Africa; however, the bulk of capital flow was concentrated in the hands of European banks and merchants.

In order to facilitate the attainment of colonial objectives, modern social infrastructures such as railways, roads, ports and airways were provided by the colonizers. This stimulated development and growth of urban centers and the consequent rural-urban drift in many parts of Africa. The provision of Western-type education in many parts of Africa for the greater part of the colonial era was the preserve of the European missionaries. However, as it has been noted, embedded in colonialism was the seed of its own destruction. The crises generated by colonialism, as well as its modernizing influence, stimulated the development of nationalism, which eventually sounded the death knell of colonialism.[33]

Nationalism and Decolonization

Karl Deutsch defined Nationalism as:

> … an attitude of mind, a pattern of attention and desires. It arises in response to a condition of a society and to a particular stage in its development. It is a predisposition to

pay far more attention to messages from its members than to messages from or about any other people.[34]

The colonized peoples of Africa did not succumb meekly to all whims and caprices of the colonizers. Colonial policies and practices, whether political, economic, or cultural, once deemed to be detrimental to the welfare of the colonized peoples of Africa, were criticized in various ways by the educated elites of Africa. The thrust of nationalist protests against colonial policies before the outbreak of the Second World War was basically for reforms of colonial policies. In the British-administered territories, the 1930s have been identified as the period when traditional nationalism transformed to modern nationalism. Before this period, protests against colonial policies were haphazard, short-lived, and localized. Certain developments internal and external to Africa stimulated the spread of nationalism and the change in the form and thrust of nationalist agitations in the post–Second World War Africa. Political and social developments during and after the Second World War in Europe and other parts of the world rendered colonialism an obsolete practice. Constitutional reforms became more or less unavoidable following nationalist agitations and the wave of anti-imperialism movement for national self-determination blowing across the globe after the Second World War.[35] The nature and mood of the post-war world had become a factor that cannot be overlooked. It dawned on the world that the Second World War and its consequential material and psychological impacts had turned nineteenth- and twentieth-century colonialism into an Old Colonial System.

The prewar status quo of the colonial system in which subject peoples were denied participation in the management of their affairs could no longer be tolerated or sustained. Thus, the colonial powers including Britain embarked on liberalization of colonial philosophy by creating representative assemblies,[36] a move to which the nationalists responded by transforming existing nationalist movements to political parties or by creating new political parties out of tribal cultural unions and ethnic associations. The African nationalists began to demand self-government and independence from colonial control.

The nature of decolonization of the various colonized African nations was informed by various factors including the political ideology of the colonizer, the type of colony involved, and the reactions of the colonized peoples. The process of transfer of power to Africans was generally peaceful in colonies where constitutional channels were provided to address the demands of the nationalists. In most white-settler colonies such as Algeria, Angola, and Mozambique, transfer of power to Africans was achieved through the barrel of the gun.[37] Most African nations achieved independence by 1960. Exceptions were Portugal-administered Angola and Mozambique, which succeeded in breaking off the colonial yoke only in 1975.[38]

Postindependence Africa

Leadership and Governance

The nationalists who took over power from the colonizers had nurtured dreams of rapid socioeconomic transformation of independent African states, but this was frustrated by certain developments within and outside Africa. It has been argued that the African nations were only granted independence after the establishment of structures for the co-optation of the would-be independent African states into the European-fashioned neocolonial network.[39] The attribution of the crises of underdevelopment and political instability of independent African states to neocolonialism alone is hardly justifiable. While it is true that most African leaders demonstrated strong leanings toward reliance on external models and institutions, the failure of African leaders to achieve political stability and economic development of their states demands more than a monocausal explanation.[40]

Africa since independence has been bedeviled with myriad problems internally generated and externally influenced. Some of the challenges confronting and frustrating the development of the continent and of its component units include domestic economic mismanagement, tyrannical military dictatorships, authoritarian and sit-tight leaders, political crises and conflicts, policy failures, foreign domination, as well as unequal exchange and foreign-debt crisis. Within the first decade after independence, most African nations had either descended into civil wars or had been brought under military rule. The floodgate was opened in 1952 by the Lt. Colonel Gamal Abdel Nasser coup that overthrew the government of King Farouk of Egypt. Subsequently, the wave of military coups and counter-coups began to blow over the African continent. Nigeria, the Republic of Benin, and Zaire came under military rule in 1965, Ghana, Burundi, and Burkina Faso in 1966, Sierra-Leone and Togo in 1967, and Congo Republic in 1968 to mention a few.[41] The outbreak of ethnic crises and civil wars in countries such as Nigeria, Liberia, Rwanda, Sierra-Leone, and Sudan became impediments to political stability and socioeconomic development.

In the quest for the industrialization and development of the economies of the African states, the reliance on foreign capital, aid and loans brought African nations under crushing foreign debts, which increased drastically toward the close of the twentieth century. The African debt portfolio stood at $81.7 billion in 1984; five years later the figure had risen to $256.9 billion, which was almost equal to the total African GDP and 328.4 percent of her exports in the same year. The collapse of commodity trade, a rapidly rising population, and widespread corruption and financial improprieties have contributed to the impoverishment of the largest segment of the African populace. The problem of corruption in many African states appears not only to be staggering and intractable, but also has become the albatross that some scholars have alleged many foreign financial agencies to be sustaining. For instance, Mobutu Sese Seko the former ruler of Zaire, was reputed to be richer than his country. Mobutu possessed foreign assets worth about $5 billion in the mid-1980s while his country was indebted to foreign lending agencies to the tune of about $4 billion.[42]

The commonality of challenges facing the African states had motivated the establishment of regional and continental institutions to address issues of unity and peaceful coexistence, conflict resolution, development, and protection of sovereignty and territorial integrity. The Organization of African Unity (O.A.U), now known as the African Union (A.U), was established in 1963. The Economic Community of West African States emerged in 1975 to promote the rapid economic development of member-states. ECOMOG, the military arm of ECOWAS had at various times played important roles in peacekeeping and peace enforcement in the African sub-region. However, incidences of wars, border closures, crimes, and bewildering insecurity have been impeding the progress of multinational cooperation. In addition to the multifarious challenges of nation building, environmental problems and the AIDS/HIV scourge have been confronting Africa in recent decades. Increasing desertification, deforestation, drought, soil erosion, urban congestion and pollution, as well as health problems such as "child, maternal mortality" and communicable diseases are issues African states are currently grappling with.[43]

Review Questions

1. Account for the emergence of centers of civilization in Africa.

2. Discuss how the complexities and diversity of societies and cultures in modern Africa are traceable in part to a series of incursions of aliens and their impacts on African societies.

3. Identify and discuss the major decisions of the Berlin Conference of 1884–1885.

4. How did Britain impose colonial domination over the area later called Nigeria?

5. Discuss the French policies of Assimilation and Association.

6. Discuss early reactions to British rule in West Africa before 1949.

7. How did the Second World War affect nationalism in Africa?

8. Discuss the impact of colonial rule on African countries.

Bibliography

Anene, J. C., and Godfrey Brown, eds. 1966. *Africa in the Nineteenth and Twentieth Centuries*. Ibadan: Ibadan Univ. Press.

Curtin, Philip, et al. 1978. *African History*. New York: Longman.

Davidson, Basil. 2001. *Africa in History*. London: Phoenix Press.

Deutsch, K. W. 1970. *Politics and Government: How People Decide Their Fate*. Boston: Houghton Mifflin.

Ehret, Christopher. 2002. *The Civilizations of Africa*. Charlottesville: Univ. Press of Virginia.

Falola, Toyin. 2000. *Africa*. Vol. 1. Durham: Carolina Academic Press.

Falola, Toyin. 2002. *Africa*. Vol. 4. Durham: Carolina Academic Press.

Kiwanuka, S. 1972. *From Colonialism to Independence: A Reappraisal of Colonial Policies and African Reactions, 1870–1960*. Nairobi: East African Lit. Bureau.

Oguntomisin, G. O., and V. O. Edo. 2007. *African Civilisation from the Earliest Times to 1500 A.D.* Ibadan: John Archers Pub.

Olomola, Isola. 1969. *Main Trends in African History from Earliest Times to 1900*. Ado Ekiti: Omolayo Standard Press.

Onimode, Bade. 2000. *Africa in the World of the 21ˢᵗ Century*. Ibadan: Ibadan Univ. Press.

Onwuejeogwu, M. A., et al. 2000. *African Civilizations: Origin, Growth & Development*. Lagos: UTO Pub.

Oyegoke, Bisi. 2002. *An Outline History of Africa*. Ibadan: Footprints Pub.

Reader, John. 1999. *Africa: A Biography of the Continent*. New York: Vintage Books.

Walter, Rodney. 1972. *How Europe Underdeveloped Africa*. Abuja: Panaf Press.

Notes and References

1. Ibid.
2. See Basil Davidson, *Africa in History* (London: Phoenix Press, 2001) 7–13, and Christopher Ehret, *The Civilizations of Africa* (Charlottesville, VA: Univ. Press of Virginia, 2002) 17–21.
3. M. A. Onwuejeogwu et al., *African Civilizations*, 65–69, and Oguntomisin G. O. and Edo V. O., *African Civilisation from the Earliest Times*, 31–39.
4. Ibid.
5. M. A. Onwuejeogwu et al., *African Civilizations*, 68–73.
6. G. O. Oguntomisin and V. O. Edo, *African Civilisation from the Earliest Times*, 39–42.
7. Christopher Ehret, *The Civilizations of Africa*, 6–7.
8. Ibid.
9. G. O. Oguntomisin and V. O. Edo, *African Civilisation from the Earliest Times*, 49–53, Bisi Oyegoke, *An Outline History of Africa*, 13–15, Basil Davidson, *Africa in History*, 25–34, and Funso Afolayan, "Civilizations

of the Upper Nile and North Africa" in *Africa*, Vol 1, ed. Toyin Falola (Durham: Carolina Academic Press, 2000) 73–96.

10. Funso Afolayan, "Civilizations of the Upper Nile and North Africa," 96–97, and G. O. Oguntomisin and V. O. Edo, *African Civilisation from the Earliest Times*, 53–57.

11. Funso Afolayan, "Civilizations of the Upper Nile and North Africa," 106–108 and G. O. Oguntomisin and V. O. Edo, *African Civilisation from the Earliest Times*, 59–63.

12. For details see Isola Olomola, *Main Trends in African History from Earliest Times to 1900* (Ado Ekiti: Omolayo Standard Press, 1969) 46–63 and G. O. Oguntomisin G. O. and V. O. Edo, *African Civilisation from the Earliest Times*, 64–72.

13. G. O. Oguntomisin and V. O. Edo, *African Civilisation from the Earliest Times*, 73–77.

14. Toyin Falola, ed., *Africa*, Vol 1, 111.

15. G. O. Oguntomisin and V. O. Edo, *African Civilisation from the Earliest Times*, 88–100.

16. Funso Afolayan, "Civilizations of the Upper Nile and North Africa," 102.

17. Funso Afolayan, "Civilizations of the Upper Nile and North Africa," 100–105 and Isola Olomola, *Main Trends in African History*, 64–69.

18. Isola Olomola, *Main Trends in African History*, 92–98, 115–128.

19. Joel E. Tishken, "North Africa: Peoples and States to circa 1880" in *Africa*, Vol. 1, 257–259.

20. Joel E. Tishken, "North Africa, 260–262.

21. For details, see Funso Afolayan, "Bantu Expansion and Its Consequences" in *Africa*, Vol. 1, 113–136 and Oguntomisin G. O. and Edo V. O., *African Civilisation from the Earliest Times*, 43–46.

22. Basil Davidson, *Africa in History*, 244–253.

23. Bisi Oyegoke, *An Outline History of Africa*, 104.

24. See Philip Curtin et al., *African History* (New York: Longman Inc., 1978) 445, Bisi Oyegoke, *An Outline History of Africa*, 29–33 and Isola Olomola, *Main Trends in African History*, 51–55.

25. See Walter Rodney, *How Europe Underdeveloped Africa* (Abuja: Panaf Press, 1972) 2009 ed., 108–122, Bisi Oyegoke, *An Outline History of Africa*, 32–34 and J. C. Anene, "Slavery and the Slave Trade" in *Africa in the Nineteenth and Twentieth Centuries*, ed., Joseph C. Anene and Godfrey Brown, (Ibadan: Ibadan Univ. Press, 1966) 92–102.

26. Isola Olomola, *Main Trends in African History*, 268–271 and Bisi Oyegoke, *An Outline History of Africa*, 30–32, 90–95.

27. John Reader, *Africa: A Biography of the Continent* (New York: Vintage Books, 1999) 525–544 and Bisi Oyegoke, *An Outline History of Africa*, 97–100.

28. John Reader, *Africa: A Biography*, 579–586.

29. Bisi Oyegoke, *An Outline History of Africa*, 96.

30. Basil Davidson, *Africa in History*, 287–294 and Bisi Oyegoke, *An Outline History of Africa*, 101–104.

31. Ibid.

32. W. Rodney, *How Europe Underdeveloped Africa*, 16.

33. For details, see Philip Curtin et al., *African History*, 498–521, 532–536, 562–568, W. Rodney, *How Europe Underdeveloped Africa*, 246–284 and Bisi Oyegoke, *An Outline History of Africa*, 106–110.

34. K. W. Deutsch, *Politics and Government: How People Decide Their Fate* (Boston: Houghton Mifflin, 1970) 80.

35. S. Kiwanuka, *From Colonialism to Independence: A Reappraisal of Colonial Policies and African Reactions, 1870–1960* (Nairobi: East African Lit. Bureau, 1972) 97–101. For details on the inter-war and post-war developments that influenced nationalists aspirations and agitations for self-determination, and subsequent establishment of political parties for the realization of political objectives.

36. Ibid.

37. Basil Davidson, *Africa in History*, 325–341 and Bisi Oyegoke, *An Outline History of Africa*, 115–125.

38. Ibid.

39. Adejumobi S. A., "Neocolonialism" in *Africa*, Vol. 4, ed., Toyin Falola (Durham: Carolina Academic Press, 2002) 483.

40. Iweriebor E. E. G., "The Psychology of Colonialism" in *Africa*, Vol. 4, 481–482.

41. Bade Onimode, *Africa in the World of the 21ˢᵗ Century* (Ibadan: Ibadan Univ. Press, 2000) 77–95 and Bisi Oyegoke, *An Outline History of Africa*, 135–139.

42. Bade Onimode, *Africa in the World*, 77–97 and Basil Davidson, *Africa in History*, 368–371.

43. Bade Onimode, *Africa in the World*, 239–253.

Chapter Four

Introduction To Language In Africa

By Akinloye Ojo and Willie Udo Willie

Introduction[1]

It is not gainsaying that a deeper understanding of the linguistic issues and the entire linguistic landscape of a people is germane to an understanding of the sociopolitical, cultural, and historical system of the people. Therefore, in this chapter we present a discussion of a generalized introduction to language on the continent of Africa, including some definitions of key terms relating to multilingualism prevalent on the continent. A section is devoted to illustrating how the multitude of languages spoken in Africa is classified and to examining the role of language in the cultural, social, and ethnic identities of most Africans. Finally, given the linguistic diversity on the continent, the cogent issue of language planning is presented in the last section.

Language in Africa

Linguistic diversity is arguably the best illustration of the diversity that exists on the African continent. As illustrated in the preceding chapters, the African continent is a very diverse continent that manifests a lot of variation in many areas. A significant number of languages are spoken on the continent. Many of these languages are straightforwardly categorized as indigenous. Examples of these languages include Amharic, Bambara, Chaga, Ewe, Ibibio, Kikuyu, Luo, Shona, Wolof, Yoruba, and Zulu. Some other languages are generally considered nonindigenous but have had tremendous impact on the African sociocultural landscape. Examples of these languages include Arabic, English, French, and Portuguese. The linguistic diversity with its indubitable cultural enrichment is a celebrated feature of life on the African continent. However, the multiplicity of languages brings not only benefits but challenges as well. These challenges are related directly to the enormous number of languages coexisting on the continent as well as the challenges related to the complex roles of language within the society at large. The value of Africa's linguistic diversity is just one of the many complex issues associated with language in Africa.

In order to obtain an introductory understanding of the linguistic situation in Africa, some questions must be addressed. A peculiar question that is often asked in the discussion about language in Africa is whether there is an African language. That is, is there a common language spoken by the nearly one billion inhabitants of the African continent? The answer to this question is an unambiguous no; there is no single language spoken by most or all of Africa. The unfortunate error is presuming that Afrikaans is the language spoken by all Africans. This is not true. Afrikaans is a hybrid language that evolved from the prolonged contact between Dutch and various South African indigenous languages. There is no single language that all Africans speak; rather, there are regional languages that serve the linguistic needs of different peoples in different regions. These include Swahili, spoken widely in East Africa; Yoruba and Hausa, spoken widely in West Africa; and Zulu, common to many areas in the southern region of the continent.

Another important question often asked is whether there are languages indigenous to the African continent and if there are, how many. It has been estimated that over 30 percent of the approximately 6,600 languages spoken in the world are indigenous to Africa. Some examples of these languages, especially those that have over five million speakers each, include Amharic, Berber, Fula/Fulfulde, Hausa, Igbo, Bamana, Swahili, Wolof, Yoruba, and Zulu (see map 1).

Scholars have been brainstorming on the the issue of the exact number of languages spoken on the African continent. This has been a very controversial issue because of certain extra-linguistic factors concerning the use of mutual intelligibility as a yardstick to determining the differences between a language and a dialect as we shall discuss shortly. Though the exact number of languages is not known, scholars have estimated that between 2,000 to 2,500 languages are spoken on the continent (Crystal, 1997, and Webb and Kembo-Sure, 2004). No matter the variation in number, it is commonly held that the approximately one billion people in Africa speak about one-third of the world's languages.

The uncertainty surrounding the number of languages arises from many factors including the challenges in the use of mutual intelligibility with its concomitant sociopolitical and socioethnic bottlenecks. Another factor is the variation in interpretation of mutual intelligibility by dialectologists (linguistic fieldworkers) themselves. Language endangerment and language death or extinction also contribute to this uncertainty. The challenge of determining what should be regarded as a language and what should be considered a dialect is an enormous one, especially when mutual intelligibility is the only criterion used. Language has been variously defined based on the immediate need of the researchers. Some of the definitions include "a means of communication," "an expression of culture," "a set of symbols and sounds that are representative of referents," "a speech form used to convey meaning," etc. But it is generally accepted that a dialect is a variant of a language. Essentially, for most linguists, the degree of mutual intelligibility (i.e., mutual understanding) between the speakers of two speech forms

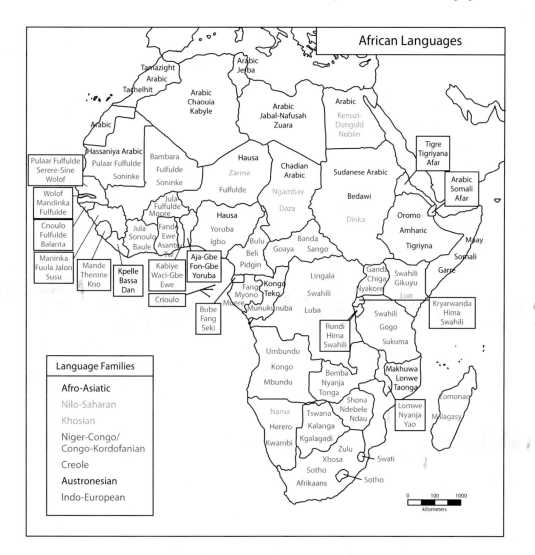

MAP 1: Examples of African Languages

will go a long way in determining whether they are dialects of the same language or distinct languages.

The use of mutual intelligibility in this way is more scientific because it presents a pure descriptive linguistic perspective on the language situation of any community without any extra-linguistic biases. However, extra-linguistics (and therefore nonscientific) factors such as historical issues, struggle for nationalism, national boundaries, prestige of the speakers, and other sociopolitical concerns can affect the definition of language vis-à-vis dialect. For instance, speech forms that can be linguistically considered as dialects of the same language are considered distinct languages due to the nationality concerns of their speakers as is the case with Swedish, Danish, and Dutch in Europe. These speech forms are largely mutually intelligible; however, because they are the official languages of three different countries, they must therefore be considered distinct languages. The same linguistic situation exists among Sotho, Swazi, and Tswana in southern Africa. Sometimes the speech forms that are mutually intelligible are spoken within the same country or regions of a country, but the speakers consider themselves ethnically and linguistically different as is the case among speakers of Ibibio and Oro, and speakers of Annang and Ekit, four languages found in Nigeria's Akwa Ibom State. A similar linguistic situation is found among the speakers of Pima and the Papago here in the United States.

On the other side of the coin are those speech forms that are mutually unintelligible but are considered to be dialects of the same language as is the case with Mandarin and Cantonese spoken in the northern and southern regions of China respectively. Another example is the case of the speech forms or dialects within the Yoruba dialect continuum in West Africa. As Bloomfield (revised 1958:51) noted in his discussion of such a geographical area of gradual transition (such as Yoruba land) known as **dialect continuum or dialect area**, "The difference from place to place is small, but, as one travels in any one direction, the differences accumulate, until speakers, say from opposite ends … cannot understand each other." Many of the Yoruba speech forms across West Africa are not mutually intelligible, but because of their sociocultural and historical links and the existence of a written standard, these speech forms are considered dialects of the Yoruba language and not separate languages. In technical linguistics terms, the variation of language over geographical space (or **dialect**) is not the only way language varies. Others variations include **idiolects,** which are language variations of the individual speaker; **sociolects,** which are language variations of a particular social group, or in some cases gender or racial groups; and **jargons,** which are language variations used by a specific profession or vocation.

A second reason for the variation in the number of languages is found in the differences in the way that dialectologists interpret the concept of mutual intelligibility. In using the scale of mutual intelligibility, these fieldworkers consider language variation differently. Some split speech forms into distinct languages based on limited differences, while others lump speech forms together as languages unless a significantly high level of differences is noted. The phenomena of language endangerment and language extinction or death are the last reasons for the variation in the number of languages on the African continent. Two major factors can cause language endangerment and language death. These include the death of the language's native speakers and/or the process of language shift. Language shift is a linguistic situation where the native speakers of a less prestigious or less dominant language abandon their language in favor of a more prestigious and dominant language for various reasons. These reasons may include lack of economic opportunities in their native language, government regulations, fear of scorn, lack of formal instruction in their native language, and even lack of other natives to speak the language with. Languages pass through different stages on the route to extinction. A language is said to be safe if it is growing in use and additive in that it is creating and integrating new words and concepts. A safe language also possesses young native speakers. Conversely, a language is said to be endangered if it is no longer inherited, learned, and spoken by the children and younger

Table 1: An inventory of the foreign languages spoken in Africa

Foreign language	"Newer" African identity	Location spoken
English	Anglophone	Mostly Eastern and Southern Africa, with the exception of Angola and Mozambique
French	Francophone	Mostly Central Africa and parts of West and North Africa, with the exception of countries such as Ghana, Nigeria, Sierra Leone, and Liberia
Portuguese	Lusophone	Angola, Mozambique, Cape Verde
Arabic	Arabic/Afro-Arab	Most of North Africa, including Sudan and Egypt
Spanish	Hispanophone	Equatorial Guinea, Western Sahara

generation who are native to that speech community. A language is said to be moribund if only a handful of elderly members of the speech community can speak it; a language is extinct when there are no living native speakers.

Interestingly, globalization associated with international languages such as English and French also contribute to language endangerment and death on the continent as the people commonly abandon their native languages in favor of these sociopolitically prestigious and economically promising languages. Though linguists have over the years sounded a note of warning that once a language is lost, the culture, the history, the knowledge, and the worldview of the speakers of that language are also lost, Africans are increasing the challenges facing indigenous languages. Africans are adding a fresh layer to their sociolinguistic identity. For example, due to colonialism and the established linguistic ties to the colonial nations, Africans identify themselves as Anglophone, Francophone, and so on, in addition to their ethnic, national, and regional identities.

Thanks to the focus on these foreign languages in the educational system (established in the colonial era), Africans are increasingly highly proficient in these languages and, conversely, make significant efforts to downgrade the focus on their indigenous languages. An inventory of the foreign languages spoken on the continent of Africa together with the new sociolinguistic identity created by each and the locations where they are spoken is presented in table 1.

These foreign languages are convenient options for official languages in the multilingual African setting. The multilingual situation on the continent has further supported their presumed indispensability. In addition, colonialism and contact with foreigners has brought about other hybrid languages such as pidgins, creoles, or foreign languages spoken by settlers in Africa. Examples of such languages include Krio, West African Pidgin, Afrikaans, German, Dutch, etc. The next section will discuss the African multilingual situation in more detail. But first, map 2 below illustrates the spread of the colonial languages on the African continent.

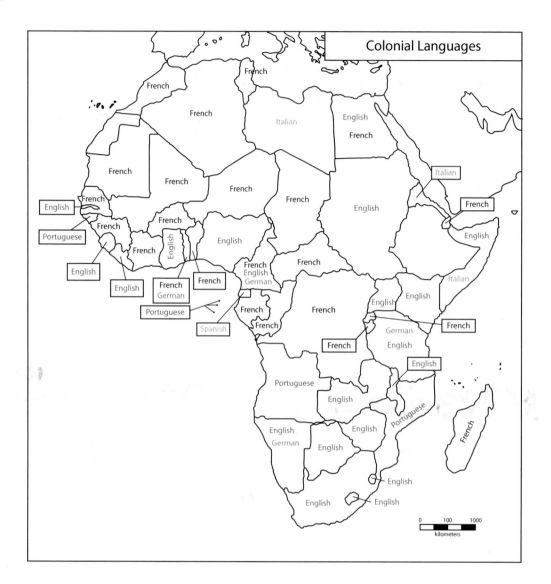

Map 2: Spread of colonial languages in Africa

Multilingual Africa: Key Definitions and Concepts

The importance of language to the overall socioethnic identity and national development of a people cannot be overstated. It is therefore imperative to clarify some of the technical terms associated with the prevalence of multilingualism and other issues relating to language in Africa in this section. The extraordinarily pluralistic number of languages spoken on the continent has resulted in a situation where the majority of Africans and other residents of the continent are multilingual. In addition to the existence of a large number of languages on the continent, there are many other reasons why Africans are multilingual. These include the following.

(1) Trade: Africans are forced to learn many languages because two or more languages are often required for a functioning trading environment particularly when that environment includes the urban areas of Africa as well as the different regions of the continent where international trading occurs.

(2) Colonialism: The colonial experiences and history are captured in the linguistic classifications that illustrate Africa's linguistic ties to colonial rulers. These foreign languages appear as linguistic solutions within the multiethnic and multilingual African societies, thus adding a new layer to the sociocultural identity of most Africans as noted earlier. Most Africans identify themselves either as Anglophone, Francophone, Hispanophone, or Lusophone.

(3) Western education: A by-product of colonialism is Western education, which brings the radical process of assimilation of educated Africans into Western cultural values as a result of the imperative need for them to add the European languages to their repertoire.

(4) Intercultural communication: The existence of multiple ethnic groups with their distinct languages in many African countries and regions make it imperative for Africans to learn, speak, and understand the languages of the other groups in order to foster harmonious coexistence.

(5) Travel and migration: These arise not only from voluntary migration but also from forced migration caused by crises situations arising from both interethnic and intra-ethnic wars. Voluntary migration is not uncommon on the continent.

In essence, multilingualism tends to become simply a function of life in most African societies. In order to develop a viable network of contacts in the larger society, an average African would need to speak the "mother tongue," the "national language," and maybe the "official language," and any other speech forms for which he may have a need in order to ensure a rewarding interaction with others in the larger multilingual society. It is very rare for one language to serve all these roles, because in most cases different languages serve specific communication needs arising in different situations in society. Suffice it at this point for us to define some of the linguistic terms relating to multilingualism and language in Africa. These terms include the following:

a. **Lingua Franca**: This is the language of communication between speakers of mutually unintelligible languages. It is essentially, the language of intercultural communication and trade.

b. **Mother Tongue**: This is the first language acquired by a child at home (the home language). It is also referred to as the native language. This is in contrast with the **ethnic language,** the language of ethnic identity, often the patrimonial language.

c. **Pidgins and Creoles**: A pidgin is a language that evolves out of contact (such as in trade situations) between speakers of two or more mutually unintelligible languages. Pidgin is said to be creolized (become a creole language) through continuous contact, which leads to the development of the speech form and to the acquisition of the pidgin by children speaking it as if it were their native language. Pidgin languages have simple grammatical structures and very limited lexicons, and usually they do not have any native speakers. No children have acquired a pidgin language as their first language or mother tongue. Creole languages, on the other hand, have more complex grammatical structures coupled with a more expanded lexicon, and children acquire it natively as their mother tongue (Bergmann et al., 2007).

d. **National and Official Language**: A language with the widest distribution and the highest number of speakers is said to be the national language, whereas a language that is legislated (mandated by law) for official government business and other administrative purposes is said to be the official language. The official language can be **endoglossic,** in which case an indigenous language is chosen. It can be **exoglossic,** in which case a nonindigenous language is chosen. An official language could be **sole,** in which case only one official language is legally recognized; or it could be **joint,** in which case more than one official language is legally recognized. In Africa, European languages commonly serve as official languages. For example, French serves as the official language of about nineteen countries in Africa; English serves as the official language of about seventeen countries; Portuguese serves as the official language of five countries; Arabic and Spanish serve as official languages of four and two African countries respectively. Only eight African countries have indigenous African languages as their official languages.

e. **Language Planning:** Language planning is government-authorized, long-term, sustained, activity and conscious efforts are made to alter a language's function and form in a society for the purpose of solving communication problems (Weinstein, 1980). There are two major components or a set of activities involved in the process of language planning; both are predominant in the ever-changing language planning processes in most African countries. These include status planning and corpus planning. Status planning has to do with changing the role and function of a particular language in a speech community, and this has a concomitant result in the change in the level of prestige and rights of the speakers of that language. Corpus planning, on the other hand, has to do with the formal or structural development of the language with regard to the development of orthography for the language, writing of primers and grammar books, etc., all leading the process of standardization of the language.

f. **Language of Wider Communication (LWC)**: A language of wider communication is the one spoken by the majority of the speakers in a country and possibly across national borders (Bamgbose, 1991). For example, Hausa, Igbo, and Yoruba can be said to be languages of wider communication in Nigeria. Also the languages of globalization such as English and French are examples of languages of wider communication in most African countries.

g. **Language of Narrower Communication (LNC):** Conversely, a language of narrower communication is one spoken by only a few speakers in a country (Bamgbose, 1991). Most African languages can be described as languages of narrower communication even within their homeland.

Classification of African languages

In this section, we discuss the classification of the multitude of languages spoken in Africa. The classification of African languages into language families is based on the pioneering fieldwork of Joseph H. Greenberg (1915–2000) in the 1950s. His book *Languages of Africa*, published in 1963, became the springboard for historical linguistics studies in Africa. Greenberg was born in Brooklyn, New York, in 1915. He became a classical pianist by age fourteen and taught himself Hebrew, Arabic, Greek, and Latin, along with the German and Yiddish spoken in his home. He was an anthropologist and World War II army veteran with duties in North Africa and Italy; he also taught at Stanford University from 1962 until his death in 2001. Greenberg (1963) used the "mass comparison of languages and words" to classify African languages because of the dearth of historical records on those languages. Mass comparison of words and sounds is a version of the comparative method that does not reconstruct the protoforms of related languages. Instead of recreating proto-languages to affirm genetic relationships between genetically related languages, he created his African linguistic family trees based on shared resemblances. Through this method, he arrived at the classification by comparing massive numbers of words and sounds of several African languages. Other scholars such as Lionel Bendor, Edgar Gregersen, Kay Williamson, Christopher Ehret, Ben Elugbe, among others, have improved on his classification, but his work was the foundation for African historical linguistics and African language classification.

Based on Greenberg's pioneering work and current consensus within the field of African historical linguistics, African languages can be classified or grouped into four major language phyla. A phylum or phyla consists of languages with a shared ancestor. The ancestor is the often reconstructed proto-language/form which is a hypothetical linguistics form arrived at by the historical linguist through the process of comparative reconstruction. Below is a discussion of the four language families, including the estimated number of languages in each, some of the language family's significant features, and examples of languages in each family (See Heine and Nurse, 2000 *and* Vic Webb and Kembo Sure, 2004):

Phylum One: Niger-Congo or Niger Kordofania

This language phylum has about 1,436 languages. It is the largest language phylum in the world with it members having the largest number of speakers in Africa. Members of this phylum are the most widespread throughout the continent, having about 360 to 400 million speakers. One of the most popular subgroup of languages in this phylum is the Benue Congo subgroup because of the Bantoid/Bantu languages that are widespread across Eastern and Southern Africa. Such Bantu languages include Swahili, Zulu, Ndebele, Xhosa, and Tiv (Tiv is spoken in Nigeria, West Africa). One basic feature of the Niger-Congo languages is the well-developed noun class systems. Most members of this phylum have this feature, with the exception of Mande, Ijo, and the Western Kwa languages such as Yoruba. Another basic feature of languages in this phylum is that they are highly tonal, attesting both lexically and grammatically contrastive tones, with the exception of Swahili and Fulani, which are non-tonal. Another important feature of these languages is the presence of clicks, especially in southern Bantu languages such as Zulu and Xhosa. Finally, most members of this language phylum have subject-verb-object (SVO) surface word order structures, with the exception of Ojo, Mande, and Gur. Examples of languages in this phylum include Akan, Akoko, Bembe, Bemba, Comorian, Dagaari, Duala, Edo, Ewondo, Fang, Fon-Gbe, Fulfulde/Fula, Gogo, Gurma, Herero, Ibibio, Igbo, Ijo, Jen-Bikwin, Kamba, Kikong, Kikuyu, Kinyarwanda, Kirundi, Lega, Lingala, Lozi, Luba, Luhiya, Moore, Nkore-Kiga, Nupe, Nyanja-ChiChewa, Oko, Shona, Soninke, Sotho (Southern and Northern), Sukuma, Swahili, Teke, Tonga, Tswana, Ukaan, Vai, Wolof, Xhosa, Yoruba and Zulu.

Phylum Two: Afro-Asiatic

This language phylum has about 300 to 500 members. It is the least controversial language phylum and the only one with members from outside the continent (e.g., Arabic). Languages in this phylum can be found all over North Africa, Central and West Africa including Chad Republic, Cameroon, Niger, Nigeria, Central African Republic, and South Africa. Phylum Afro-Asiatic has six major subgroups of language namely Chadic, Berber, Egyptian, Semitic, Cushitic, and Omotic. The basic linguistic features of most members of this phylum include the fact that they are nontonal languages with two or more pitch levels, they mark grammatical gender, they have varying surface word order (SVO, VSO, SOV), and most members have pharyngeal and uvular sounds. Examples of languages in this phylum include Amharic, Arabic, Basketo, Berber, Gurage, Hausa, Kefa, Masa, Nefusi, Oromo, Siwi, Somali, Taureg, Tigré, Tigrinya, Wolaytta and Zenaga.

Phylum Three: Khoisan (Khoesan)

This language phylum has about 25 to 35 languages. This is one of the least studied groups and is not necessarily an accepted linguistic-genetic group. The languages in this family are dominantly found in South Africa (Mbuti, Khoi, Sans) and Tanzania (Sandawe, Hatsa). The basic linguistic features of languages in this phylum include the fact that most of them are tonal languages with preferences for contour tone patterns. They also mark grammatical gender, and most of them have at least three types of clicks as clicks can form roots of words in these languages. It is believed that these languages were the original sources of clicks. Examples of languages in phylum Khoisan include Hadza/Hatsa, Hua (East), Khoekhoe, !Kung, Kwadi, Kwi, Nama, Sandawe, Tuu, !Ui-Taa, and !Xóo.

Phylum Four: Nilo-Saharan

The Nilo-Saharan phylum has about 190 to 250 members and is said to be the most controversial language family on the continent because some scholars consider it a collection of unrelated languages. Languages in this phylum are spoken in countries such as Sudan, Republic of Congo, Ethiopia, Uganda, Tanzania, and West Africa (for example Songay spoken in the Old Songhai Empire). The basic linguistic features of members of this phylum include four types of word order attested by languages in this group. These include (a) SVO; (b) partly SVO and partly SOV (this is the dominant or primary word order); (c) VSO and (d) SOV (this scarcely serves as the dominant word order). These languages are also known for their central vowels, a feature that is not common among other African languages. Examples of Nilo-Saharan languages include Berta, Daza, Dinka, Foran, Gumuz, Kado/Kadugli, Kenuzi-Dangoid, Koman, Kuliak, Kunama, Maban, Ngambay, Nobiin, Songai, and Zarma.

Others

The only African language (a language spoken indigenously on the African continent) not classified into any of the four families is Malagasy or Malgache, spoken on the island of Madagascar. It belongs to the **Austronesian or Malayo-Polynesian** language family, which includes 1,200 to 1,500 languages. In addition, some languages on the African continent have remained unclassified. Unclassified languages are languages whose genetic affiliation has not been established due to the lack of reliable data. Languages that do not get linked with genetically related languages over a long period of time are termed language isolates. Languages can remain unclassified for a variety of reasons including absence of data and paucity of data. Examples of such languages on the African continent include Weyto, Ongota and Shabo spoken in Ethiopia; Bete, Lufu, Atta Luo, Jalaa and Bauchi Mawa spoken in Nigeria; Bung spoken in Cameroon; Kujarge and Laal spoken in Chad Republic; Mpre spoken in Ghana and Oropom spoken in Uganda.

A Different Classification

A possible alternative to the foregoing genetic classification of African languages can be found in Mazrui and Mazrui (1998). This work used sociopolitical considerations or factors to classify African languages. According to this work, in spite of the astronomical number of languages in Africa the continent has made a successful transition from oral tradition to written words. Africa is credited for inventing the human language; Asia is credited for making it sacred (the cradle of institutionalized religion gave language a sacred imprint), and Europe is credited for universalizing the human language (international capitalism contributed to globalization of language). The classification is therefore based on the African triple heritage notion. African triple heritage includes the European influences such as Christianity and Western cultural practices, African influences such as traditional religion and indigenous cultural practices, and Arabic influences

Table 2: An inventory of near monolingual nations in Africa

Country	Language	Population % that are primary speakers	Official language(s) and examples of other languages
Botswana	Setswana	90%	- Setswana and English - Birwa, Herero, Ndebele, Afrikaans
Burundi	Kirundi	95%	- Kirundi and French - Swahili and Kinyarwanda
Lesotho	Sotho	99%	- Sesotho and English - Xhosa and Zulu
Madagascar	Malagasy	98%	- Malagasy and French - Maore and Comorian
Mauritius	Morisyen (Creole)	94%	- English and French - Bhojpuri, Tamil and Urdu
Rwanda	Kinyarwanda	98%	- Kinyarwanda and French - English, Swahili, Rundi and Hema
Seychelles	Seselwa Creole French	95%	- English and French Creole - English and French
Somalia	Somali	98%	- Somali and Arabic - Arabic, Swahili, English, Boni, Boon, Dabarre, Garre, Jiiddu, Maay, Mushungulu, Oromo, Tunni
Swaziland	SiSwati	91%	- SiSwati and English - Tsonga, Zulu and Afrikaans

(Sources: Bamgbose, 1991; Ethnologue.com; and Webb and Kembo-Sure, 2004).

such as Islam and Eastern cultural practices. It is the interplay of these traditions with Africa's history that brings about a sociocultural typology presented in that work.

These categorizations include the following.

Afro-ethnic Languages

This typological group has about 800 to 2,000 languages whose native speakers are predominantly Africans. These languages have been shaped only minimally, if at all, by either the Arab-Islamic or Euro-Christian impact. The least documented languages on the continent belong to this group. They are mostly rural in nature and are subnational and geographically limited to specific regions within nation-state boundaries. Some still function as lingua franca or national languages, though they were marginalized during colonialism. Examples include Kalabari, Yoruba, Pokot, Luganda, Zulu, Ethiopian languages, Berber, Amharic, etc. In analogy with the

Table 3a: African and Non-African languages serving as official languages in Africa

Major African Languages	8
French	19
English	17
Portuguese	5
Arabic	4
Spanish	1

Table 3b: African and Non-African languages serving as sole official languages:

Languages	No. of Countries	Countries
Major African languages	2	Somalia and Ethiopia
English	13	Gambia, Sierra Leone, Liberia, Ghana, Nigeria, Uganda, Kenya, Malawi, Zambia, Zimbabwe, Swaziland, Mauritius and Seychelles
French	13	Guinea Republic, Senegal, Mali, Niger, Chad, Burkina Faso, Ivory Coast, Togo, Benin, Central African Republic, Congo, Gabon and Zaire
Portuguese	5	Guinea Bissau, Sao Tome and Principe, Cape Verde, Angola and Mozambique
Spanish	1	Equatorial Guinea
Arabic	2	Mauritania and Sudan

Table 3c: African and Non-African languages serving as joint official languages

Languages	No. of Countries	Countries
French and Arabic	2	Djibouti and Comoros
English and major African language	3	Tanzania (Swahili), Lesotho (Sotho), Botswana (Setswana)
French and major African language	3	Burundi (Kirundi), Rwanda (Kinyarwanda), Madagascar (Malagasy)
French and English	1	Cameroon

historical linguistics classification, these would be considered indigenous African languages predominantly within the Niger-Congo and the Khoisan language families.

Afro-Islamic Languages

These are languages native to Africa in terms of the ethnic origins of the speakers but influenced by Islam due to the Islamic identity of the native speakers and the sustained contact with the Arab-Islamic world over the centuries. These cultures have been infused with the Islamic ethos and traditions, many of which are reflected in the language. The most prominent language that has exerted tremendous influence on African languages is Arabic. The speakers of these languages constitute a third of Muslims in Africa, and they tend to be urban. Examples include Swahili, Somali, Nubi, Hausa, Fulfude, Mandinka, etc. In analogy with the genetic classification, these would be considered the Islamic languages predominantly within the Afro-Asiatic and Nilo-Saharan families with the dominant denominator being the influence of Islam and Arabic.

Western and Afro-Western Languages

Western languages are languages whose native speakers are located predominantly in Europe and the Americas. Their presence in Africa is linked directly to the transatlantic slave trade and colonial experiences. These languages are spoken as additional languages throughout Africa and this has, over time, weakened the indigenous languages. They have the widest geographical spread in terms of use and are the most successful lingua franca for interethnic communication, presumably helping to solve the problem associated with multilingualism on the continent. Examples of these languages include English, French, Portuguese, Italian, Spanish, and German. Afro-Western languages on the other hand are predominantly emergent languages from contact between African and a subset of Western languages. These are essentially pidgin and creole languages spoken on the African continent.

Language, Ethnic Identity, and Multilingualism in Africa

Language is one of the components of a people's sociocultural identity. The other components may include religion, gender, locality, and other cultural aggregates. More importantly, language plays a critical role in the formation and maintenance of both individual and community or national cultural, social, and ethnic identity. In this section we discuss some of the topical issues relating to language and individual as well as national identity in Africa. Language acts as a vital sociocultural marker in many African societies such that there are variations depending on age, gender, vocation, social status, education level, economic class, social bond or intimacy, and so on. Ethnic identity in Africa is often "linguistically marked" though language is not exclusively responsible in establishing and maintaining such ethnic identity.

There are three possible positions on the role of language in establishing and maintaining ethnic identity in Africa. The first position is that language is crucial to ethnic identity. This position holds that while language may be only one of the factors that determine ethnic identity, it is the most powerful factor in maintaining it. For example, some Africans, especially from large majority groups, equate their ethnic identity with their linguistic identity so that a Yoruba person equals a Yoruba speaker, or an Igbo person is the same as an Igbo speaker, etc. The second position holds that language is important but in conjunction with other factors: The role of language as one of the features of ethnic identity is crucial but not to the exclusion of other features such as lifestyle, vocation, social class, etc. The third position holds that language plays a variable role. According to this view, the role of language in establishing and maintaining ethnic identity varies according to the social, cultural, and political status of the particular ethnic group depending on whether their language is regarded as a minority or a majority language.

As already noted, most Africans are multilingual, using two or more languages for various reasons. Some of the results of multilingualism include code mixing, code switching, borrowing, Diglossia, language choice and use, among others. Multilingualism can be both societal and individual as most African nation-states are multilingual. Some examples of African countries with a high number of languages are Nigeria with about 350 to 505 languages, Tanzania with about 135 languages, Kenya with about 46 languages, and South Africa with about 31 languages. However, there are counties in Africa that can be said to be highly monolingual where 70 to 90 percent of the population speaks the same language as either a first or second language. Examples of such languages are presented in table 2 below.

Even before contact with any Europeans or Arabs, certain African languages served as lingua franca in the multilingual regions of the continent. Examples of African languages that served as lingua franca before contact with the Europeans include Amharic in Ethiopia, Songay and Hausa in West Africa, and Sango and Ewondo in Central Africa. During the colonial period, Arabic, English, French, Portuguese, and Dutch became the lingua franca. This had enormous consequences such as language shift, loss of linguistic identity, and language death that are widespread throughout the continent. The Post-contact lingua franca languages are mostly hybrid languages such as pidgins and creoles formed either from combining two or more African languages or from a blend of African languages with the contact languages. Examples of the post-contact lingua franca in Africa that are hybrids of two or more African languages include Barikanci, which is a hybrid of Hausa and other Chadic and Afro-asiatic languages, Ewondo Populaire, a combination of Ewondo and other Cameroonian languages, Zambian Pidgins which is a Bantu-based pidgin spoken in the Copper belt region of Zambia. Examples of the post-contact lingua franca that are hybrids of the colonial or contact languages with the native African languages include Sierra Leone Krio, which is a hybrid of English and Sierra Leonean languages; Petit-Negre, which is a combination of French and West African languages; Tekrur, which is a mixture of Arabic and Chadic languages spoken around Lake Chad in Nigeria and the Niger Republic; Nigerian Pidgin English, which is a mixture of English and Nigerian languages.

In the multilingual setting of Africa, there is generally a need for an official language. The multiplicity of languages and the challenges they have over language use in education and other official matters demand the selection of one or more official languages. However, there are five factors that must be considered in the selection of an official language (Bamgbose, 1991). These include the following. (1) **Nationalism versus Nationism**: This deals with the question of whether the choice will serve the general national interest of the country or whether the choice will highlight the importance of some ethnic groups within the country. (2) **Vertical Integration**: This focuses on the ability of the chosen language or language variety to bring about integration among all the social strata in the society. For example, it is concerned with whether the educated and the noneducated members of the society feel the same way about using the chosen variety. (3) **Population**: This is in reference to the number of speakers already using the language. Some choices will focus on the language(s) with a lot of speakers whereas others will focus on the languages with a small number of speakers. (4) **Acceptability**: Acceptability depends on the other factors already mentioned. It has to do with how well the selected language will be tolerated by citizens in the country. (5) **Language Development Status**: This relates to the level of development and status of the chosen variety in the country.

As we stated earlier, one language may be chosen as the official language because it best accommodates dealing with particular "official" situations. Another language may be more suitable for another situation. The need to accommodate different situations may lead to their being joint official languages in one country rather than a sole official language. Tables 3a–c present an overview of the possible types of official languages. Table 3a shows the African and non-African languages serving as official languages. Table 3b shows the distribution and locations of African and non-African languages serving as sole official languages. And finally, table 3c shows the distribution and locations of African and non-African languages serving as joint official languages:

Language Planning in Africa: Terminology and Methodology

In this section we turn our attention to the very important issue of language planning in the multilingual African environment. The discussion here benefits from the definitive work done in Bamgbose (2000). As noted earlier in the chapter, language planning involves two major activities namely the status planning and the corpus planning. The major challenge for the multilingual African continent is language standardization, which is a by-product of both status planning and corpus planning. The goal of standardization is turning a linguistic variety (a dialect, a sociolect, and so on) into a standard language. This goal can be achieved through two related methods. One method is by creating an aggregate norm for generalized and normative usage in domains such as literature, science, higher education, the mass media, churches, and the public sector. The other method is by regularizing and codifying the system of reference through a standard orthography, standard reference grammars, and standard dictionaries.

Status planning is the social or the external planning of the language achievable through specifying the social functions or roles of language within a country. A language may be chosen to serve as the official language, the language for education and other cultural purposes, the language of the mass media, the language of religion, etc. In most African countries the language choice is supported by legislation enshrined in the constitution and or in the National Policy on Language in Education.

The two kinds of language policies in most African countries are the **unstated language policy** and the **stated language policy.** The unstated language policy is based on existing norms of practice and usage whereas the stated language policy entails the presence of a policy document. Such documents vary with respect to the contents and application. The variation range from vague statements with no clear plan of compliance to very grand and idea-laden statements that pose enormous challenges to implementation.

A major element of language planning in Africa is the role of language in education. This has been a challenge since the introduction of colonial education, which was geared toward reading and writing. The chief purpose of literacy was Bible reading and translation, translation of classic religious works, and service in the colonial labor system. Though the purpose of literacy has expanded to include African creativity, particularly in Anglophone Africa, a significant effort at cultural catch-up was still needed in some parts of the continent, particularly in the Francophone areas. At independence, education reform was high on the plans of most African governments. This was motivated by the need to increase access to formal education and the adaptation of formal education to national realities, including the desires to "domesticate" the inherited colonial educational system and to promote indigenous languages.

These reforms proceeded in four stages as follows: (1) Sensitization: This involved getting the Africans to accept the fact that their mother tongue should be developed for educational purposes. (2) Corpus Development: This involved practical work on the development of orthographies and school manuals (in Francophone Africa) and the reform of orthographies and encouragement of creative writing and pedagogic writing in the mother tongue (in Anglophone Africa). (3) Bold Effort: This involved making bold policy initiatives by deciding on national languages and providing for their full development for use in basic education and literacy as in Tanzania, Ethiopia, Somalia, Madagascar, and Guinea. Examples of such policy initiative are the six-year primary project in Nigeria and the six national languages policy in Guinea. (4) Stalling: This refers to the point at which African leaders appear to be afraid to implement the language policies they have formulated. The implementation of language policies in most African countries is stalled for various reasons. These include the fear of the psycho-pedagogical inappropriateness of the mother tongue in education, fear of the challenges to national unity, and the fear of the purported damaging effects of the mother-tongue education on achieving fluency in English/French for higher education.

These fears should not pose any serious impediments to the implementation of the language policies. But, unfortunately, the bold initiatives, even the successful ones, have not gone beyond the experimental phases. Another setback to the implementation is the "big man syndrome" in language planning: A situation where a charismatic leader might push for a regional or a national language in multilingual countries but the effort is stalled upon their departure from office. The prevailing pattern of policy on language in education across the continent is as follows: (1) The mother tongue is used as the language of education in the early years of primary education, as well as in adult and nonformal literacy programs, but it is taught as a subject at higher levels of education. This is the situation in most of the English speaking countries like Nigeria. (2) The mother tongue is the language of the basic cycle of education as in Tanzania, Madagascar, Burundi, Rwanda, Somalia, and Ethiopia. (3) The mother tongue is taught as a subject of learning but is not a language of formal instruction as in most of the French- and Portuguese-speaking countries. (4) The colonial language serves as the language of higher education as is the case in virtually all African countries.

The second aspect of language planning is corpus planning. This often involves activities intended to result in standardization of the chosen variety. Corpus planning is often geared toward developing the norms of spellings and grammar and expansion of the lexicon and other linguistics modification. There are six aspects of corpus planning, namely determination, codification, elaboration, implementation, cultivation, and harmonization. Determination involves the choice of a norm or a code to serve as a standard frame of reference for any chosen variety or language. Codification entails the provision of a writing system and a standard orthography for the chosen variety or language. The process of elaboration has to do with attempts to expand the vocabulary and the grammar and to strengthen the code and increase the range of usage of the chosen variety or language. Metalanguage workshops and conferences may be hosted to convene experts to brainstorm the formulation of scientific terminologies, writing of reference grammars and dictionaries. The process of implementation is the promotion of acceptance of the chosen variety of language in the speech community. The process of cultivation involves monitoring the corpus planning activities to enhance of the chosen variety. This may be done by language association, the mass media, sociolinguists, language policy makers and educators. And lastly harmonization involves unifying all the variations in the chosen variety or language and may be in the form of a national harmonization, an international harmonization, or a cross-language harmonization.

Conclusion

It is a daunting task to provide an all-encompassing introduction to language and its many impacts and processes on the African continent in a single chapter. What we have attempted to do in this chapter is to provide a succinct introduction to some of the critical aspects of language in the society and a few language processes. We have considered the number of languages spoken on the continent and reasons for the variation in the numbers. We have also provided introductory discussions on issues of multilingualism and language planning on the African continent, among other topics. Our attempt here at answering a few topical questions often asked about language in Africa should not be seen as an exhaustive discussion of all the roles played by language, all the impacts of language on the different African societies, or all the individual and communal language-related processes that occur on the continent.

Review Questions

1. Multilingualism is prevalent on the African continent with almost all Africans speaking more than one language. What are the factors responsible for the prevalence of multilingualism in Africa?

2. What are the three transformations that happen to a pidgin language before it becomes a creole?

3. Discuss the classification of African languages as discussed in the chapter based on the work of Greenberg. Can you attempt to research and provide the classification of one African language?

4. What are the four persistent patterns of language in education policy on the African continent?

5. Discuss the overview of official languages found on the African continent. In your discussion, define "official language" and list the five factors that affect the choice of an official language.

6. What are two important facts about the largest African language phylum?

7. What are two of the three possible positions regarding language and identity in Africa?

8. Would you consider Mazrui & Mazrui's (1998) categorization of African languages socio-cultural or sociopolitical? Discuss the basis and contents of this categorization, including possible harmonization with the historical linguistic classification based on Greenberg's work.

9. A significant aspect of language planning is status planning. Discuss the process of status planning on the African continent, including existing language policies and the efforts at reform.

Bibliography

Bamgbose, Ayo. 2000. *Language and Exclusion: The Consequences of Language Policies in Africa.* Hamburg: LIT.

Bamgbose, Ayo. 1991. *Language and the Nation: The Language Question in Sub-Saharan Africa.* Edinburgh: University Press.

Batibo, Herman M. 2005. *Language Decline and Death in Africa: Causes, Consequences and Challenges*, 62–86. Clevedon, UK: Multilingual Matters.

Bergmann, A., K. Hall, and S. Ross. 2007. Language Files: Material for an Introduction to Language and Linguistics. Ohio: Ohio University Press.

Bloomfield, Leonard. 1935. *Language.* London: George Allen & Unwin.

Campbell, Lyle, and William J. Poser. 2008. *Language Classification: History and Method.* Cambridge: Cambridge University Press.

Childs, G. Tucker. 2003. *An Introduction to African Languages.* Amsterdam: John Benjamins.

Cooper, Robert Leon. 1989. *Language Planning and Social Change.* Cambridge: Cambridge University Press.

Crystal, David. 1997. *The Cambridge Encyclopedia of Language.* Cambridge: Cambridge University Press.

Fardon, Richard, and Graham Furniss, eds. 1994. *African Languages, Development and the State.* New York: Routledge.

Greenberg, Joseph. 1948. "The Classification of African Languages." In *American Anthropologist Journal.* No 1, Part 1.

Greenberg, Joseph H. 1963. The Languages of Africa. The Hague: Mouton; JAL 29.1 Publication 25 of the Indiana University Research Center in Anthropology, Folklore, and Linguistics. Bloomington: Indiana University Press.

Heine, Bernd, and Derek Nurse, eds. 2000. *African Languages: An Introduction.* Cambridge: Cambridge University Press.

Herbert, Robert K. 1992. *Language and Society in Africa: The Theory and Practice of Sociolinguistics.* Johannesburg: Witwatersrand University Press.

Lewis, M. Paul, ed.. 2009. Ethnologue: Languages of the World. Retrieved from www.ethnologue.com.

Mazrui, Ali A., and Alamin M. Mazrui. 1998. *The Power of Babel: Language & Governance in the African Experience.* Binghamton University, Binghamton, NY: IGCS Publications.

Moshi, Lioba, and Akinloye Ojo, eds. 2009. *Language Pedagogy and Language Use in Africa.* London, UK: Adonis & Abbey Publishers.

Ong, Walter J. 1982. *Orality and Literacy: The Technologizing of the Word.* New York: Routledge.

Simpson, Andrew. 2008. *Language and National Identity in Africa.* Oxford: Oxford University Press.

Webb, Vic, and Kembo Sure, eds. 2004. *African Languages: An Introduction to the Languages and Linguistics of Africa.* Cape Town: Oxford University Press.

Weinstein, Brian. 1980. "Language Planning in Francophone Africa." *Language Problems and Language Planning.* 4.1:55–77.

Wolff, H. Ekkehard. 2000. Language and Society. in Heine, Bernd and Derek Nurse, eds. African Languages: An Introduction. Cambridge: Cambridge Univ. Press. 298–347.

Chapter Five

Religions In Africa

By Ibigbolade S. Aderibigbe

Introduction

The triple heritage of Africa is vividly captured in the continent's three main religious traditions. This heritage, though contemporarily more dynamically evidenced, has a long history and influence that can be traced back to the very beginning of the emergence of African peoples in the case of African traditional religion, the very first century AD, and maybe beyond, in the case of Christianity, and the seventh century in the case of Islam. The central place of religion that becomes so evident in coming to any meaningful understanding of African life in all its ramifications—social, economic, and political—gives credence to Mbiti's statement that African people are "notoriously religious" (Mbiti, J.S. 1969:1). Consequently, Africans have evolved and sustained religiously conscious communities, either devotees of the traditional religion or as followers of the two "converting religions" (Christianity and Islam).

Africa is a massive continent with diverse religious traditions, to the extent that within the same tradition there have been variations. It would be an impossible task to cover in this chapter the totality of all religious traditions in Africa. Consequently, the effort here can only be an exploration of the three principal religious traditions on the continent, namely: African indigenous religious beliefs and practices, which African scholarship has "christened" African Traditional Religion(s) (Idowu, B. 1971:3), Christianity, and Islam. The focus, therefore, is on the African experience(s) of the religious traditions within the contexts of their origins, beliefs, doctrines and practices as worldviews permeating and influencing various aspects of the African people's life.

In exploring the worldviews of the three religions in Africa, it is imperative to indicate certain initial operating parameters that may affect the discourses. First, African traditional religion has no sacred scriptures or clearly defined documents. Indeed, serious studies in the religion have only recently developed (Moyo, A. 2007:319). Even then, the studies have been largely carried out by sociologists, anthropologists, and theologians, who are "outsiders" to the religion either as "non-Africans" or Africans who are Christians, and most times have very limited knowledge of the experiences of the actual devotees of the religion. Consequently, the "authentic" source of information about the religion is embedded in oral traditions found in myths, rituals, folktales, proverbs, etc., and non-oral sources, such as archaeological findings, African arts of paintings, sculptures, music, and dance.

The studies of the Christian and Islamic traditions pose no difficulties with regard to sources of information. Both religions have sacred books. In addition, the founders, geographical origins, and organizational structures are well articulated and remain largely the same for the adherents, regardless of the different interpretations. However, both Christianity and Islam are regarded as "foreign" to the African continent and it peoples. For example, Christianity's advent into Africa in the first century, majorly in North Africa, was cut short by the advent of Islam in the seventh century. Its attempts in sub-Saharan religion only became successful with the involvement of the missionaries under the protection and impetus of the colonialists in the eighteenth and nineteenth centuries. Though Islam gained the control of North Africa from the seventh century, it, however, had very little impact, if any, in the sub-Saharan regions until the later part of the eighteenth century and more effectively in the eighteenth and nineteenth centuries, just like its Christian counterpart.

However, these limitations, found in varying degrees in the three principal African religious traditions as identified above up until the seventeenth century, did not necessarily diminish the growing impacts of the three religions in shaping the spiritual thoughts, beliefs, and practices of Africans, and eventually blossoming and becoming the predominant religions on the continent. This is true particularly with regard to Christianity and Islam. We begin our exploration with the African traditional religion drawing substantially from the sub-Saharan experience.

African Traditional Religion

African traditional religion(s) evidently has no sacred books or definitive creed upon which to base any organized or systematic analysis; yet there are unique basic characteristics that clearly designate the religion as a universal religious phenomenon all over Africa. A very unique characteristic of the religion is its embellishment in the heritage of the African people. This heritage, of which African religion is not just a part, but it's very symbolic manifestation, is ultimately concretized in a religious belief system discernible through common components. The African heritage is rich culturally and has been sustained through a long lineage of forefathers (Mbiti, J. S. 1991:3). Though, in historical perspective, many of its elements have been lost and others have undergone changes due to the dynamics of other internal modifications and expansions at contacts with influences from outside cultures, the basic or fundamental believes and practices have remained intact. One other important element of African heritage is its diversity, characterized by both similarities and local differences. This makes it a unique agency of a people's "world outlook" steeped in unity and diversity. Thus, the popular dictum, "Africans are in all things religious" (Mbiti, J.S. 1969:1). The religion actually designates the traditional worldview of Africans, manifesting both the philosophical and practical experiences developed, sustained, and passed on from one generation to the other.

The sustainability of the character and the existence of the African society are located in the traditional component of the nomenclature of the religion. This has been demonstrated in the dynamic evolution of "ancient" thoughts and practices, adapting to succeeding situations borne out of personal and communal experiences of the people, linking forefathers to their descendants. Even though these thoughts and experiences Africans were "born into" have witnessed changes, the essential distinctive elements that make African traditional religion a "living" religion have remained not only unchanged but universally influential to Africans. These elements are laid out in the salient features of African religions located in an inclusive dynamic of beliefs and practices. These can be compressed under three headings: belief structure, functional components, and religious officials and sacred places.

Belief structure

The belief structure of African traditional religion(s) has been presented in diverse forms by different scholars of religion. For example, P. A. Talbot propagated a four-element structure consisting of polytheism, anthropomorphism, animism, and ancestral worship (Talbot, P. A.:14). For E. G. Parrinder, the structural elements are made up of Supreme Being, Chief divinities, cult of divinized ancestors, and charms and amulets (Parrinder, E. G. 1914:11–12). However, the most acceptable belief structure of the religion has been the five hierarchical structure advocated by Bolaji Idowu. These are made up of the Supreme Being, divinities, spirits, ancestors, and magic and medicine (Idowu, B.1973:85).

(i) Supreme Being

The belief in the Supreme Being constitutes not just a universal belief among all Africans, but also represents the center and apex of the African religious belief system. Three forms of the dynamics of this belief have been identified among different peoples of Africa. First, there is belief without practical demonstration, such as having a cult of the Supreme Being represented by religious officials and designated locations of worship. The Yoruba people of Nigeria are a model of this kind of belief. Second, there is belief with partial worship. Here, some members of an African tribe may believe without outwardly practicing the religion while another segment of the tribe operates as a cult of worshipers of the Supreme Being. An example of such a tribe is the Ewe of Togo, where it is only in the Abomey community of the tribe that there are altars and religious officials dedicated to the Supreme Being, Plawu. The third form of belief is belief with practice. The Ashanti of Ghana are a model of this form of practice. According to P. S. Rattray, "It is hardly an exaggeration holding that every compound in Ashanti has an altar for Nyame called Nyame dua (God's tree)" (Aderibigbe, I.S. & Oguntola, D. 1997:1).

Whatever the form of the religion and the demonstration of the belief, there is no doubt that against the claim of some scholars, long before the introduction of Christianity and Islam, Africans not only knew and acknowledged the existence of a supreme being, but their religious worldview was built around his being the source of all beings. Through his creative activities, humanity was believed to be inseparably bound together with all other creatures, indebted to this source of all life (Moyo, A. 2007:319). This perception is vividly demonstrated in various ways by African religious thoughts and practices. In most cases, the perception is captured in the names and attributes given to the Supreme Being by different African peoples. For example, in West Africa, the Yoruba people of Nigeria have many names for the Supreme Being. The most distinctive ones of these are Olorun, which means "owner of the heavens", and the ritual one Olodumare. This means "one who owns power and authority" (Abioye, S.O. 2001:194). In terms of attributes, the Yoruba describe the Supreme Being as Eleda, meaning the creator, "Oba Mimo" the Holy king, "Oba awon oba," King of kings. In addition, he is the Supreme Being, who is assisted by lesser deities called orisas. These serve as his assistants to look after his creation (Awolalu, J.O. & Dopamu, P .A. 1976:51).

In East Africa, the Akola people of Uganda call the Supreme Being "Bagyendanwa," which means the source of all things (Aderibigbe, I. S. & Oguntola, D. 1997:7). In southern Africa, the people of Zimbabwe call the Supreme Being "Musikawanhu" (creator of humankind). This affirms that the Supreme Being is the originator of all there is. (Moyo, A. 2007:319). Ultimately, the African belief in the Supreme Being must be understood within the context of variations, in emphasizing the local sociological complexions. Thus, while some African groups portray an anthropomorphic image of the Supreme Being, for some it is in masculine terms, some others have adopted the feminine terms; yet for others, there is no specific image (Awolalu, J.O. & Dopamu, P.A. 1976:53).

(ii) Divinities

The belief in divinities stands next in rank to the Supreme Being. Indeed, the influence and sometimes inappropriate devotion to the divinities in African traditional religion have triggered the notion that the religion is polytheistic. However, the authentic African belief about divinities totally falsifies this claim. Africans regard divinities as assistants to the Supreme Being. They are what could be regarded as "ministers" in the "theocratic government" of the Supreme Being. All over Africa, there are three identified categories of divinities. There are the primordial ones, believed to have been with the Supreme Being since the creation of the universe, and to have actually participated in the creative task. For example, the Yoruba people believe that Orisanla has been given the duty of making human bodies before Olodumare puts souls into them (Abioye, S.O. 2001: 194).

There is also the category of deified divinities; these are human beings, who after their death were raised to the level of gods. A divinity that belongs to this category in Yoruba belief is Sango, the god of thunder. The third category is made up of divinities associated with natural objects such as rivers, mountains, rocks, forests, and so on (Idowu, B. 1962:26). The nature, number, and formation of the divinities vary from one locality to the other. Also, they may be either male or female. They also attract different appellations depending on the local language. For example, the Akan of Ghana call them "Bosom" whereas the Yoruba call them "Orisas." The name for the divinities among the Ewe of Togo is "Tovo" or "Trowo" whereas the Fon of Sierra Leone refer to them as "Vodu Nudu" (Aderibigbe, I.S. & Oguntola, D. 1997:7).

However, these diverse tendencies in no way diminish the African common and central belief in the nature, importance, and functions of the divinities. By nature they are not to be compared in rank to the Supreme Being. They are his subordinates, actually created at his pleasure to assist him in specific areas of responsibility. Ultimately, the divinities are regarded as intermediaries between the Supreme Being and humanity. They constitute the channels through which the Africans believe they can successfully approach the Supreme Being.

(iii) Spirits

The Africans are also conscious of the existence of nonhuman beings, which are not also divinities by nature, description, and functions. These are known as spirits. The spirits usually make natural phenomenon their abodes. However, they are distinct from the material objects and are not affected by whatever happens to the objects. By nature the spirits are immaterial beings, though some of them may possess abstract powers through which they may take both human and nonhuman forms, and assume various dimensions at will (Abioye, S. O. 2001:192). Two types of spirits are identified: nature spirits and human spirits. Nature spirits habituate trees, rivers, mountains and other natural objects. For example, human spirits among the Yoruba are called "Iwin" or "Irunmole." They could either be benevolent or malevolent.

The malevolent types are associated with the Abiku (born to die) syndrome in Yoruba land. The Abiku spirits are accredited with the power of removing the fetus inside a pregnant woman and replacing it with one of themselves. This is why pregnant women in traditional Yoruba societies are not allowed to walk about at noontime and midnight. These are considered to be the periods when the Abiku spirits wander about looking for prey. It is also interesting to note that long-dead ancestors ultimately become spirits, roaming the spirit world and awaiting the chance of reincarnation through family or tribal descendants. These are generally regarded as benevolent and are actually courted to be born again into the family or community.

(iv) Ancestors

The African belief in ancestors symbolizes and actually gives meaning to the immortality of humans, or life after death. It is a belief that underlines the definition of the African community of comprising both the living and the dead. It also justifies not only the practice of many African tribes burying their dead at home (so as to be assured of their continuous presence) but also the elaborate funeral ceremonies that are conducted as full burial rites. The full burial rites ensure that the dead are properly sent off and received in the ancestral community in the other world. It also provides the guarantee for the ancestor to be well disposed to those still alive, and therefore look after their well-being. An inferior burial may incur the anger of the dead ancestor and may ensure dire consequences for the living. The calamities resulting from such a situation can only be mitigated after due consultation with traditional diviners and once a proper and satisfactory burial ceremony, is reconducted.

The ancestors are called different names by different peoples of Africa. The Igbo and Yoruba of Nigeria call them "Ndichie" and "Baba-nla" respectively. The Ashanti call them "Samanto" while the Ewe call them "Neshuwe." Ancestors are called "Vadzium" among the Shona of Zimbabwe. The Zulu address them as "Amadhozi" while among the Zezuru they are called "Kurova Guva." The high level of significance enjoyed by the ancestral cult among Africans has led to the erroneous conception that Africans worship their ancestors. This is far from the truth. Ancestors are never objects of worship for Africans. Rather, they perform the functions of guardian spirits and consultants. Their roles are principally to be intermediaries between the living and the spiritual world. Within this context, the ancestors are venerated as a demonstration of respect for elders and forefathers. Because the ancestors exist in the spiritual world, they are regarded as more knowledgeable and not subject to the limitations of time and space. They consequently become protectors of the family. They also symbolize ideal communal existence, acting as agents of social control and communal discipline.

It should be stressed, however, that not all people who die will automatically attain the status of an ancestor. Certain qualifications must be met. These generally include but are not limited to, dying in ripe old age, dying a good death (not death from suicide and illness such as smallpox, and others considered as moral-sanction induced). Also, the full burial ceremonies must have been conducted. The individual must have been adjudged morally upright while alive so that he could serve as a character model for the individual, family, or community.

The ancestors are venerated in different forms and at different levels across Africa. They may be venerated by pouring of libation, offerings of food, and through elaborate ceremonies. The veneration may also be done by individuals, family, or, as happens occasionally, on behalf of a community by religious officials. For example, among the Yoruba, the communal veneration of ancestors is annually observed in different localities in the Egungun (masquerade) festivals. The festivals are a time for visitation of the ancestors called "Ara orun" (visitors from the spiritual world). They masquerade as ancestral spirits visiting the living to bring blessings of prosperity, health, and other social benefits for the continued well-being, order, and peace within their social structure. In some, the central belief of Africans is that life would be of no value without the presence and power of the ancestors.

(v) Magic and Medicine

The belief in magic and medicine has been sometimes elevated to disproportionate status in African traditional religion. This has largely been due to the visibility of daily practical engagement in their practices by Africans. Also, most times the two practices have been taken to be synonymous. For example, the Yoruba call the two phenomena "Oogun," thereby suggesting that they are one and the same. However, this is not the case either in belief or practice, though they may sometimes overlap as the agencies addressing human life situations. The distinctive natures and functionalities of magic and medicine are vividly brought out in the definitions that indicate different subject matter, attitude, and approach (Aderibigbe, I. S. 2006:365). For instance, magic may be defined as:

> The act of using the available resources of nature to produce a nontherapeutic need of man. It is the art of influencing course of events by means of supernatural control of nature and invocation of particular spirit aids (Hallgren, R. 1991:67).

Medicine, on the other hand, can be generally defined as:

> The traditional art and science of the prevention, and cure of diseases. It is the use of natural substances to prevent, treat, and cure diseases. It can also mean medicament used internally or externally (Dopamu, P. A. 1979:4).

Magic in African belief can be used to protect or to harm. However, it is widely ascribed to the employment of spiritual powers for evil to harm. Even when it is used for protection, it is generally for the purpose of fighting evil forces. The most widely acknowledged evil forces in Africa are witches (female) and sorcerers (male). These are regarded as wicked human beings who employ their magical powers through witchcraft to intentionally kill people. It is believed that the magical powers of the witches equip them with the ability to fly at night, attend motional meetings, become invisible, and metaphysically consume human flesh and blood even when the victim is still physically alive.

Medicine in African belief is inextricably intertwined with religion. It can also be approached in two forms. The first is the simple notion of medicine. This is the healing system employed to treat minor illnesses, such as headaches, stomachache, and other forms of illnesses, curable through easily available herbs. These can be administered by anybody within the social structure. The second form is complex medicine. This deals with serious illnesses. The illnesses are treated using both physical and metaphysical components. Also, the administration of the "medical process" here is reserved for the professionals as custodians of traditional healing system. The intertwined relationship between religion and medicine in African belief comes from the notion that illnesses are never seen as just psychological but also spiritual. Thus the diagnosis, prescription, and treatment must be physical and, more important, metaphysical. Thus, in Yoruba land, for example, the professional medicine man sees his profession in the realm of religion. He performs rituals, invokes spirits, and offers sacrifices for the efficacy and potency of his medicine (Awolalu, J.O. 1979:73). The divinity he has to placate to ensure these outcomes is Osanyin. The diagnosing process for the Yoruba medicine man is Ifa divination, through which the cause of the illness is established. The prescription and treatment are shared between performances of necessary sacrifices followed by physical medication.

Functional Components

The devotees of African traditional religion usually express their religious beliefs in practical terms through dynamics sometimes individualistic, but mostly communal. The expressions are significantly located in prayers, sacrifices, offerings, and rituals. The media of these are the family or communal festivals and ceremonies celebrated in honor of divinities, harvest periods, and significant landmarks such as birth, marriage, burial rites, and so on. The festivals and ceremonies that are agencies of these activities are manifested in rituals made up of cosmic liturgy and religious language. These manifestations are vividly expressed in music, drumming, dancing, and various forms of arts in drums dressing and other paraphernalia of liturgical celebrations. Both music and art have always had a significant and sustained cultural impact on African traditional religion. These have tremendously represented concrete means of relaying abstract themes of African religious worship. Sounds produced from songs and drumming are regarded as vehicles for articulating abstract ideas in concrete forms. This becomes very relevant in the African dependence on oral and non-oral traditions in the absence of written documents (Adegbite, A. 1991:38).

For the African, music and religion are seen as a singular enterprise. African religious music is often rendered in a "call and response" format. This is more vividly demonstrated in the rituals of spirit possession, where singing, drumming, and dancing become a trancelike performance, invoking the direct correspondence between the divinities and the people symbolized in the possessed as the messengers of the divinities. Music for Africans and the traditional religions not only gives "live" expression to the beliefs of the people, but also and more important serves as means of prayers, the language of communication with the divine entities, the divinities, and ultimately through them indirectly to the Supreme Being.

Art, just as music, drumming, and dancing, has always empowered African people in fulfilling various aspects of their religious obligations. For example, according to Robert Thomson, the Yoruba people regard art as avatars of "ashe" (divine energy), in ceremonial bowls, stilts, and iron sculptures. These materials are no longer regarded as ordinary works of art, but have been transferred to being sacred, by the conferment of "ashe," the divine force (Adegbola, I. O. 1983:34). Also, the undertone of the importance of arts to African religion is discernible in inscriptions found on materials used for religious ceremonies such as drums, headdresses, garments, and paraphernalia of different divinities and their devotees. Most important, African art in different forms, has given credence to the religious content of African historical heritage. Thus, temples or shrines of divinities, images of kings, and royal persons, as well as infrastructures of palaces have largely been represented in religious artifacts. Indeed, historians, anthropologists, and archaeologists have relied heavily on these to obtain a meaningful and "factual" depiction of the African people's different ways of life.

Religious Officials and Sacred Places

Religious officials are central to the practice of African traditional religion. This is because as religious leaders, they constitute the custodians of religious knowledge and practices. Within these contexts, the officials conduct religious rituals and act as intermediaries between the devotees and the spiritual sphere of the divinities and Supreme Being. The religious officials can be either male or female, but they are of different kinds. There are those who are cultic officials. These are priests and priestesses who preside over activities at the shrines of the divinities. The Akan and Yoruba peoples have a sizable number of these officials. They are officially responsible for offering sacrifices and petitioning divinities on behalf of the devotees.

Another category of religious officials is that of diviners. They are also usually of both genders. The main function of diviners is to communicate with the spirit world. This is very important to Africans because it is through such communication that they are in communion with the ancestors, divinities, and ultimately with the Supreme Being. The subject matter of the communication may be for the purpose of determining the cause of problems such as misfortunes, sicknesses, diseases, death, and other forms of calamities, and also seek for solutions. At other times, it may be for guidance as to the course of action to be undertaken concerning, for example, the future of a newborn baby, a marriage, the building of a house, or the embarking on a journey or trade.

There are different methods of divination in different parts of Africa. Some of these include the case of wooden dice, sea shells, pieces of ivory, palm nuts, and a bowl of water. The most famous method among the Yoruba is Ifa divination, which adopts a very elaborate system of palm nuts usage. The Yoruba Ifa diviners are usually priests and priestesses of Orunmila, the Yoruba divinity of knowledge and wisdom.

One other category of traditional religious officials, and perhaps considered to be the most powerful, are the spirit mediums. These are people through whom the spirits of ancestors communicate with their descendants. Most spirit mediums are females, and they may be associated with family, tribe, or territory. Through them, Africans, at the individual, family, or communal level, discern the will of the ancestors, and obtain explanations for all situations affecting them, either for good or evil. The mediums also provide solutions to problems and steps to be taken to preserve good fortunes.

Due to their office and traditional functions they perform, kings are also regarded as religious leaders. For example, the kings as community heads are responsible for the consultation of community spirits. They are also responsible for ensuring that all religious functions and observances, such as festivals, are carried out by various religious officers. Indeed for the Yoruba, the king called "Oba" is referred to as "Alase ekeji orisa"—second in command to the deity—from whom he derives his authority. Consequently, his authority is not just political but divine in source and sustenance. The Oba is therefore regarded as not only the number one religious official, but he also must partake in devotions to all divinities of his community.

Sacred places are central and vital to the practical expression and functions of religious leaders in African traditional religion. Perhaps the most prominent of these are the shrines, where the divinities may be located in family compounds or places communally dedicated to the divinities. The Ashanti of Ghana, for instance, have a familial sacred place for the Supreme Being—Nyame. This is usually in the form of a forked branch cut from a certain tree, called "Nyame dua." The Zulus of South Africa have elevated portions of a hut called "Umsamu." This is where ancestor-related rituals are conducted. In addition, mountains, rivers, forest groves and caves, are regarded as sacred based on the notion of their being inhabited by spirits, divinities, or even the Supreme Being. These usually serve as venues of prayers, where religious officials visit. For example, in Zimbabwe, there are several such sacred places, which have become venues of prayers, particularly for petitions for rains in times of drought.

Sacred places, particularly the shrines, are very important as sources of information for African religion because they provide traditional non-oral knowledge and understanding of the African people and their religion. Artifacts of various instruments used in worship have provided archaeologists with valuable insights into not only the religious, but also the social, political, and overall cultural history as well as the worldviews of Africans.

In summary, before the advent and influence of Christianity and Islam, and particularly in precolonial Africa, the beliefs and the practices of African indigenous religion were firmly rooted in the cosmological and cosmogenial worldviews in a number of fundamental, philosophical, and theological concepts. These were based on the African people's observation of the world around them, and consequent reflections on its existence and workings. To begin with, Africans believed that the world was created, and that it was created by the Supreme Being. Different myths, from different parts of Africa, portrayed diverse methods and processes through which the world came into existence. Though there may not be uniformity on these, there is the universality of looking at the world from the religious perspective and explaining it theoretically.

Africans also believe in the duality of the universe as comprising the visible (the earth) and the invincible (the heavens). However, the two are linked through the religious activities of humans linking the world to the Supreme Being. The origin, distribution, and subsequent reinstatement of this link through close relationships with the Supreme Being are narrated in many creation stories. The stories also indicate that though the universe is created, it has assumed an unending existence in terms of space and time.

Also, central to African cosmological thoughts, is the belief in the order in the universe. This order, which is inclusively morally and religiously based, depicts a mystical order responsible for governing the universe. The attempts to relate and sometimes control this order have resulted in practices such as medicine, magic, witchcraft, and other religious activities discussed earlier. The general belief is that, though the divinities and other spiritual beings may exercise mystical power, the ultimate source of the power is the Supreme Being.

Perhaps the most important cosmological belief of the African peoples is that man is the center of the universe. Indeed, the whole world is seen as existing for his sake (Mbiti, J. S. 1991:43). Consequently, the world and all in it must function for the ultimate benefit of man. This may account for ascribing sacredness to even physical and natural objects in the universe.

Consequently, man considers it necessary to live in harmony with nature. Though he realizes that he is not the master, but rather the beneficiary end user, he has the obligation to preserve it and use it wisely. This is the only way his survival can be guaranteed (Mbiti, J. S. 1991:44).

Contemporary Status of African Traditional religion(s)

Over the centuries, African traditional religion has faced many challenges that have significantly diminished the practice and influence of the religion on the continent. These challenges are found in what could be termed internal and external factors. The internal factors, associated with the location and internal workings of the religion, have acted as barriers to its development in consonance with evolving developmental realities. External challenges arose and are still arising from the continent's contacts with the outside world, principally the Western influence through the slave trade, colonialism, and missionary activities.

The internal challenges are mainly derived from factors such as geographical expansiveness of the continent, which makes uniformity of beliefs and practices in the religion impossible. This obvious diversity has been unfortunately employed to insinuate or even assert that Africans have practiced different or tribal religions. Another internal factor militating against the religion is the lack of written documents in the form of a scripture as available in other religious traditions. In depending exclusively on oral sources, its claims have been usually dismissed as products of superstitious and "unintelligible" stipulations. One other internal factor, which is directly linked with lack of written documents, is the secret nature of the religion. Religious officials of different categories in African traditional religion often for various reasons keep to themselves vital information and knowledge pertaining to the contents, processes, and methods of the beliefs and practices of the religion. Coupled with a nonwritten tradition, these pieces of information and knowledge die with the officials and are therefore lost to present and future generations.

The external challenges faced by African traditional religion in terms of Africa's contact with the outside world substantially began with the transatlantic slave trade when significant numbers of its adherents were transported across the ocean, many of them never to return, and the few who returned after the trade, converted to other religions. This challenge was compounded by the two-dimensional and competitive evangelical "invasions" of Christianity and Islam. The propagations of the two religions have been so effective that the African continent is today split almost down the line by both religious traditions. Finally the colonial impact became a major challenge to African traditional religion. In collaboration with the Christian missionaries, Western education and civilization were introduced. The combination of these two phenomena created "elitist" consciousness in the followers of religions in the continent. Those who practice Christianity and Islam regard themselves as civilized and educated, while those who practice the traditional religion are regarded as largely illiterate and uncivilized.

The aforementioned having been said, it should, however, be stated that in spite of these challenges, African traditional religion still has a future in global religious space. This position is evidenced by a number of factors that have emerged and are contemporarily emerging. Principal among these factors are first, the increased attention in studies and scholarships being paid to African traditional religion, not only in Africa but all over the world. Courses in the religion are being offered in both public and private higher institutions in all parts of the world. Numerous books have been and are being written on the religion. Also, conferences, symposia, and other forms of scholarly meetings deliberate on themes based on the religion. Second, many African nations are beginning to show significant commitment to the spirit and letter of nationalism in the search for African self-identity. African traditional religion as the centerpiece and sustainer of African culture is being directly or indirectly promoted to meet this objective. Third, even with the almost total conversion of Africans to Christianity and Islam, the traditional practices of the African people continue to be relevant and observed as cultural values in their everyday engagements. Again African traditional religion is mirrored as a basic component of the values. Fourth, through the process of acculturation, enculturation, and so on, African traditional religious values have become part and parcel of the practices of both Christianity and Islam on the African continent to the extent that the practices of these religions in Africa today are not in the original form in which they were introduced into the continent. As a result of the factors enumerated above, African traditional religion has become visible as a competitive religion in African and global religious spaces.

Christian Religious Tradition in Africa

As a religious tradition, it has been generally accepted that Christianity grew out of Judaism. This is evidenced and established by many studies and literatures. Foremost among these is the three-volume study of the Bible by Wilfred J. Harrington. The volume is titled *The Record of Revelation: The Bible; The Record of Promise: The Old Testament; The Record of the fulfillment: The New Testament* (Walsh, H. H. 1962:230). Within this context, Christianity right from inception has regarded itself as the direct succession of the Old Testament Tradition. This claim has been vividly demonstrated in first, the origin of its name and second, the historical and theological configurations of its founder, Jesus Christ.

The word Christ, from which Christianity is derived, comes from the Greek word "Christos." This is equivalent to the Hebrew word Mashiah which, when translated to English, is Messiah. The etymological meaning of the word in the three languages is "the anointed one." It denotes someone who is given a specific mandate of undertaking a national responsibility. Second, the name Christian was first used in Antioch to describe the followers of Christ through the observation of their behaviors.

Jesus, the founder of Christianity, historically lived in Galilee in Palestine in the early first century BC. Facts about his birth and mission come almost exclusively from the Christian Bible (the New Testament). His birth is claimed to be a miraculous one, since he is believed to have been conceived of the Holy Spirit and born of the Virgin Mary. He is, however, regarded as a descendant of David through lineage with Joseph his foster father to whom his mother, Mary, was betrothed. The mission of Christ, which became the foundation of Christianity, lasted about three years. During this period, Jesus traveled throughout Judea. He chose twelve men, who became his apostles. In their company, he preached about the kingdom of God.

The kingdom was distinguished from an earthly one. Though it was a Messianic kingdom foretold by the prophets, it was a heavenly one, contrary to the expectation of the Jewish people. The central message of Christ was that in this heavenly kingdom; salvation is spiritual rather than physical or political. The members would worship God as heavenly king. The worship would be spiritual in nature. In addition, the members would live by the truth and have brotherly love toward one another. In addition, Jesus in words and actions presented himself as the expected Messiah foretold by the prophets. His principal mission was to save the world and establish the heavenly kingdom. He was credited with many miracles (mighty works) to give credence to his messianic power. Ironically, it was the messianic claim of Jesus (the Son of God) that got him into trouble with the official Jewish establishment, and eventually had him delivered to the Roman authorities and executed.

Apart from his disciples and retinues of other followers, Jesus, had no organized group as such. In addition, he did not write anything down. However his preaching and activities became perpetuated in the New Testament consisting of the Gospels, the Acts of the Apostles, and the Epistles. It is instructive that the violent death of Jesus on the cross was initially disappointing to his disciples; however, his resurrection, reappearance, and ascension reassured them of his power and truth of his promises. Finally, the events of the Pentecost through which the apostles experienced the coming of the Holy Spirit as promised by Christ not only emboldened them but also and more significantly "officially" constituted the first winning of souls to the movement later to be called Christianity.

Though the mainstream doctrines of Christianity are located in the Apostles' Creed, the various interpretations they have witnessed have created controversies that have resulted in heresies and eventual schisms (Walker, W. 1970:61). In spite of this situation, which has led to denominations in Christianity, the central doctrines as theological foundations of the Christian faith have remained, with the Christian Bible as the point of reference. Based on the Apostles' Creed and the scriptures, the Christian faith is presented in a number of beliefs and practices. As indicated earlier, the splitting of Christianity into denominations makes a comprehensive or universal Christian worldview very difficult, if at all achievable and definitely not within the context and space of a chapter. In spite of the obvious denominational challenges of the Christian faith, there are some basic beliefs and practices universally common to all Christians. These beliefs and practices are stated in the "official Christian" Apostles' Creed. They mainly consist of belief in one God, belief in the Holy Trinity, belief in Jesus, belief in the church as the kingdom of God on Earth, the concept of man, concept of worship, and concept of eschatology.

History and Influence in Africa.

As a religious tradition, Christianity became part of Africa from the first century AD. There is no doubt, as earlier pointed out, that Christianity had to wait until the late 1800s and early 1900s to become fully established as one of two most practiced religions on the continent. From its introduction in the first century to the present period, Christianity has undergone different fortunes in African history. Nevertheless, its presence, importance, and influence have always been felt significantly within African religious space. The presence and influences of Christianity in Africa historically may be divided into three main segments. The first comprises the earliest contacts in North Africa. The second spans the precolonial and colonial periods consisting of Portuguese traders and later Christian missionaries' efforts with the support of the colonial governments. The third includes the postcolonial and contemporary period. Within these contexts, this chapter attempts to explore the Christian religion from the perspectives of its advent, development in different regions, the leaders with their expansion methods, their worldviews as represented by doctrinal peculiarities and artistic influences, as well as the contemporary facets of the religion.

Christianity in North Africa, Ethiopia—Early Contacts

In symbolic terms, Christianity may be said to have been in early contact with Africa in two ways. The first, going by the biblical narrative, was the taking of the child Jesus to Egypt to avoid his being killed by King Herod. The second was the possibility of the infiltration of the message of Jesus into North Africa, which at the time was part of the Roman Empire, just as was Palestine, where Jesus carried out his ministry. However, historically as an organized religion, Christianity came to Egypt in the first century AD. This is believed to have occurred simultaneously as Christianity was making its way into northern Europe. According to the church historian Eusebius, the Christian church in Egypt was founded by St. Mark, the writer of the fourth Gospel. The location was in Alexandria. From Alexandria, Christianity spread to other parts of Egypt. Indeed, by the end of the first century, the religion had penetrated into even the rural parts of Egypt and had actually become the religion of the majority of the people. As King points out, the strong presence of Christianity in Egypt in the early history of the church is indicated in the fact that apart from Rome, it is only Egypt that has one of the oldest churches and also longevity of tradition and continuity in the same locality (King, N. 1991:1). Also, the city of Alexandria became an outstanding theological center, producing figures such as Origen, Cyprian, Clement, and others, who influenced the church for all time through their theological writings. The spread and vibrancy of Christianity in Egypt continued until the seventh century when it was conquered by the Muslims. Even then, Christianity was still practiced as a minority religion.

Other parts of North Africa that had early contact with the Christian faith are modern-day countries such as Tunisia, Morocco, and Algeria. They were known as Roman Africa, during the period of the Roman Empire. The area had a very strong following of Christians in the early second century. In addition, the area produced influential theologians of early Christendom. These included Tertullian, who first used the term Trinity to describe and explain the Godhead. There was also St. Augustine, the Bishop of Hippo, who produced significant theological works. His theological writings were reputed for shaping Western Catholicism as well as the Protestant Reformation. They also continued to be relevant and central to Christian thoughts of all ages. Unfortunately, Christianity in this area did not survive the onslaught of the Islamic conquest of the seventh century, and thereafter Christianity became totally extinct in the region.

Beginning from the first and through the fourth centuries, Ethiopia, which was south of Egypt and was greatly impacted by the Alexandria church, also witnessed the advent and spread of Christianity. Ethiopia's acceptance of Christianity has been accounted for in two but not necessarily exclusive fashions. The first is legendary and is reported in the Acts of the Apostles. The narrative centered on the conversion through baptism of an unnamed Ethiopian eunuch by Philip, an apostle of Jesus. The eunuch, a high official to the queen of Ethiopia, Candace, after his conversion returned to his home kingdom to propagate Christianity among the Ethiopians. The second, from independent sources and more historic, ascribed the Christianization of Ethiopia to the efforts of two Syrian Greek brothers, Frumentius and Aedesius. The two were believed to have been shipwrecked off the Eritrean coastline. They were spared and aided by the royal court of the Axumite kingdom, and thereafter gained tremendous power in the kingdom. They were also much loved by the people of the Axumite kingdom of Ethiopia so much that Frumentius was called "revealer of light" (Kesate Birhen), and Aedesius "father of peace" (Abbeselema). The two brothers were not only able to convert King Ezna, the ruler of the kingdom, to Christianity, but also persuaded him to make Christianity the official religion of the Axumite kingdom. Subsequently, Frumentius was appointed the first official bishop of the Ethiopian church by St. Athanasius, the patriarch of Alexandria at the time.

Christianity in Sub-Saharan Africa

With all its spread and impact in North Africa and Ethiopia in the early centuries, unfortunately there is no indication of any attempts to take Christianity into the region south of the Sahara. Consequently, the first advent of Christianity into that region, in precolonial Africa, had to wait until the fifteenth century. The principal harbingers of the religion to Africa's eastern, western, and southern regions, were mainly the Roman Catholic missionaries. They belonged to the Jesuit and Dominican orders, who accompanied Portuguese traders along the coastal regions of Africa. For example, by 1490, the missionaries had started to build Christian communities in the Congo and Angola. Also by 1560, Father Gonzalo da Silveira, had along with other Portuguese missionaries established a Christian community of about 450 persons in the empire of Mwanamtupa, today's Zimbabwe. Also along the coast of West Africa, the same Portuguese missionaries brought Christianity to southern parts of today's Nigeria, of Calabar, and the Benin kingdoms. In addition, the Gold Coast, now called Ghana, witnessed the presence of Christian missionaries and some conversions.

However, these efforts eventually proved unsuccessful for a number of reasons. Prominent among these was the issue of health. Most of the missionaries died of malaria. The death toll was so enormous that Africa came to be referred to as the "white man's grave." Also, there was the issue of the slave trade. It was ironic that the missionaries, who came to preach the Christian message of love of neighbor, were in collaboration with Portuguese traders, whose main business soon changed from seeking and transportation of gold and ivory to human slaves. It soon became obviously difficult, if not impossible, to sell the contradictory messages of "love" of Christianity and "cruel inhumanity" of the slave trade. In addition, there was the competition of Islam, which had actually predated Christianity into the region. Muslim trading partners of traders in these areas resisted the threat of the Portuguese traders and their trade monopoly through Portuguese missionaries. For example, Father Gonzalo da Silveira was actually executed by the emperor of Mwanamtupa, whom he had earlier converted to Christianity and baptized. This act was ascribed to pressure from Arab Muslims who were trading partners to the emperor, in order to protect their trade monopoly (Moyo, A. 2007:329). With the failure of these efforts, Sub-Saharan Africa had to wait until the nineteenth century and early twentieth century for Christianity to take root and grow.

The late nineteenth and early twentieth centuries actually witnessed the advent and spread of Christianity in sub-Saharan Africa. The success of this "project" is traceable to a number of favorable developments. These involved, for example, the discovery of quinine, effective against death from malaria. Also, the slave trade had ended. Thus, the moral dilemma of preaching Christian love while at the same time capturing and transporting slaves to Europe and the Americas was no longer a burden. In addition, the propagation of Christianity was then taken as a full-time campaign rather than at the part-time leisure of Portuguese traders in the coastal regions of Africa. Then, most important of all, the success was basically the product of the painstaking efforts of different Christian missionaries in Europe, who not only pioneered, but also helped to sustain missionary evangelism in different parts of Africa, by making both the finance and the personnel available. The period also coincided with the colonization of the African continent. Consequently, colonial governments contributed significantly, through various means and at different stages, to the Christianization of Africa. In addition, freed slaves from American and European nations, who settled in different parts of Africa, particularly, in West Africa, were also great catalysts in the propagation of Christianity in Africa. A combination of these dynamics took the Christian faith to the nooks and crannies of the eastern, western, and southern regions of Africa. Indeed, by the middle and definitely before African countries began to gain independence in the 1950s, the Christian religion with its counterpart, Islam, had become a dominating religion on the African continent.

Leadership, Worldviews, and Artistic Influences

From the first century through the middle centuries, Christianity in North Africa and Ethiopia became central and influential in the "evolving" and later "matured" Christendom in terms of leadership, personnel, and doctrinal worldviews. Many leading theologians as church leaders, who shaped the doctrinal worldviews of Christianity, not only in the early and middle centuries, but for all time, were leading figures in the Alexandria church, the Ethiopian church, and Roman African churches. These were achieved through their numerous writings, establishment of schools, and propagation of doctrines.

Beginning with the Egyptian Coptic Church in Alexandria, there emerged a substantial number of church leaders from the first century to the seventh century. This crop of church leaders started with Mark, the founder of Christianity in Egypt. He was the writer of the fourth Gospel. St. Mark not only established the church but also created the catechetical school in Alexandria. The school was the oldest catechetical school in the world. The first manager of the school was St. Justus, who later became the sixth bishop of Alexandria. Panaterious was the first teacher, and after him came many renowned church scholars such as Clement, Didymus, and Anthenagoras. The school became not only a center for theological scholarship but also mathematics, science, and humanities. However, the most well-known teacher and scholar of the school was Origen. He produced the famous Hexpla and more than six thousand commentaries. Saint Jerome, who first translated the Bible into Latin, also visited the school in AD 600. The catechetical school has also been credited with developing a system of utilizing wood carving as a means of reading and writing for blind students.

The Alexandria church, also in searching for authentic Christian life, devoid of all fleshy desires and serving God through a life of self-denial, prayer, and worship, introduced the first monastic movement in Christendom. The nearby caves and desert areas provided ideal locations for the ascetic pursuits (Moyo, A. 2007:328). The movement was introduced by St. Macarius the great in the fourth century. The principal figures he used were St. Pachomius the lenolbite and Anthony the Great. The monasteries ended up producing prominent leaders and teachers, known as the "great fathers of Egypt desert," and their works played a significant role in shaping the characteristics for which the Coptic Orthodox Church is historically known. They also greatly influenced the formation of early and growing Christian doctrinal and practical worldviews, becoming models for Christianity in other parts of the world such as Asia Minor.

As mentioned earlier, prominent church leaders known as African church fathers, also emerged in what was then the "Roman Africa." Among these were figures such as Tertullian of Carthage and St. Augustine of Hippo. The works of these African church fathers tremendously shaped Christian theological worldviews in their lifetimes and thereafter for centuries.

The Ethiopian Orthodox Church leaders also contributed immensely to the theological issues from its inception and well into the midcenturies. Indeed, its propagation of the "Tewahedo" doctrine, the idea that the nature of Christ is single and united, became a reference point in Christian theological development. Not only did it become a subject of controversy; it actually ultimately led to the East-West schism of 1054. The schism occurred when the Patriarchs of Alexandria, leading the Ethiopian Coptic Church, along with his counterparts in Antioch and Jerusalem, went against the historic council of Chalcedon doctrine of "two natures of Christ," and insisted on the one unified nature of Christ. Subsequently, the Orthodox Tewahedo Church and their Oriental counterparts were called Monophysite, symbolizing their adherence to the belief that Christ was of a single nature.

Interestingly, the basic beliefs of the Orthodox Ethiopian Church actually depicted some aspects of the indigenous Miaphysite beliefs. This was symbolically reflected in the general religious beliefs and practices coordinated by the local priests of the church. For instance, the belief system was founded around a belief in God, angels, and saints. The belief system definitely resonated with the indigenous religious belief in the Supreme Being, divinities, and ancestors respectively. Also, the role of the priests as the spokespersons for the devotees before God found commonality with functions of priests and priestesses in the indigenous religion. Another area is the practice of the priests being permitted to enter the inner sanctum of the circular church where the Ark (or Tabot) devoted to the church patron saint lies. This would find concurrence with the indigenous religious priests' functions in the shrines of the divinities and ancestors. There were also the festivities of singing, drumming, and dancing to mark special days devoted to angels and saints. Finally, the idea of a "trinate monotheist" belief would not have been too strange to the converted indigenous people with their notion of "diffused monotheism."

Christianity's advent and expansion in Africa, particularly in North Africa and Ethiopia, were phenomenal, starting from the first century and through the midcenturies AD. However, beginning from the seventh century, it began a decline. Thus, by the eve of colonization, with the exception of the Coptic Church in Ethiopia, it had become almost extinct. Notwithstanding, certain legacies survived, and it was upon these that Christianity built a strong and lasting reemergence in colonial and postcolonial Africa. A significant part of these were architectural masterpieces of the Monolithic Church buildings in Ethiopia. Examples of these are the churches at Lalibala. They included two key types of artistic architecture made up of basilicas and native forms. A model of the basilican type is the Church of Our Lady of Zion in Axum. The native churches were impressively constructed with sanctuaries surrounded by a courtyard as well as walls covered with frescos. (Documents, School of Alexandria, Part 1).

Contemporary Facet

As stated above, Christianity today, is one the two dominating religions in Africa. It is estimated that there are close to 390 million Christians in Africa. Also the religion has continued to grow at the estimated rate of 2.65 percent yearly. The phenomenal growth of Christianity, without diminishing the pioneering contributions of the missionaries, has been traced to the innovations through enculturation which have become the hallmark of Christianity on the African continent. Consequently, the Christianity practiced in Africa today, though still essentially subscribes to the fundamental beliefs, doctrines, and practices of universal Christianity, is remarkably unique and different in terms of methods and applications.

The departure from the method of propagation, application of contents, and enculturation of values actually began in the early 1920s with the establishments of African Independent Churches. These churches introduced many African cultural values and beliefs that made the belief and practice of Christianity African in responding and addressing the heart of African spirituality, known to be all encompassing and spontaneous, as different from the exclusive and abstract natures of the mission of Christianity. Over the decades, indigenous African churches have expanded with the injection of the Pentecostal mode of Christianity to become the dominating Christian denominations in many parts of Africa. These denominations have become so popular because of the premium they place on existential issues of everyday Africa such as healing, poverty, witchcraft, marriage, bareness, and so on alongside spiritual concerns.

Islamic Religious Tradition in Africa

As a religious tradition, Islam postulates a worldview of an entirely monotheistic religion. This is the belief in a single indivisible God, called Allah. The faith grew out of the teachings of Mohammed in Arabia in the seventh century AD. It is regarded as the third fiscal card in the monotheistic Abrahamic religions. The major themes of Islam are peace and submission. It is also a religious tradition that is named after a concept, rather than a person. The unique practices required of devotees are found in the five pillars of Islam—the Shahada (creed), the salat (daily prayers), the sawm (fasting through Ramadan), the zakat (giving alms), and the hajj (pilgrimage to Mecca at least once in a lifetime). The overall Islamic doctrines and practices are based on its holy scripture, the Qur'an and religious traditions—the Hadith. The discourse on Islamic religious tradition in this section focuses on the history of the advent and spread of the religion, its distinctive African features, the influences on African indigenous religion in particular, and all facets of African life in general.

Advent and Spread in Africa

The advent and spread of Islam in Africa can be traced to two distinct waves from the seventh century to the early nineteenth century—the eve of African colonization. There are indications that the first wave of the seventh century may have actually accommodated Islamic contact with Africa during the lifetime of Mohammed. This is reported in connection with the migration ordered by Mohammed that his followers should flee to the Christian kingdom of Abyssinia, present-day Ethiopia. The order was given so that these dedicated followers could escape the persecution of the pagan non-Muslim rulers of their homelands. (Cleaveland, T., 2001).

However, what has been strictly regarded as the first wave of Islam as an organized religion occurred after the death of Mohammed in AD 632. The advent and spread was through wars of conquest. By AD 640, Egypt, whose rulers were supported and influenced by the Byzantine Orthodox Church, had been overrun. The seeming ease with which the Muslims conquered Egypt has been attributed in part to the face-off between the Byzantine Orthodox Church supported by Egyptian rulers, and the majority of Egyptians who were Coptic Christians. The Coptic Christians did not accept the teachings and authority of the Orthodox Church, and in addition held the Egyptian rulers responsible for their religious oppression. They consequently welcomed the Arab rule as liberation and freedom from their Egyptian overlords.

The Islamic takeover of "Roman North Africa" was through both conquest and persuasion. First, the Christians, who were based in the towns, were defeated. Second, the Arabs gradually converted the Berbers who lived in the rural areas. This was done mostly through intermarriages. Eventually, the Berbers, Islamized and incorporated into the Arab armies, fully participated in the military campaigns for the conquests of other parts of North Africa, particularly the Maghreb. (Trimingham, J. S., 1962:18).

The military option employed for Islamizing most of North Africa was not adopted for Islam's advent and spread in the regions south of the Sahara. Here, Islam was propagated mainly through peaceful means. The method was essentially informal "missionary," and the missionaries were actually the Arabized Berber merchants. They traded in manufactured goods from the Mediterranean, exchanging them for raw materials, such as gum, gold, slaves, and ivory. However wherever they went, they became proselytes of the Islamic faith. It was through this method that the West African region became Islamized. For instance, Gold Coast (now Ghana), was an already established Islamic center by 1076. This is also true of the Yoruba nation (part of present-day Nigeria). Indeed, by the fifteenth and sixteenth centuries, Islam had become the official religion of rulers and elites in many West African kingdoms. Also in the eastern part of Africa, Islam had been introduced by the beginning of the seventh century. This was done by the Persian and Arab merchants. Though their activities were confined to the coastal trading towns, the religion also spread downward to South Africa. Its great assets of spread and popularity were intermarriages, commercial contacts, and the eventual development and adoption of the Swahili language.

The second wave of Islam in Africa can be properly located in both the western and eastern regions of Africa. Again, both military and missionary methods were employed. For example, in the precolonial periods of the seventeenth and eighteenth centuries, African Muslims undertook mass military movements through Jihads (Holy wars) to Islamize West Africa. A very prominent Jihad was that of Uthman dan Fodio in the area now known as Northern Nigeria. He attempted to impose religious reforms through the Jihad. The goal was to establish a more rigorous Islamic theocratic state. In the process, this became a justification for military campaigns, conquests, and political dominance (Mazrui, A. A., 34).

However, there were also a lot of missionary efforts at Islamizing the areas. For instance, the Sufi religious movements (Brotherhoods) were in the forefront of propagating Islam through teachings. One of these such Brotherhoods, the Qadiriyya, was brought to the great Muslim center of learning in Timbuktu in the sixteenth century. The work of this group enormously impacted the efforts of Uthman Dan Fodio in carrying out his Jihad and founding the Sokoto Caliphate. (Voll, J. O., 1982:250).

Overall, the Islamic advent and spread in Africa in the first centuries witnessed diverse history of movements, and even dynasties competing for power and control of different regions of the continent. In addition, the advance moved both southward and northward, until the final years of the eleventh century when the religion became a dominant religion and political force across the continent. Also in terms of leadership positions, in the Islamic world, Africans did enjoy prominent status. For instance, the very first Muezzin (privileged person to lead the adhan- call to prayer), was a North African called Bilal ibn Rilah. He was of the Habasha descent. Also throughout the history of Islam, numerous empires led by figures from West Africa emerged. Such empires, which had tremendous influences, included the Mali Empire, and the Songhai Empire under the leaderships of Sonni Ali and Askia Mohammed respectively (Davidson, B., 1991:25). There was also the Sokoto Caliphate established by Uthman dan Fodio.

Islamic Features and Cultural Influences

Although military conquests constituted the main method of Islamizing different parts of Africa, it was more readily accepted by Africans than its main rival, Christianity, particularly in precolonial Africa. A number of factors have been identified for this situation. Two of these fac- tors are distinctive. The first, and the most touted, is the accommodating nature of the Islamic beliefs and practices in relation to African indigenous beliefs and practices. Africans found Islamic beliefs and practices compatible with or at least tolerant of, their religion and cultural values and practices. For instance, religiously Islam resonated with African beliefs in ancestral veneration, magical use of objects, divinities, and spirits. Culturally, Islam also allowed po- lygamy, whereby a man could have more than one wife at a time, provided he could support and care equally for each wife. Circumcision, a very important practice among most African peoples, was also allowed. The Islamic religion also found common ground with Africans in terms of clear gender roles for men and women. Consequently, Africans were more comfort- able converting to and practicing Islam rather than Christianity. In preaching Islam, African Muslims were more committed to observing the five pillars of faith than to the elements of Sharia, which were incompatible with African social and political customs.

The second factor had to do with the Islamic civilization contributions to African cultural developments. Islam is practiced as a way of life. It affects all aspects of human endeavor, just as African religion permeates the totality of the African life. Islam also stressed community living as its followers lived as communities of believers. As the religion took root on the African soil, its emphasis on literacy and scholarship became attractive to Africans. Its Islamic law (Sharia) became the framework and model for theocratic governance, legitimizing religious leadership of rulers and regulating the relationship between the rulers and the ruled. In addition, Islam bequeathed to Africa many great architectural models, spread across the continent. One of these was the great Mosque of Ketchaoua in Tunisia. This mosque is regarded as the "ancestor" of all mosques, even in Western Islamic communities. Finally, it is quite evident that Islamic civilization in Africa, as part of the global one, was highly advanced. Thus as the religion spread across Africa, it made major impacts on Africans and their everyday lives, both in precolonial and postcolonial African settings.

Contemporary Status

In conjunction with its counterpart-Christianity, Islam even though it is predominantly practiced in the northern part of Africa, also has substantial followers in sub-Saharan Africa. In 1985, the total population of Muslims in Africa was estimated to be 215 million. However, by 2003, the number of Muslims in sub-Saharan Africa alone was estimated to be 150–160 million. In 2004, the Muslims population in Africa was estimated to be 402 million.

Summary and Conclusion

This chapter has explored the "worlds" of the religious traditions in Africa. The discourse centered on the three principal religious traditions—the African indigenous religion, Christianity, and Islam. The indigenous religion has been in competition with the other two religions since the time of their introduction and developmental years on the continent. Notwithstanding the challenges they have posed and are posing to it, it has struggled to withstand their strong intimidations. Consequently, it has continued to provide religious responses born out of African cultural heritage. The responses have not only defined the world views of Africans but also and, more important, have sustained the unique identity of Africans as a people vast in religious values.

The advents and developments of Christianity and Islam have introduced alternative religious dynamics into the African religious space. These have ultimately influenced the religious beliefs and practices of the African people. However, their impacts on the indigenous religion and its devotees in terms of acceptability and affiliations of the "new religions" evoked different responses. These were inadvertently based on the approaches adopted by the two religions in practicing accommodation and enculturation over the centuries. Today, both religions have become the two most practiced religions in Africa and have had a huge impact with enormous influences and holds on the totality of the African life—to the extent that they have become, so to say, "African religions."

Review Questions

1. Highlight and explain the reasons for the state of the three main religions in Africa today.

2. What factors (external and internal) currently constitute major challenges for African "Traditional Religion" in Africa?

3. Why is it no longer "practical" to refer to Christianity and Islam as "foreign religions" in Africa today?

4. How have Christianity and Islam impacted African sociopolitical and economic spaces?

5. What future awaits collaboration and inter-religious relations among followers of the Traditional, Christian, and Islamic religions in Africa?

6. What cultural dynamics constitute the main "drives" of African religiosity?

Bibliography

Aderibigbe, G., and D. Oguntola. 1997. *Topics in African Religion*. Lagos: Adelad Educational Publishers.

Aderibigbe, G., and D. Aiyegboyin, eds. 2001. *Religion: Study and Practice*. Ibadan: Olu-Akin Press.

Awolalu, J. O. 1979. *Yoruba Belief and Sacrificial Rites*. London: Longman.

Awolalu, J. O., and P. A. Dopamu.1979. *West African Traditional Religion*. Ibadan: Onibonje Press.

Baur, John. 1998. *200 Years of Christianity in Africa: An African Church History*, 2nd ed. Kenya: Pauline Publication Africa.

Cleaveland, T. *Becoming Walata: A History of Saharan Social Formation and Transformation*. Heinemann.

Davidson, Basil. 1991. *African Civilization Revisited*. Trenton, NJ: African World Press.

Falola, Toyin, and M. Heaton. eds. 2006. *Tradition and Modern Health System in Nigeria*. Trenton, NJ: African World Press.

Floyd, Doudshafer. 1952. *Liturgy: Worship and Work*. USA: Division Christian Education of National Council of Churches.

Gordon, A., and D. Gordon. eds. 2007. *Understanding Contemporary Africa*. London: Lynne Rienner.

Grooves, C. P. 1948. *The Planting of Christianity in Africa*. London: Luther-Worth Press.

Hildebrand, Jonathan. 1970. *History of the Church in Africa: A Survey*. 3rd ed. England: African Christian Press.

Holt, P. M. 1961. *History of the Sudan*. New York: Groove Press.

Idowu, E. B. 1971. *African Traditional Religion: A Definition*. New York: Orbits.

Idowu, E. B. 1973. *African Traditional Religion*. London: SCM, 1973.

Idowu, E. B. 1962. *Olodumare: God in Yoruba Belief*. Ikeja: Longman, 1962.

King, Noel. 1971. *Christians and Muslims in Africa*. New York: Harper and Row.

Latourette, K. S. 1953. *The History of Christianity*. New York: Harpers.

Levtzion, L., and R. Pouwels, eds. 2000. *The History of Islam in Africa*. Ohio: Ohio University Press.

Mazrui, A. A. 1982. *The Africans: A Triple Heritage*. London: BBC Publications.

Masiri, I. H. 1978. *The Story of the Copts*. Cairo: The Middle East Council of Churches.

Mbiti, J. S. 1969. *African Religions and Philosophy*. London: Heinemann.

Okure, Teresa, Van Theil, et al. 1990. *32 Articles Evaluating Enculturation of Christianity in Africa*. Kenya: Amecea Gaba Publications.

Parrinder, E. G. 1949. *West African Religion*. London: Epworth Press.

Talbot, P. A. *The People of Southern Nigeria,* Vol. 11.

Trimingham, J. S. 1962. *A History of Islam in West Africa.* London: Oxford University Press.

Voll, J. O. 1981. *Islam: Continuity and Change in Modern world.* Boulder, CO: Westview Press.

Whithman, A. R. 1968. *The History of the Christian Church.* London: Livingstones.

Chapter Six

Social Institutions In African Oral Societies

By Akinloye Ojo

Introduction

The majority of societies on the African continent can be considered oral or oral dominated as a large amount of the societies' knowledge base is shared by word of mouth. These societies present unique challenges for researchers interested in their social institutions. As Ong (1982) notes, "Primary orality fosters personality structures that in certain ways are more communal and externalized, and less introspective than those common among literates." A significant characteristic evident in all oral or oral-dominated societies and which appear to transcend cultural differences is group orientation (Kayongo-Male & Onyango, 1984, Mosha, 2000, Ampim, 2003, Lawal et al., 2004, Abdi, 2007). It determines their cultural values as well as the social, political, educational, spiritual, and economic activities of each person in the community. In all of these things the group is in focus, and not the individual. Group orientation also affects the decision-making processes as group decisions are usually regarded as more important and more binding on the individual than their own personal decisions. This essential value is well illustrated by works on aspects of socialization among several African societies such as the Yoruba people in Nigeria (Bascom, 1969, Lawal et al., 2004), the Kasena people in Ghana (Awedoba, 2000), and the Chaga people in Tanzania (Mosha, 2000).

In this chapter, we begin with the discussion of six practical sources of information on comprehending oral societies (following Nyembezi, 1963, Kayongo-Male & Onyango, 1984, Olatunji, 1984, Boateng, 1985, Mutisya, 1996, Siegel, 1996, Mosha, 2000, Ojo, 2000, Wane, 2000, Lawal et al., 2004, Nsamenang, 2004, Oyedipe, 2004, Tiumelissan, 2006, Abdi, 2007, Shanklin, 2007, among others). This is followed by a brief consideration of the indigenous systems of instruction in various oral and oral-dominated African societies and a summative discussion of the rites of passage across Africa with illustrations from different parts of the continent. We end the chapter with the extended examination of some of the possible generalities about kinship systems and marriage across the continent.

Comprehending Oral Societies

The predominance of oral or oral-dominated societies in Africa (Isola, 1992), however, necessitates an inaugural, even if pithy discussion of some of the ways to best understand these oral societies. Here, we provide an inventory of six of these sources for information on the social institutions within oral societies, particularly in Africa. The first source is the arts to be found within the society. These include not only the visual arts, the decorative arts, but also the performance arts including dances and other acts at festivals. It also includes what has been labeled as "religious" arts. As can be deduced from Campbell's (2008) discussion of "religious" arts among the Yoruba people, the focus on sacred paintings found in the shrines and revered spaces of divinities, honors and celebrates the divinities and epitomizes the salient qualities of the venerated divinity. Aspects of the oral tradition form the second set and are probably the richest sources for information on oral societies. These include riddles (to teach and sharpen minds), folktales (to entertain and instruct in morality), legend tales (significant stories of the culture told in story form), idioms and poetry (language and phraseology), taboos (cultural and health restrictions), prayers (supplication and attesting to higher powers) and curses (teaching of natural and cultural repercussions).

Two other closely related sources are the myths and proverbs. These are, for most people, forms of the oral tradition. Notwithstanding, these sources, combined, dominate the existence of the members of any oral or oral-dominated society, and they will most likely produce the most information and comprehension about such societies. Myths are revered and well-regarded tales socially considered nonfiction, never (or seldom) to be questioned or debated. They are the society's objectives and permanent philosophy of life. Myth serves as a clear presentation of the culture's outlook on life. They are an energetic means of conceptualizing the past, present, and future social and political orders Proverbs, on the other hand, are the societies' encyclopedia or body of reference for constant and evolving knowledge. Essentially, proverbs capture the truth for a society. The fifth source of information on oral societies is the onomastics or onomatology of the society. Among other things, naming practices often reveal a society's expectations, fears, hope, and outlook on life. The final sets of sources for information on most oral and oral-dominated societies are the revered institutions. These include traditions, mores, rites and observances that the society regards as sacred, perpetual, and fundamental. We will discuss two such institutions that appear to traverse the entire continent. These are the kinship systems and marriage, and the rites of passage.

All six identified sources in this section, along with many others, are valuable sources of information when considering the worldview of oral or oral-dominated societies. Significantly, in most of these societies in Africa, the society's worldview is the people's conceptions and assumptions about their place or the place of humanity as a whole in the universe and in nature as well as the limits to and workings of the natural and spiritual world. A society's basis for interpreting the world and for illuminating all of their interactions within it is their worldview.

Existing in this worldview are their belief system, ideologies, ontology, metaphysics, philosophy, religion, and, more important, their social order.

Indigenous Systems of Instructing

In this section, we turn our focus to the indigenous systems in place for instructing children and shepherding young people into maturity and responsibility. It is common throughout Africa to see the child as possessing a rather wild nature that must be tamed and controlled through proper supervision and training. Without this monitoring and education into proper conduct, the child will not develop into a responsible and worthy adult. This has been carried out in the home, the village, and community associations, such as age-sets, vocation leagues or secret societies. Many people make a distinction between that which was knowledge open to everyone and that which one had to be initiated into or rites of passage discussed in the next section. Indigenous education also involved apprenticeships to learn such tasks as metal working, building, and medicinal practice (Vontress, 1999). In essence, indigenous education refers to the transfer of (indigenous) knowledge, that is, local know-how, from one generation to the other. It is mostly oral, practical, and effective. More important, it is always relevant to the learner and the environment in which the learning is being done.

At the end, the learner acquires education (knowledge) and enlightenment (wisdom) about family and community traditions, philosophies, worldview, beliefs, and practices. At the family and work level, education concerns the transfer of vocational and family-trade skills and knowledge to new generations. The ultimate goal of indigenous education is survival. It provides critical knowledge for surviving in the community, the environment, and the world at large. Other goals of indigenous systems of education include character development, environmental awareness, molding behavior, developing skills, integrating moral and ethical values, empowering, and knowing gender roles within the society (Boateng, 1985; Mosha, 2000; Wane; 2000; Nsemenang, 2004). African children are often given housekeeping and other work responsibilities at a very young age. There is often, but not always, a a gender-based division of labor, with girls more typically given work related to child care and cooking. Boys, on the other hand, are more commonly called upon to leave the house to tend livestock.

This is the case with several groups, such as the Bukoba of Northwestern Tanzania. Among the Fulani of northern Senegal, children start pastoral duties at a very young age (five or six), progressing naturally from play to actually guarding calves in the compound. In almost all groups, the father teaches his sons by going out with them first, then giving hands-on responsibility; the knowledge is firmly established by age nine or ten. The knowledge of livestock range and husbandry among the Somali is passed on when young boys, seven to eight years old, are taken to camel camps to learn firsthand which grasses are good, noxious, etc. At eight to ten years old, Wodaabe children start to learn about herding by being assigned to watch over calves near the camp. Between ten and twelve years of age, they start to herd shoats alone in the bush, and at fifteen they herd cattle on their own. Wodaabe girls start at nine or ten to make butter; at eleven or twelve years to pound millet; and at fourteen or fifteen to milk cows. Among the Lozi of Zimbabwe, young boys and girls would go to the cattle posts in the wet season to herd cattle and to be "hardened and taught morals and tribal law."

Some of the methods of teaching include storytelling, direct instruction, gestures, body language, games, myths and fables, real-life activities, and so on (Boateng, 1985; Mosha, 2000; Wane, 2000; Nsemenang, 2004). The methods of learning therefore include imitation, repetition, participation in activities, and strict observance of rules and regulations (Boateng, 1985; Mosha, 2000; Wane, 2000; Nsemenang, 2004). Monitoring and punishment in the traditional education system is done by all groups of "teachers" because "the child must be raised by all." Punishments often are "weighted," based on the principle that children are allowed to make mistakes so that they can learn from them, but they are not allowed to make the same mistake repeatedly. The key injunction is to "Fold the fish while it is still wet," which in essence means teach children while they are still young. Once the fish is dry, it becomes difficult to bend without breaking it.

As the Yoruba people say, managing the roots of a timber tree is best done when it is still young because once it becomes a full-grown tree, it becomes almost impossible to adjust. Finally, indigenous education provided the young with the needed skills and ideology for social participation. It meant the "survival of society through the survival and perpetuation of customs, norms, and the old tried ways of doing things. It was supported by the social system and was natural, nonformal, practical, effective, and diverse." It combines what we would see today as home training, survival-skill training, and lessons in history and worldview for all children, plus additional specialized skill or trade training for a selected view. Allied to this is the knowledge that one had to be initiated through the system of rites of passage (Mosha, 2000; Wane, 2000; and Nsamenang 2004).

Rites of passage

Rites of passage are of varied forms and are common across the continent. These rites are seen to have positive value for the individual in relieving stress at times when great changes or upheaval in his or her life occur, such as those brought by coming of age, entering marriage, having children, and dying (moving into the other realm). These rites are not peculiar to African societies; graduation ceremonies, bar or bat mitzvahs, baptisms, and bridal or baby showers are rites of passage, too. Rites of passage regularly involve transition into a newer, often higher status, but they also signify the ending or exiting of a lower status within the society (Ronald, 1992; Doyle, 2005). Rites of passage, no matter how they are classified, are very symbolic, often elaborate, and rich in imagery. Most common among these markers of new status are alterations and embellishments of visible or hidden parts of the body. The societies that base their social hierarchy on these rites of passage perceive these ceremonies as also involving achieved status based on personal effort. There are very few places where this grand symbolism is more discernible than in Africa, with its various emblematic rites of passage.

Rites of passage in Africa

Characteristically, most African societies have five major initiation rites. These rites, at various stages of life, are seen as basic and essential for the growth, development, and well-being of an individual within the society. As Manu Ampim (2003) noted:

> Initiation rites are a natural and necessary part of a community....These rites are critical to individual and community development, and it should not be taken for granted that people automatically grow and develop into responsible, community-oriented adults. The process of *initiation* concerns undergoing a fundamental set of rites to start a new phase or beginning in life. It marks the passing from one phase in life to the next more mature phase. *Initiation* fundamentally has to do with transformation, and has been a central component of traditional African cultures since time immemorial. The details of the rites vary among the different societies, but these rites are nevertheless basic components of the society as they help guide the person from one stage in life into the next stage of one's life and development, that is, from birth to death and beyond.

Essentially, an understanding of a society's rites of passage or initiation rites can provide indispensable information on the society regarding issues such as:

a. Stratification of a society:
The rites of passage highlight the varied ways in which a society is stratified socially. Certain customs surrounding these rites of passage and the very occurrence of these rites will reflect how the society categorizes its individuals into groups such as children vs. adult vs. elders or women vs. men or even age-sets or age-mates as with the Nuers of Sudan and the Maasai of Kenya/Tanzania. In many societies with age-sets, these are often men and women who were initiated into adulthood together.

b. Worldview and belief system:
Among other things, the rites of passage provide an in-depth view of the core elements of a society's worldview and belief system, including their beliefs concerning such things as the role of ancestors, reincarnation, ownership and individual rights, and so on.

c. System of traditional education and incorporation of values:
While the rites of passage appear as specific shifting points, the process involved in the different categories of rites highlights the lifelong learning or system of indigenous education within

the society as these all involve the preparation of the individual for ascension or movement into the next social role/grouping.

d. The extent to which a society values individual achievement allows community interest to prevail over these achievements:

The different types of rites of passage in many African societies generally involve the surrender of individual privileges in the attainment of newer, more group-focused roles or positions in the society.

Purposes of Rites of Passage

In most African societies, the rites of passage serve several social and spiritual purposes including the following:

1. Linking the individual concretely to the community and through the community to the all-encompassing and ever-present spiritual world.
2. Conferring privileges and responsibilities that come with the latest social membership (A Yoruba proverb which basically says that "an elder behaves as an elder" or that "only childhood makes one act like a child" makes this point more clearly).
3. Acquisition and transferring of indigenous knowledge, especially about cultural and environmental adaptation.
4. Demonstration of acquired knowledge and the performance of cultural competence.
5. Preparation of children and young people for future roles as they first learn, simultaneously learning to teach and then teaching (Ronald, 1992, Doyle, 2005).
6. Provision of a model of consistency and inter-generational unity through the ritual structure. (Another common West African saying states this point better: "That which makes us who we are should be done today as it has always been done.")
7. Prevention of conflicts between age groups and the methodical abuse of women, children, and the elderly through the array of ritual procedures.

The five major categories of rites of passage in most African societies, following Manu Ampim's (2003) classification are the following: rites of passage associated with *birth*; rites of passage associated with *adulthood*; rites of passage associated with *marriage*; rites of passage associated with *elderhood*, and rites of passage associated with ancestorhood.

The rites associated with birth or rites of birth (Ampim, 2003) is a category of rites of passage that is often a complex of distinct rituals that prescribe different behavior on the part of the mother, father, other relatives, and nonfamilial members of the society with respect to the newborn. Observances may begin when pregnancy is first noted and may continue until the time of delivery, when the full rite of passage is performed in the naming ceremony. Being the first rite, it is primarily about initiating the infant into the world through a ritual and naming ceremony (Ojo, 2000). These ceremonies vary from simple to elaborate, but it is often centered on extended family and community participation. The time from birth to the naming ceremony varies from society to society. It could be immediately after birth (especially with societies with preordained sequence of naming children as with the Luo people in East Africa) to a customary set period after birth. Traditionally, these set periods had varied across the continent as much as from three days (as with the Akamba people of Kenya or the Sara people of Chad) or four to five days (as with the Gikuyu of Kenya), up to forty days (as with the Somali people), up to three months (as with the Ishan people of Nigeria), and even up to a year (as with the Massai people in East Africa).

However, in contemporary times, with the widespread adaptation of the seven-day work week, the commonly set periods are now often a week in many African cultures. Among the Igbo people of Nigeria, the set period used to be twenty-eight days, but now the naming ceremony is commonly done on the eighth day. Societies that have now switched to seven days as the set period between birth and naming ceremonies include the Tutsi people (of Rwanda); the Wolof people (of Senegal); the Ndebele people (of Zimbabwe); and the Edo people (of Nigeria). There are also societies that determine the set periods based on the gender of the child. Among the Yoruba people of Nigeria, female children are named after the seventh day, male children after the ninth day, and twins are named on the eighth day. Cultures with similar practices are the Goun people of Benin and the Bassa people of Cameroon. In all these places where a time is set aside before the naming ceremony, societies adapt different appellations for the child that will translate into newborn; infant; and child. Among the Yoruba people, it is *ìkókó* and *omo ofu* among the Igbo people. During these periods, the mother is also expected to remain indoors recuperating and observing various social and health-based restrictions (or taboos). There are actually some societies such as the Somali people of Somalia and the Yoruba people of Nigeria that allow longer "incubatory" periods of forty days for new mothers beyond the period set aside between birth and the naming ceremony.

In addition to the actual naming ceremony, the birth rites often involve discovering the new community member's unique mission in the world. Nearly all African cultures hold that the infant has come from the spirit world with important information from that world and is bringing unique talents and gifts to offer to the community. The infant, in fact, is believed to have been commissioned to come to the world and accomplish a particular mission or project or deliver a great message. Therefore, it is the responsibility of the family and community to discover the infant's unique mission through consultations with a diviner and to have rituals and a birth chart done. This is done to clearly determine the new community member's mission in order to guide him or her through life. Among the Yoruba people, the process is known as *Wíwo Esèntayé*. The infant's name is given after the determination of the mission and reflection of the infant's personality or the life mission itself.

The rites associated with adulthood or rites of adulthood (Ampim, 2003) are the most popular category of rites of passage found among most African societies. Therefore, most people today assume that "rite of passage" refers only to initiation into adulthood, and they are often not aware that adulthood rites are only one set of rites within a larger system of rites in most African societies (Ampim, 2003). As the stronghold of social structuring (who becomes an adult and who does not), the rites may involve secret or private procedures and/or painful and difficult trials before the initiate can become a "real" or "accepted" member bonded to the community. Such rites vary greatly (from endurance rituals to circumcision) and often involve a shepherding process, where those who are at a higher level guide the initiate through increasing exposure to knowledge. This may include the revelation of secrets, usually reserved for those at the higher level of understanding. As in many societies, coming of age rites (or puberty rites) are usually done at the onset of puberty (around twelve to fourteen years of age), and they are done to ensure the shaping of productive, community-oriented, responsible adults. There is nothing automatic about youth becoming productive members of society, nor is there anything particularly difficult about transitioning from a child to an adult.

Most African societies often take the young initiates out of the community and away from the concerns of everyday life to teach them all the ways of adulthood, including the rules and taboos of the society, moral instruction and social responsibility, and further clarification of his or her mission or calling in life. Initiation rites also create a common bond of experience that unites all who make it through the ordeal. Generally, it is possible to divide most of these rites into two: ceremonies without circumcision and ceremonies with circumcision. Ceremonies without circumcision include those found among the Khoi people of Namibia featuring the Choma (puberty) dance and tattooing for boys and the Choa (puberty) dance and sequestering for girls; ceremonies among the Mbuti of the Congo feature killing games in which boys are roughed up by girls and girls are sequestered in the forest, all during the Elima festival; ceremonies among the Krobo people in Ghana feature three weeks of sequestering and training for young girls and no circumcision but the back being tattooed.

Among the Waikiriki people in Nigeria, the rite of passage known as *iria* involves young virgin females in the community spending five weeks in seclusion in what is known as "fattening" rooms. In these rooms, the young women's heads are shaved and their bodies are painted and powdered while their entire family honors them by waiting on their every need. As Ngozi Onwurah reported in her 1993 video, *Monday's Girls*, the five-week-long iria ritual is overseen by postmenopausal women in the Egbereneme society. The girls are paraded bare-breasted before the entire community so their nipples can be examined to determine whether they are still virgins. They are then confined to the "fattening rooms," their legs immobilized in copper impala rings, where they are pampered and fed. Finally, the girls, now women, are presented to society, wearing yards of fabric around their waists indicating each family's wealth—and suggesting pregnancy. A young woman who refuses to participate in the Iria ceremony or is found not to be a virgin at the time of the ceremony brings shame to her family within the community and is not considered honorable.

Examples of ceremonies with circumcision include those found among the Merina people in Madagascar, the Sukus people in Congo and the Gussi in Kenya. These ceremonies for boys provide training on social roles in addition to the physical circumcision ritual. This is also true of ceremonies with circumcision for girls as those found among the Nandi people in Kenya, the Afikpo Igbo people in Nigeria, the Kalenjin people in Kenya, and the Maasai people. The initiates are often identifiable by their special clothing or ornaments such as wearing only black clothes for three to four months among the Maasai. In most of these societies, circumcision is done without medications or numbing agents and often, part of the test is for the initiate not to flinch or show any sign of pain, especially among male initiates. And for these societies, too, circumcision and its associated shedding of blood serves the ethno-religious task of cleansing and reincorporation. After the shedding ritual, the child, male or female, has been transformed into a mature being and with the other rituals and education, can move into the social roles of men and women within the society.

Although female circumcision has been widely criticized because of its long-term health risks, perpetuation of women's subordination to men, and repression of female sexuality, not all female initiation involves genital cutting. Instead, some other test is required. The entire community, from parents, relatives, friends, to members of the wider society, is expected to be part of the instruction within the system. This is true of most African societies, including the Kikuyu of Kenya, the Manus of Guinea, and most groups in Nigeria (Igbo, Yoruba). The demand, therefore, is on all members of the immediate family, extended family, and the community to provide instruction (to transfer knowledge) to the young people whenever and however an opportunity presents itself.

Among the Zulu in southern Africa, the rite of passage known as *umemulo* involves young boys going through whitewashing their body and discarding regular clothing for nothing but a thin blanket used for cover regardless of the weather. The process involves these boys congregating in what is known as a circumcision hut along with adult circumcised men who perform the circumcision procedure. This procedure, which primarily involves the removal of the foreskin, is done in the company of other young boys and each initiate is expected (or does his best) not to show fear or pain. The young boys' foreheads are smeared with blood while their wounds are covered with eucalyptus leaves. The group must then trek into the woods to get rid (or leave behind) their removed foreskins. This is followed by four to six weeks of sequestering and training in social roles and duties. This sequestering allows their wounds to heal and for them to be physically and mentally prepared for their new roles within society. At the end of the period, the nascent young men go to the river for a group washing followed by their reintroduction into their families and community amidst great celebration (Doyle, 2005).

If marriage is one of the earliest social institutions invented, then Africans seem to be the best at understanding the anticipated purpose of the institution. Accordingly, they have developed rites (and ceremonies) that highlight their understanding of the institution. The category of rites associated with marriage or the rite of marriage (Ampim, 2003) in many African societies represents not only the joining of two families but also the joining of the two missions of the new couple. In other words, the marriage rites are performed not only for the coming together of males and females to procreate and perpetuate life and the coming together of families, but also for creating an institution that helps both the husband and wife to best fulfill their mission and objectives in life. Still, in many African societies, the basic focus of marriage is on building families and communities—the collective more than the individual (Kayongo-Male and Onyango, 1984).

Hence, a person is not generally considered an adult until he has married (and had children). In fact, for many African groups such as the Zulu of South Africa and the Amhara of Ethiopia, marriage signifies full adulthood. For the Zulu, a girl who has gone through the puberty rite is ready for marriage and for the men, in addition to going through the umemulo rituals to become men, marriage confirms their adulthood. Similarly for the Amhara, the best signification of full adult status is marriage, which allows a man to assume the required maintenance of his home and family (Messing, 1996).

The various rituals associated with marriage can generally be divided into at least three groups of rituals and rites. These are the courtship ritual; the bridal rituals; and the marriage rites. The courtship rituals often involve activities to show stamina, grace, wealth and/or ability, among other things. The demonstration of these qualities is often expected of the male. Among the Fulani people of West Africa and the Surma people of Ethiopia, men engage in stick fights to impress young women who will eventually make their choices among these men. There is the painting and body adornment for all male beauty contests among the Wodaabe people of Niger. Young women, who are ready to select their grooms, are mostly the judges at these contests. The bridal rituals are ceremonies and activities designed to prepare, honor and/or spotlight the bride. These include the tradition of *Ekun iyawo* (bridal poetry recitation) among the Yoruba people of Nigeria (Babatunde, 2004), the weeklong body treatment and henna painting among the Swahili in Zanzibar, and the Hoop ceremony, which also includes body adornment with beaded hoops around hips and legs among the Ndebele people of Southern Africa. Finally, the marriage rites are ceremonies and rituals that mark the actual unification of the couple and the families as well as the actual transfer of the bride.

The rites associated with elderhood or rites of eldership (Ampim, 2003) are important rites that involve most of the aged and experienced custodians of the society's indigenous knowledge, tradition, and ancient practices. The participants in the rites associated with elderhood are not just members of the society that are more biologically advanced in age than many others, but they are mature members of the society who are known to have lived a model life of achievements, service, and selflessness. The life of an elder is centered in the best tradition of the community—an elder has gone through all of the previous three rites and is a living model for the other groups in the society to emulate (Ampim, 2003). Elders occupy the loftiest position in most African societies as they have participated, gained increased knowledge, and achieved all the social status associated with all the preceding rites and rituals. They are highly regarded because they are moving closer to the ancestral realm after having survived the majority of life's challenges. As a Yoruba adage says, no matter how much children or young people have clothes just or even more than elders, they cannot have rags as the elders. Rags, in this case, being experiences acquired in life.

The rites associated with elderhood are often related to the induction or initiation of an elderly or fully matured individual into a group or society, often secret societies. It is notable that many of these rites often coincide with biological stages of life or age markers in the society. Illustrations of such rites include Orngesherr ceremonies among the Maasai people in East Africa or the initiation of postmenopausal women into the Egbereneme society among the Waikiriki people in Nigeria (Onwurah, 1993). Other illustrations are initiation or "advanced" rituals in secret societies such as the *Ogboni* (among the Yoruba people of Nigeria), *Ogo* (among the Afikpo Igbo people of Nigeria), and *Poro* (among the Kpelle people of Liberia.)

The rites associated with *ancestorhood* or *the rite of ancestorship* (Ampim, 2003) are in the final category of rites of passage in most African societies according to Ampim's postulation. All human societies have beliefs in souls or spirits and an afterlife, and all conduct rituals when people die. For most African societies, the final initiation rite is an extension of the elder/older—one's status in life will affect one's status in the afterlife. There is virtually no African society that believes that death ends all ties and communication with the living. Rather, the prevalent African worldview agrees that the spirit of the deceased is still with the living community, and that a distinction must be made in the status of the various spirits, as there are distinctions made in the status of the living. These rites are often part of the preparation of the body for burial and the rituals performed based on the beliefs about afterlife. A respected elder who passes on becomes a respected ancestor and is given the highest honor. These groups of ancestors wield great power and are often called upon in matters of trouble or uncertainty to help influence a favorable outcome. Thus, ancestors are respected elders who continue to serve as an extension of the family and community. In most of these societies also, the death of a young(er) person is generally considered a tragedy. As such, there are prayers and sacrifices that are continually offered in most societies to ward off death of young people. Funeral ceremonies are performed, in most societies, for young people who have been moral and have made contributions to the society (or have children) before their death. These are, however, devoid of death rites or elaborate rituals.

In most societies on the continent, death is generally perceived as a journey to another realm, and the beliefs about the destination determine the handling of the dead. Generally, death rites are concerned with the transition of the aged deceased individual to the ancestral world and include rituals and observations from the death pronouncements until burial. As such, an assortment of rules govern different aspects of how the dead are buried from preparing their body; what to bury with them; and where to bury them. In fact, many societies such as the Yoruba people, the Urhobo people, and the Igbo people, all of Nigeria, believe that if funeral rites and rituals are not performed, the spirit of the departed elder will not be able to "rest," that is take its rightful place among the ancestral spirits. Depending on age, gender, and socioeconomic status, different societies have different requirements for how the death is announced and the number of days (mourning days) between the death pronouncements and the commencement of the funeral rites and ceremonies. The Bara people of Madagascar have three days of mourning, and on each day, female relatives of the deceased come in to weep and mourn three times a day. On the third day of mourning, the actual funeral takes place, and the deceased is declared a new ancestor through libation ceremonies at the entrance to the family abode. Dance rituals are also commonly performed across the continent. These vary from gloomy performances of mourning to forceful dance rituals meant to symbolize the engagement of death and the afterlife. Among the Kenga people of Sudan, there are mourning dances during the *Dodi* ceremony.

The Dogon people of Mali have masked dances ceremonies such as the *Dama* that marks the end of a mourning period for the dead and can be seen as a form of confrontation with death as well as a culminating rite of passage for those relocating to the ancestral world. The Dama, like other masked ceremonies of the Dogon, involve male initiates who can take on the personality of Dogon spirits. Some of these dance rituals and ceremonies include the performance of vocational and ordinary dirges such as the hunters' dirge ceremonies among the Yoruba people of Nigeria (known as *Iremoje*) and the Mande people of West Africa. Other parts of the dance rituals and ceremonies might include masquerades and the performance of reserved roles by elder societies. An illustration is the Kita ceremony among the Suku people of the Congo. In addition to the variety of mourning days and dance rituals, the number of days for the actual funeral also varies. In most cases, the burial is on the last day of the mourning period but in some other societies, funerals can last from just a day to longer. Among the Yoruba people of Nigeria, funeral rites and rituals last at least a week with various ceremonies and rituals on each day.

Finally, considerable thought is devoted to burial places. Some societies bury their dead underneath the compound or the house. For others, it is important to remove the body to a burial ground some distance away. Among the Baganda people of Uganda, graves are prepared in childhood and can be continually maintained throughout life. Among the Dogon people of Mali, bodies are wrapped in cloth and hauled by rope 300 feet up a sheer cliff face to centuries-old burial caves. However, there are many changes to these indigenous practices in contemporary African societies due to many influences including the nonindigenous religions as Christianity and Islam.

Kinship Systems and Marriage

Anthropologists have done most studies about kinship systems and marriage practices around the world. In the course of their studies, they have developed a number of terms that help us to understand the many different varieties of kinship forms in Africa and other parts of the world. From these studies, things that might at first appear to be simple processes based on our experiences start to appear more complicated when the experiences of other people begin to factor into our consideration. Is our own understanding of our relationships good enough to define similar relationships for all people, everywhere? For example, simple relationships and institutions such as family, marriage, fatherhood, cousin, and so on and so forth become difficult to define without one sounding prejudiced or biased by one's own way of thinking about things.

With the exception of society-specific discussions or studies, what are often presented are generalizations rather than complete representations of all African societies. This is especially true when it comes to the discussions of various social institutions across the African continent. African family or kinship descent systems are unique to each geographic region; and many Africans do not appreciate generalizations about Africa. Akin to any sociocultural discussion about Africa, there is the issue of traditional versus contemporary, especially within (long) urbanized societies. Precolonial stateless societies were governed by kinship systems that divided largely along family lines. Even with the emergence of central authorities in state societies, there was still heavy reliance on familial relationships. There have been constant and continuous changes in practices, but commonalities persist, especially since every group in Africa seems to have a migration story. Significantly, the most common social order in traditional precolonial Africa was the "dual-sex system" in which each sex governed its own affairs and shared power to varying degrees on major decisions. This was overlooked by the colonizers due to their social biases in favor of male domination; unfortunately, it is also often missed by researchers who have predetermined theories of social/gender relations that Africans are expected to illustrate readily.

Although all African societies are different, sharing is a greatly valued trait. There is a common traditional perception that the "self" is not complete when other related or connected "selves" are not complete. African marriage and kinship systems are more about preserving choices, not individual preference. In many societies, choice is considered a burden, and members are glad to give up this "burden" to the community. *When Africans talk about families, they often have in mind something other than the contemporary Western emphasis on nuclear/immediate families.* The form and format of families varies with a society's type and level of development. In most of Africa, nuclear families serve more like units within the extended family. The combinations of these units (either within a physical locale or in various places) constitute an extended family. The purpose of the extended family is to provide a "social" solution to most (if not all) human challenges/problems. It is also for sharing and for group survival. Essentially, it is a means of adaptation to economic, social, and political conditions that require great cooperation.

Kinship Relations

Universally, people are related to one another in various ways, but it is the kinship systems that define how these people are related to one another within their community and even beyond. Kinship systems encompass the formation of family ties, types of families, marriage and its duties, lineage or descent, family residency, as well as social structures that emerge from families and the division of power within them. Kinship terms, based on the system of relationships, can be limited (common in more African societies) or extensive (less common and in most contemporary/urban centers). There are three types of kinship relations. Consanguine relationships are blood relations (consanguineal kins), while affinal relationships are marriage relations. These are often generic and highly descriptive in many African societies. An additional type of relationships, common in the West and emerging among urbanized Africans and Africans in Diaspora, is fictive relationships, which are established relationships other than blood or marriage ties. Examples include godparenthood and the emergence of "uncles" and "aunties" (through this process, Africans from the same ethnic group country or region but residents abroad in places such as America establish close friendships through which their children become "nephews" and "nieces").

Rules of descent are rules or links that connect individuals within particular sets of kin because of known or presumed shared ancestry. Europeans and Americans have kinship systems that reckon descent from grandparents on both sides. In other words, one's mother's parents and one's father's parents are considered to be the same category of kin: a grandfather is a grandfather, a grandchild is a grandchild. In Africa and in many other parts of the world, however, people often have what are called lineages. There are three types; patrilineal system; matrilineal descent; and dual descent. The patrilineal descent system is the most common in Africa. Descent, in this system, is traced over generations to a male founding ancestor. Relatives are traced by who their fathers were. In this system, mothers are important, but they do belong to one's lineage and neither do the children of female relatives. And so while one's siblings, both male and female, are in one's patrilineage, the status of one's cousins will depend on whether they are related to one through the mother or father. If the relationship is through one's mother, chances are high that they do not belong to one's patrilineage.

Matrilineal descent systems are virtually the opposite of the patrilineal systems. Descent is traced over generations to a female founding ancestor. The identity of the mothers is the basis of tracing one's relatives. Everything else said above is true, but the focus is on relatives who share connection through a set of mothers. Children born into a matrilineal society cannot be "illegitimate." If a man should choose not to claim his child, the mother's brother will fill the role. The relationships with the mother's brothers are therefore highly valuable in these societies. Examples are found among the Asante and Akan of Ghana; the Lemba people of Zambia; the Ngulu and Nata of Tanzania; and the Yako of Nigeria. Although no society granted women control over everything, matrilineal systems did often give women opportunities to achieve higher status. While men were the political leaders, women were often very important leaders and advisors.

The system of dual descent exists only in a few African societies and is also not a popular descent system universally. It is called a dual system because for some purposes descent is matrilineal for some purposes and patrilineal for others. This is often called ambilineal descent because both male and female genealogical links are valued. Two often-cited societies in Africa with the dual descent system are the Tongo people in Zambia and the Yako people in Nigeria. Among the Tongo people, birth and inheritance are reckoned by patrilineal descent, but marriage is reckoned by matrilineal descent. Among the Yako people, on the other hand, land inheritance is conducted through patrilineal descent while movable property such as livestock is inherited through matrilineal descent.

Comparatively, Africans mostly have unilineal descent through either paternal or maternal sides, and the descent system produces kinsmen (and kinswomen) whereas Western societies (as in America in particular) mostly have the bilineal or bilateral descent in which descent is traced through both the paternal and maternal sides. These descent systems produce kindred. In addition to kin (versus kindred), there are other expressions or terms that can be challenging in connection to kinship systems in African societies. Three of these include lineages, clans, and totems. Lineages are the set of kin whose members trace descent from a common ancestor through known links (patrilineages or matrilineages). Clans are the set of kin whose members believe they are descended from a common ancestor but without specified or known links (patriclans vs. matriclans). In popular discourse, it is often noted that following the shift from statelessness to organized state systems in the early history of the African continent, lineages became clans. However, this is highly improbable, especially when lineage poetries and histories are considered. Prior to colonialism, many African societies formed small, autonomous communities that did not have chiefs, kings, or a large centralized government. When this was the case, societies were organized along kinship lines, with lineage systems being the most common.

Lineages had political functions in terms of group decision-making, settling disputes, and the organization of people for war and common defense. They had economic functions in that they often acted like corporations, pooling resources—land, for example. In other words, individuals didn't own and allocate land; the lineage did. Lineage systems could become very large and break up into segments. The Nuers and Dinka (East African pastoralists in places such as Sudan) are organized in this way. It is often thought that a collection of lineages constitutes a clan. Size (villages or towns descending from a true lineage) or spread (people of shared lineage migrating away from other lineage members) does not alter the definition or representation of lineages and clans. Keeping track of lineages and clans is addressed through the oral traditions. Totems are signifiers of a clan or an object/animal/plant representing a clan. It has special significance to the clan and is a means of group identification.

Creation of family ties

As with other parts of the world, family ties are created through blood and marriage relationships. Many African societies believe blood ties (parent/child) are much more important than marriage ties (husband/wife). Other non-blood relationships (friendship and age sets) do carry weight and sometimes can challenge the importance of blood relationships. To better understand marital arrangements in most African societies, certain questions must be answered and some issues addressed. The questions regarding marriage in Africa will include what, when, who, and how. Let us address these and related issues in sequence.

What is marriage in most African societies?

Marriage, if we can define it, is a socially approved sexual and economic union, usually between a woman and a man. We must remember that different social institutions have social functions.

Most people around the world do not get married just because they felt like it or because they suddenly fell in love. Marriages establish relationships of responsibility of adults toward children and provide for legal inheritance of property. Marriage has usually been a matter of kin groups and communities making arrangements with each other, using marriage to cement social ties and relationships between groups. When this aspect of the marriage function is emphasized, anthropologists talk of "alliance theory." On the other hand, kin groups need to have children to maintain themselves. For most Africans, the importance of children cannot be overemphasized; procreation is generally considered the primary reason for marriage.

In agricultural societies, having many children can be useful because they soon become economic assets, working the land or tending livestock. Parents also look to their children to care for them in their old age. In Africa, children were often so important to a marriage that without them the marriage was not really considered valid. This is especially so in patrilineal societies. For this reason, wives gain status in their husband's lineage by having sons to carry on the lineage. This is why a lot of Africans appear obsessed with the notion of having male children. Generally, the desire for children has led to the development of various surrogacy practices, levirate systems, and, in a few societies, of same-sex marriage and what has been called "ghost marriage" and/or "female husbands" (Nandi of Kenya, the Igbo of Nigeria, and the Kikuyu of Kenya are examples of societies with these same-sex marriages.) In one form of same-sex marriage, a woman could pay bride wealth to marry another woman. This other woman would then have children with a man not considered to be her husband. The woman who paid bride wealth would then be considered the "female father" of these children. The female father would usually be an older woman who had failed to conceive in her "normal" heterosexual marriage. Any children conceived by her wife are considered to be the children of the female father and her male husband. Because of this, some argue that this is not purely woman-to-woman marriage because it is done to bequeath children to the male husband. Either way, the "female husband" retains control. The advantage for her is that the children are responsible for her well-being, as they would be for any father. The advantage for the mother is that she may have had difficulty contracting another marriage, perhaps because of premarital pregnancy or other factors. For a perspective on woman marriage and ghost marriage from the point of view of an Igbo scholar, see Celestine Obi's *'Marriage among the Igbo of Nigeria,'* at http://www.afrikaworld.net/afrel/igbo-marriage.htm. For findings on these practices among the Kikuyu, please see the work of Wairimu Ngaruiya Njambi and William E. O'Brien.

When do you marry, and whom do you marry?

In most traditional societies, there are economic and natural markers for an individual's readiness to marry. In most cases, a young person is ready for marriage after becoming an adult via initiation rites and acquiring the necessary resources to provide for a family (for example, among the Yoruba of Nigeria, having a farm or unhindered access to a farm was a major requirement for marriage). In modern times, age is often presented as the determining factor for readiness.

A kinship rule that dictates marrying outside of one's group is called "exogamy." If lineages are large—they can number in the thousands—then one might be expected to marry someone else of his own lineage. This is called lineage endogamy and can be found among such groups as the Maasai warriors and some Tutsi castes. Among the Fulani of Nigeria, endogamy is practiced in which the ultimate choice of bride is a patrilateral parallel cousin. When this option is unavailable, then the bride can be a patrilateral cross-cousin or a girl who shares a great-grandfather with the groom. Interestingly, exogamy is often reported in most African societies today.

One way that many African societies keep links and relationships going between groups that tend to intermarry is the custom of bride wealth. This is an exchange of wealth, often in the form of livestock, from the groom's family to the bride's family. Examples include payment of a dowry (*Owo Ori* among the Yoruba people of Nigeria and *Lobola* among the Zulu people of Southern Africa) or a gift of livestock (among the Jie people of Uganda; the Kalenjin people of Kenya; the Tutsi people, the Hutu people, and the Twa people of Rwanda; and the Kpelle people of Liberia) or the gift of farm produce (among the Ebira people in Nigeria) or labor owed to the bride's family (among the Yoruba people, this was also expected in addition to the dowry). Bride wealth is an honorable and relevant social system in which the payment made via personal resources or labor is often used to equip the bride or benefit her family. Essentially, it provides security for the new bride. In societies where bride wealth is paid, the resources are used to empower the young wife. Among the Kalenjin people, the livestock given is the property of the bride; there will be no shared ownership with the husband or husband's family. These exchanges also help to link families because it gives them both an economic stake in the marriage's success. If divorce occurs, for example, then the bride wealth is generally expected to be returned.

Types of marriages

In Africa, there are several different types of marriage allowed besides monogamy, that is, marriage between one woman and one man at the same time. In Africa, it is also legal in most countries for a man to have more than one wife at the same time. Anthropologists refer to this as polygyny. Polygamy, in anthropology, means marriage to more than one spouse at the same time, whether male or female. So, polygamy includes both polygyny (man with two or more wives) and polyandry (a woman with two or more husbands). Polyandry is rare around the world, and this is so in Africa as well. A quite unusual form of polyandry was reported as being practiced until the 1940s among a people from the Kasai region of the Congo (DRC) called the Lele (Siegel, 2007). Most marriage was monogamous among the Lele, but there were also sometimes women who got married to a group of men who were all about the same age and belonged to an association of age-mates called an "age set." Whereas polyandry is rare, polygyny is not uncommon in Africa. Of course, in any society where there is a relative balance of men and women, it is impossible for most men to have more than one wife. Consequently, polygyny is often the privilege of chiefs, kings, and other high-status men. Historically, it was a system that helped to maximize labor in the family (consequently lineage and community).

In addition to expanding the size of their family, marrying different women from different families also helps such men establish political alliances with various groups. One of the most famous of African contemporary kings was the king of Swaziland, Sobhuza II, who reigned for sixty years from 1922 to 1982. Various numbers have been given for the number of wives the king had, but one reliable Swazi source put the number at seventy. Sobhuza II reportedly also had 210 children in the years between 1920 and 1970. One of his sons, known as Mswati II, is currently king. He is carrying on the tradition of polygyny, with more than ten wives. As with most things, there is a difference of opinion in Africa about polygyny. Some see it as an example of the exploitation of women; others see it as a tradition that provided some economic advantages for co-wives who worked together in agricultural endeavors.

The tradition has often been attacked within Christianity, but Islam allow up to four wives, provided that they are treated properly and equally. However, polygyny solved some particular problems. For instance, it was a way of compensating for postpartum sex taboos (as among the Hausa of West Africa), according to which a husband is not to have sexual relations with his wife for two years after childbirth. Also, in levirate systems (as among the Yoruba of Nigeria), a widow would be expected to marry one of the younger male kins of her deceased husband. This has been labeled as a form of inheritance, but it is essentially a means of providing security for the widow. The traditional reasons behind these practices have been somewhat eclipsed in modern times, especially among urbanized Africans. A newer practice of "pseudo-polygyny" is now the norm, with urban-dwellers having multiple (often unmarried) mistresses. This is a common practice among migrant workers in mining nations like Southern Africa. However, such behavior has contributed to the HIV/AIDS explosion in the region.

Marital Residency & Contemporary Challenges for the Extended Family

There is a connection between the types of descent systems and marriage patterns. Often, traditional marriages were arranged by elder members of one's lineage. Children were the object because it was through them that the lineage grew and could become more powerful. In patrilineal societies, a woman usually left her parent's home to get married. People were frequently prohibited from marrying into the same village or lineage. The commonest type of residency is patrilocal (brides moving into or near the family of the groom). Matrilocal residency (groom moving into or near the family of the bride) is seen in matrilineal societies and is less common in Africa. A newer practice of marital residency prevalent among urban or "modern" Africans is establishing neolocal residency by moving away from all relatives. Modern problems such as warfare, natural crises, and other sociopolitical and economic realities in Africa, have affected systems of marital residency. The extended family system is changing in most African societies and may be on the verge of demise in others. Nuclear family units are becoming more important to Africans, especially in the urban areas. Westernization (the introduction of ideas, values, and social practices from the West), increased and rapid urbanization, new religious values (especially Christianity-based), labor migration, and the prevalence of natural disasters and crises (creating refugees and breaking up extended family units) have contributed greatly to the breakdown of the extended family system. These changes notwithstanding, it is easy to affirm that the extended family system in most African societies is not going to become extinct; instead, African extended families will continue to adapt and have newer opportunities to serve the support roles in most individual's existence.

Review Questions

1. What are some of the significant sources of information for comprehending the oral and oral-dominated societies found all over the African continent?

2. Following Manu Ampim's (2003) classification, what are the five categories of rites of passage prevalent across the African continent?

3. Identify some of the indispensable information about the society that rites of passage can provide. In addition, provide some of the purposes of these rites of passage in many African societies.

4. What is marriage in most African societies? In your discussion, briefly consider the types of marriages found on the continent.

5. Attempt to provide a detailed discussion of kinship systems and marriage across the continent.

6. What is marriage in most African societies? In your discussion, briefly consider the types of marriages found on the continent.

Bibliography

Abdi, Ali. A. 2007. Oral Societies and Colonial Experiences: Sub-Saharan Africa and the de-facto Power of the Written Word. *International Education*, Vol. 37 Issue (1). Retrieved from: http://trace.tennessee.edu/internationaleducation/vol37/iss1/3

Allen, Philip M., and M. Covell. 2005. *Historical Dictionary of Madagascar*. Lanham, MD: Scarecrow Press (African Historical Dictionary Series 98).

Appiah, Kwame A., and Henry Louis Gates, Jr, eds. 2010. *Encyclopedia of Africa.* New York: Oxford University Press.

Ampim, Manu, 2003. The Five Major African Initiation Rites. Retrieved from http://www.manuampim.com/AfricanInitiationRites.html.

Awedoba, A. K. 2000. *An Introduction to Kasena Society and Culture through Their Proverbs.* Maryland: American University Press.

Babatunde, Emmanuel. 2004. "Traditional Marriage and Family." In Lawal, Nike, et al., eds. Understanding Yoruba Life and Culture. Trenton, NJ: Africa World Press.

Bascom, William. 1969. *The Yoruba of Southwestern Nigeria.* Long Grove, IL: Waveland Press.

Boateng, F. 1985. African Traditional Education: A Tool for Intergenerational Communication. In M. K. Asante & K. W. Asante, eds., *African Culture: The Rhythms of Unity* (pp. 109–122). Westport, CT: Greenwood Press.

Bolaji Campbell. (2008). Paintings for the Gods: Art and Aesthetics of Yoruba Religious Murals. Trenton, NJ: African World Press.

Booth, Alan R. 2000. *Historical Dictionary of Swaziland.* Lanham, MD: Scarecrow Press (African Historical Dictionary Series 80).

Clark, Andrew F., and Lucie C. Phillips. *Historical Dictionary of Senegal.* Lanham, MD: Scarecrow Press (African Historical Dictionary Series 65).

Decalo, Samuel. 1997. *Historical Dictionary of Chad.* Lanham, MD: Scarecrow Press (African Historical Dictionary Series 13).

Decalo Samuel, V. Thompson, R. Adloff. 1996. *Historical Dictionary of Congo.* Lanham, MD: Scarecrow Press (African Historical Dictionary Series 69).

Doyle, D. 2005. "Ritual Male Circumcision: A Brief History." In *Journal of the Royal College of Physicians of Edinburgh.* 35:279–285.

Elwood, Dunn, D. 2001. *Historical Dictionary of Liberia.* Lanham, MD: Scarecrow Press (African Historical Dictionary Series 83).

Eshleman, J. Ross. 1994. *The Family: An Introduction.* 7th ed. Boston: Allyn & Bacon.

Falola, Toyin, and Ann Genova. 2009. *Historical Dictionary of Nigeria.* Lanham, MD: Scarecrow Press (African Historical Dictionary Series 111).

Gordon, April, and D. L. Gordon. 2007. *Understanding Contemporary Africa.* 4th ed. Boulder, CO: Lynne Rienner Publishers.

Grimes, Ronald. 2000. *Deeply into the Bone: Re-Inventing Rites of Passage.* Berkeley: University of California Press.

Grotpeter, John J. 1994. *Historical Dictionary of Namibia.* Lanham, MD: Scarecrow Press (African Historical Dictionary Series 57).

Imperato, Pascal James, and G. H. Imperato. 2008. *Historical Dictionary of Mali.* Lanham, MD: Scarecrow Press (African Historical Dictionary Series 107).

Isola, Akinwumi. 1992. New Findings in Yoruba Studies. Ibadan, Nigeria: J. F. Odunjo Memorial Lecture Organizing Committee.

Kayongo-Male, Diane and P. Onyango. 1984. *The Sociology of the African Family.* New York: Longman.

Lawal, Nike, M. N. O. Sadiku, and P. A. Dopamu, eds. 2004. *Understanding Yoruba Life and Culture.* Trenton, NJ: Africa World Press.

Lobban Jr., Richard A., R. S. Kramer, and C. Fluehr-Lobban. 2002. *Historical Dictionary of the Sudan.* Lanham, MD: Scarecrow Press (African Historical Dictionary Series 85).

Maxon, Robert M., and T. P. Ofcansky. 2000. *Historical Dictionary of Kenya.* Lanham, MD: Scarecrow Press (African Historical Dictionary Series 77).

Mazrui, Ali A. 1987. *The Africans: A Triple Heritage.* New York: Little, Brown and Company.

Messing, Simon. "Amhara." *Encyclopedia of World Cultures.* 1996. Retrieved from Encyclopedia.com.

Mosha, R. S. 2000. *The Heartbeat of Indigenous Africa: A Study of the Chagga Educational System.* New York: Garland Publishing.

Mutisya, P. Masila. 1996. "Demythologization and Demystification of African Initiation Rites: A Positive and Meaningful Educational Aspect Heading for Extinction." In *Journal of Black Studies*, Vol. 27, No.1. (Sept. 1996), pp. 94–103. Sage Publications.

Mukhtar, Mohamed Haji. 2003. *Historical Dictionary of Somalia.* Lanham, MD: Scarecrow Press (African Historical Dictionary Series 87).

Nock, Steven. L. 1992. *Sociology of the Family.* 2nd ed.. New Jersey: Prentice Hall.

Nsamenang, A. B. 2004. *Cultures of Human Development and Education: Challenge to Growing up African.* New York: Nova Science.

Nyembezi Sibusiso, C. L. 1963. Zulu Proverbs. Johannesburg: Witwatersrand Univ. Press.

O'Connell, Helen. 1994. *Women and the Family.* New Jersey: Zed Books.

Ofcansky, Thomas P., and R. Yeager. 1997. *Historical Dictionary of Tanzania.* Lanham, MD: Scarecrow Press (African Historical Dictionary Series 72).

Ojo, Akinloye. 2000. "What Is in a Name? The Contents and Gender Representation of Some Yorùbá Personal Names, Praise Names, and Aliases." Unpublished manuscript.

Ojo, Akinloye, and Adeniyi, Harrison. 2004. "Family Description." In *ÀKÓYE: Yoruba Language Online Learning and Teaching Program*: Retrieved from http://www.africa.uga.edu/Yoruba/index.html.

Ojo, Akinloye, and Robert Shanefelt, 2007. *"Introduction to African Online Course."*Athens, Georgia: Georgia University System African Studies Certificate (CIASP) project.

Olatunji, Olatunde O. 1984. *Features of Yoruba Oral Poetry.* Ibadan, Nigeria: University Press.

Ong, Walter J. 1982. *Orality and Literacy: The Technologizing of the Word.* New York: Routledge.

Onwurah, Ngozi (Dir.). 1993. Monday's Girls. Documentary produced by Lloyd Gardner. United Kingdom/Nigeria.

O'Toole, Thomas (with Janice E. Baker). 2005. *Historical Dictionary of Guinea.* Lanham, MD: Scarecrow Press (African Historical Dictionary Series 94).

Owusu-Ansah, David. 2005. *Historical Dictionary of Ghana.* Lanham, MD: Scarecrow Press (African Historical Dictionary Series 97).

Oyedipe, F. P. A. 2004. "Changes in the Traditional Family System." In Lawal, Nike et al., eds. Understanding Yoruba Life and Culture. Trenton, NJ: Africa World Press.

Pirouet, M. Louise. 1995. *Historical Dictionary of Uganda.* Lanham, MD: Scarecrow Press (African Historical Dictionary Series 64).

Ronald, H. Isaacs. 1992. *Rites of Passage: A Guide to the Jewish Life Cycle*. Jersey City, NJ: KTAV Publishing House.

Rubert, Steven C., and R. K. Rasmussen. *Historical Dictionary of Zimbabwe*. Lanham, MD: Scarecrow Press (African Historical Dictionary Series 86).

Saunders, Christopher, and N. Southey. 2000. *Historical Dictionary of South Africa*. Lanham, MD: Scarecrow Press (African Historical Dictionary Series 78).

Shanklin, Eugene. 2007. Family and Kinship. In Gordon, April, and D. L. Gordon. *Understanding Contemporary Africa*. 4th ed. Boulder, CO: Lynne Rienner Publishers. 265–292.

Shinn, David H., and T. P. Ofcansky. 2004. *Historical Dictionary of Ethiopia*. Lanham, MD: Scarecrow Press (African Historical Dictionary Series 91).

Siegel, Brian. 1996. Family and Kinship. In Gordon, April, and Gordon, D. L. *Understanding Contemporary Africa*. 2nd ed. Boulder, CO: Lynne Rienner Publishers. 221–248.

Simon, David J., J. R. Pletcher, and B. V. Siegel. 2008. *Historical Dictionary of Zambia*. Lanham, MD: Scarecrow Press (African Historical Dictionary Series 106).

Tiumelissan, Agazi, et al. "Ethiopian Village Studies II." Wellbeing and Development in Ethiopia. University of Bath, February 2006. Web. 21 June 2009.

Twagilimana, Aimable. *Historical Dictionary of Rwanda*. Lanham, MD: Scarecrow Press (African Historical Dictionary Series 105).

Vontress, C. E. 1999. Interview with a traditional African healer. *Journal of Mental Health Counseling*, 21 (4), 326–336.

Wane, N. N. 2000. Indigenous Knowledge: Lessons from the Elders. In G. J. S. E. Dei, B. L. E. Hall & D. G. E. Rosenberg, eds., *Indigenous Knowledges in Global Contexts: Multiple Readings of Our World* (pp. 54–69). Ontario: OISE/UT in association with University of Toronto Press.

Chapter Seven

Gender Issues In Africa

By Felisters Jepchirchir Kropono and Janet Musimbi M'mbaha

Introduction

There are divergent perspectives on the roles and position of the African women in different historical contexts. Just as the African continent is diverse in its geographical locations, cultural practices, colonial influences and other sociopolitical factors, diverse aspects of the African women's roles and positions exist. The African women's experiences have been shaped by both the historical, cultural and environmental factors and experiences. Indeed, women's roles have differed from one community to the other, which makes it difficult to generalize (Gordon, 2007). However, certain similarities existed among many precolonial African women; it is based on these similarities that we wish to generalize. This chapter focuses on gender issues in Africa during the precolonial, colonial, and postcolonial periods. Specifically, we focus on different socioeconomic and political aspects of the African women including governance, education, and labor.

Precolonial Africa

Although very little has been written on the roles and issues of African women during the precolonial period, diverse views on the role of the African woman exist. While some researchers present the African woman as weak, dependent, and powerless, the traditional and cultural practices in some communities confirm the African women as the shapers and movers of their society. Undeniably women issues differed from one community to the others as was influenced by the society's governance system and socioeconomic status. For instance, the issues faced by young girls from rich families were different from those from middle income, or poor families. Generally, roles, rights, and responsibilities were defined by gender and age. Given the diverse historical, socioeconomic, and political factors, gender roles differed from one country to the other as well as from each cultural group. According to Sudarkasa (1986), "Women were conspicuous in 'high places'; they were queen mothers; queen sisters; princesses, chiefs and holders of other offices in towns and villages" (91). Thus women are seen as having maintained a position of power during the precolonial time as their roles were seen as complementing those of men. This is an aspect of the African women that most writers on precolonial time ignore, and instead allocate men and boys better roles than those of women and girls.

Marriage/Family Practice

The African traditional society exercised two forms of marriage; matrilineal and patrilineal. Patrilineal is a system of tracing descendants through one's father. All the property is inherited from the fathers' lineage and children are named after their fathers. Matrilineal is a system of tracing descendants through one's mother. Inheritance of property and naming are through the mother. Some communities such as in West Africa had kin groups they belonged to; under each group men and women had roles and duties toward their fellow kinsmen and kinswomen (Sudarkasa, 1986). Polygamy was a common practice in precolonial Africa. Such practices and traditions afforded men and women different roles depending on their cultural background. Polygamy is a system in African traditional society where men are allowed to marry more than one wife. Marriage, whether polygamous or nuclear, was considered a union of the family rather than that of the two couples marrying. Since roles were assigned depending on the seniority of wives, the first wife in the family had more power than the other wives in the family.

Another common practice in some communities was the woman-to-woman marriage; which is a legal marriage between two women. Essentially, this practice was commonly encouraged to give a male heir to a barren woman. The female husband pays the bride wealth to the family of her wife. Oboler (1980) defines a female husband as "a woman who pays bride wealth for, and thus marries (but does not have sexual intercourse with) another woman" (p. 69). The bride wealth gives the female husband the legal and social authority over her wife and children (Greene, 1998). All the children born by her wife will bear her name. In most cases, the female husband would choose a man for her wife, and "the man would most likely be a younger clan-mate of the female husband's husband—possibly his younger brother, his brother's son, or the son of one of his other wives" (p. 78). Generally, the institution of woman-to-woman marriage varies(d) from one country to the other. For example, among the Nandi of Kenya "the property of a woman's house could only be transferred to male heirs; as it was inappropriate for a woman to hold property, it could not be passed to daughters" (Oboler, 1980, p. 73). Female husbands took up their newly acquired status as that of "men," and they were expected to take up the role of the head of the household. Socially they were treated with respect and presided over meetings and also participated in ceremonies and meetings that women were not permitted to attend. In the case of the Nandi women, they were allowed to attend male circumcision ceremonies (Oboler, 1980). Both polygamy and woman-to-woman marriages were practiced in precolonial Africa. Polygamy afforded the male and female husbands economic power in their community through agriculture; because "the more wives they had, the more labor they controlled and then more agricultural surplus was created" (Greene, 1998, p. 402). Female husbands who could afford to practice polygamy gained financially more than those who could not.

Women in Agriculture and Labor

Farming was an activity considered essential to the survival of communities. Most communities relied on farming for food production and cattle raising. During the precolonial period, men and women worked together on the farm. Each member of the family, including children, had his share of activity in the farm. Their roles were, however, separate but interdependent. Basically, men were responsible for clearing the land, protecting and obtaining the land owing to the shifting nature of their agriculture, while women were responsible for plowing, planting, weeding, harvesting, carrying the harvest home, and preparing it for storage (Sudarkasa, 1982). Even though men and women participated in agriculture, Boserup (1970) states that approximately 30–79 percent of women did the actual physical work in agriculture.

Therefore, women generally provided agricultural labor. Agriculture crops were generally gender specific (Ekechi, 1995). Specifically, this crop-gendering practice was common among the Esan and Igbo communities in Nigeria. Crops such as cassavas, beans, melon, groundnuts, cotton and peppers were considered female crops, while yams and palm oil were men's because of the association to the kings and the chiefs (Ogbomo, 1995; Ekechi, 1995). Farming was not just limited to crop growing but included animal keeping as well. In such cases men and young boys would herd animals while women were left with the difficult role of tilling and preparing the land for harvesting. In addition, in the Kalenjin communities of Kenya, women had the responsibility of milking the cows in the evening after they come home from grazing.

In economics, the African woman is seen as being independent because she owned property, engaged in farming activities to produce crops, engaged in trade and even took care of her family. In most cases gender roles were clearly defined, and women's roles included crop farming, tending animals, craft making, and taking care of the family while those of men involved hunting and protecting the community, among others. Women were considered by the society as the driving force of the economy through their economic contribution. Agricultural cultivation was considered the main economic income for women in most African countries, while among the Yoruba of Nigeria, it was trading (Allen, 1972). Also, women from Nigeria, Ghana, Senegal and Guinea-Bissau actively engaged in trade practiced both long-distance and short-distance trade, selling vegetables, pots, baskets, mats, palm oil. That they experienced financial success (Brooks, 1976) enhanced their financial and economic power and control.

Generally, trading was preferred by women as it supplemented the income from agriculture, it required minimal finances, and most of all it was considered that the "most efficient way of connecting buyers and sellers was by bringing them together in periodic, rotating markets; and they were numerous because local trade was a generally accessible way of adding to farm incomes, since it required few managerial or technical skills and little capital" (Hopkins, 1973 p. 56). Even though selling agricultural produce was profitable for women, the majority of their proceeds (90 percent) went to family consumption. Additionally, dry seasons would result in a low harvest (Chuku, 2005). Comparatively, men profited more from their crops such as yams and palm oil because both crops were less consumed at home (Allen, 1972). While these roles may be interpreted as belittling and/or overburdening the women, they were viewed as being critical to the general welfare of the family; moreover, women prided themselves on being coworkers and coproviders for their family.

Women in Politics

Contrary to what has been presented by some writers, the African women were not as passive and powerless as depicted. In fact, Aidoo (1998) points out that the hungry, dependent, and powerless African woman is a creation of the Western media. Moreover, research on African communities has revealed women as being very powerful. Folklore from the Agikuyu community in Kenya refers to the women's former powerful position in the matriarchy system:

> According to folklore, the Kikuyu tribe was ruled based on a matriarchal system. During the rule of Wangu wa Makeeri, a leader who was said to be so fierce she held meetings seated on the backs of men, the men decide to revolt and take over leadership. One version of the story says that the revolution took place when kikuyu men organized to have all women dance marked in a Kibaata dance. The women refused and the Kikuyu men took the rule to themselves. In another version, the men conspired to make all the women pregnant at the same time. This made them vulnerable and unable to carry out leadership duties. The men then took over leadership—and never let go.
> Retrieved from http://kenyaculturegalore.org/Kikuyu.html

Although traditional myths and folklore allude to the women's abuse of their former powerful status, culminating in men overthrowing them, research studies have shown women as being in a powerful position and actively involved in the sociopolitical affairs of their community. Evidently, a reciprocal relationship with the members of the opposite sex in the traditional African society existed. For instance, among communities of Nigeria, African women were so "conspicuous, they were the queen mother; queen sister; princess, chiefs and held offices in towns and villages" (Sudarkasa, 1986). They also presided over some critical cases in their communities. Generally, the African women's role was seen as complementary to that of men.

According to Falola (1995), women always had some form of political control in various parts of their community and had special titles that recognized successful women in the system. Because society recognized women and appointed them as leaders, Falola (1995) further explains that "there was no town without a chief of some kind" (p. 28). These chiefs were men and women. The women chiefs and kings (in Yoruba) were prevented from performing female activities and contributed in male activities. These tasks include speaking in public meetings, controlling trade and engaging in the decision-making processes. For instance, in the Nandi community of Kenya, when a woman marries (d) a woman, they automatically acquire (d) the male status, "*kagotogosta komostab murenik*" (Oboler, 1980, p. 74), that affords(ed) them a political power and the ability to participate in the decision-making process with regard to issues that affect their community.

For women, formation of political organizations/institutions was one way in which women could purposively use to effectively articulate their issues as mothers, sisters, daughters and wives; their main and most important political base of power being the family. They made sure (in some cases) that their children, especially their sons, supported them before proceeding to their external political base. The *miriki* of the Igbo of Nigeria is an example of the powerful institution that was known for "sitting on a man;" they used it as a way of punishing men for their misconduct. Punishment would involve women imposing sanctions and strikes such as not cooking for their husbands until their demands were met. Similarly, all women in the community had to participate for it to be successful (Allen, 1972). Generally these women's groups had set rules that were developed by the group to be followed strictly by all members. Members appointed their group leaders, whose mutual responsibility was representing their members (women) in discussions that required a representative from women. Leadership roles were assigned according to age, wealth, and wisdom, and they varied from culture to culture. However, as noted by Allen (1972), "age combined with wisdom brought respect, but age alone carried little influence" (p. 168). Evidently, the African communities had different criteria that needed to be fulfilled by prospective community leaders. Perhaps this criterion ensured a fair system in the appointment of leaders. Additionally, the use of successful acquisition of wealth implied a society that valued hard work; hence leaders were role models.

Some women such as the Esan derived political power from the production of the ceramics due to the religious or political significance their products had in the society (Ogbomo, 1995). Sandy (1974) confirms this by stating that "in societies where control and production are linked and a competitive market exists, female power is likely to develop if females are actively engaged in producing valued market goods" (p. 200). Most women worked very hard to achieve political power using this method since most of their produce were not as profitable as men's.

Women in Education

Education was an essential part of the African traditional society, as it was the best way of preserving their cultural practices through each generation. As opposed to the dark picture painted by Western scholars of education in precolonial Africa, African society had its forms of education even before the coming of the missionaries or colonialism. Most Western scholars believed that the first form of education in Africa was through encounter with the missionaries. On the contrary, African society engaged in traditional African, community-based education; men and women educated themselves in traditional African society. They did so by having mature members of the family to guide and teach children, adolescents and their youth social, ethical, and moral values deemed important in their society. Generally learning occurred through imitation and observation; however, apprentice education provided a way of passing specials skills such as birth attendants, medicine men, carpentry. Basically, education transcended the family confines, and there was no end to education in the African society as it was considered a lifelong process. Marah (2006) notes that education of "a child in the early years of education is in the hands of the biological mother" (p. 20), but as the child matures into adulthood, he/she becomes the community's responsibility. It was expected that all mature members of the community should not hesitate to guide and educate their younger generation wherever necessary. Kenyatta (1961) best explains the African traditional education in the precolonial period using the Kikuyu of Kenya by stating the following:

> Education begins at the time of birth and ends with death. The child has to pass various stages of age-groupings with a system of education defined for every status in life. They aim at instilling into the children what the Gikuyu call "*otaari wa mocie*" or "*kerera kia mocie*," namely, educating the children in the family and clan tradition.... There is no special school building in the Gikuyu sense of the word; the homestead is the school.... This is one of the methods by which history of the people passed from generation to generation (pp. 99–100).

Since there were no buildings or books, various communities in African countries such as Tanzania, Nigeria, and Malawi believed that the older generation was the library of the younger generation. Adults were responsible for passing down the knowledge to the younger generation. This affirms the common African saying that when an old person dies, a library is burned. Precolonial education was gender based as it was meant to prepare both men and women for their diverse roles in society (Adeyemi & Adeyinka, 2003). Men and women were prepared for their corresponding masculine and feminine roles, which included planting, harvesting, taking care of the home, husband and children.

Women during Colonialism

Colonialism and capitalism are viewed as sources of gender inequality in most of Africa (Taiwo, 2010), and feminists regard both capitalism and colonialism as being conduits of the oppression of the women (Freedman, 2002). While research shows the social structures of most African societies as being patriarchal, the system had respect for various gender roles and positions, and viewed them as being reciprocal and essential to the society's welfare. In contrast, the type of patriarchy promoted and practiced by the Europeans and missionaries focused on gender-based power positions favoring hierarchical ordering of society, where men possess power and economic privilege (Eisenstein, 1999; Omwami, 2011). Sudarkasa (1982) has noted that capitalism "eroded complementary and near parity of male and female occupational roles found in many indigenous economies" (p. 281). Essentially, this colonial agenda is blamed for subordination of the women and that by selecting to prepare men for administrative roles, women were inadvertently subordinated. Consequently, men were empowered in all socioeconomic and political sectors such as education and employment.

Governance

The duplication of the European style of governance to the African continent, together with Victorian cultural practices, saw the African woman disenfranchised of her former powerful position in society. For example, the Victorian conceptions of women as frail and inferior, promoted the men over women, through assigning of leadership roles to men, while relegating women to subordinate roles of child rearing and bearing (Courtrier and Chepko, 2001). The new type of governance totally ignored the role and status of women as a critical ingredient in the functioning of society. By refusing to acknowledge them, they were clearly stating their new administrative rules that aimed at obliterating the African cultural practices. The changes in the social-structural organization during the colonization period eroded the women's authority and dissolved their former powerful positions (Freedom, 2002).

Some of the laws that were implemented by the colonialists, such as the property right law, were used to disempower the African women through open preference for the patriarchal inheritance (Cheater, 1986). For instance, in Zimbabwe, the property rights laws were used to disinherit women's property as all property was registered in the man's name. Even though marriages were conducted under Christian laws, these laws were selectively used and manipulated accordingly in certain circumstances. For example, the traditional law or African act law was applied in cases of customary inheritance (patrilineal inheritance), which effectively disinherited women upon her spouse's demise. These laws failed to take into consideration the women's role as a coinvestor in the family property. Ironically those laws that could have liberated women ended up victimizing them (Cheater, 1986). Clearly, the laws were not only segregating in terms of color but gender, too, thus creating a double tragedy for the African woman.

One school of thought suggests that political development depends on a strong economic development base. Given that African women actively engaged in economic activities and continue to contribute a larger percentage of productive labor, Africa's economic development is driven by the women in the labor force. In acknowledging the important socioeconomic roles of African women and the need to include them in governance, O'Barr (1975) asserted that "women's economic activities meant that they frequently exert political control, sometimes directly and sometimes indirectly. The economic contribution (or power) of women guarantees them a well-defined place in the process of resource allocation because they are responsible, they own valued resources...." (p. 21).

The African women's resistance to the colonial influences and imposition of laws that they viewed as being retrogressive showed that women were indeed articulating their political and economic power. For instance, the Aba riots by Igbo women were triggered by the imposition of taxes on their market products. Touted the "women's war," the 1929 riots were used to protect women's economic and political power, which was threatened by the imposition of property tax.

Other resistant protests by Nigerian women took place in 1959 to protect their declining power status (Freedman, 2002). Through their organized trade and resistance riots, women had clearly demonstrated a high propensity for leadership; yet they were denied leadership positions in the colonial administration. Instead, they had to suffer under the newly appointed leaders (men). In fact, Allen (1972) notes the following:

> Women suffered particularly under the arbitrary rule of warrant chiefs who were reported as having taken women to marry without conforming to customary process, which included the right to refuse a particular suitor. They also helped themselves to the women's agricultural produce and to their domestic animals (p. 172).

Essentially, the colonial legacy inherited by the newly elected leaders in Africa has successfully ensured that women are excluded from participating in the governance of the African states. Research on the participation of women in liberation or women's rights movement indicates that when compared to the European feminist movements, the women's rights movements in Africa have not been as robust as those of European women. Basically they have been made invisible by the sociopolitical systems that failed to acknowledge and highlight women in their roles as political players. At independence, political and administrative positions in most African states were left to men. For women, formation of women's groups was the only way through which African women could be recognized. The newly independent African states perceived the formation of women's groups as necessary for the representation of women's interests in the government. Some of those groups include Kenya's *Maendeleo Ya Wanawake* (MYW), women's development, and Tanzania's Umoja *Wa Wanawake Wa Tanzania* (UWT). These groups' objectives have been criticized as being limited to empowering women at the household levels, and not increasing their participation in leadership at the national and international levels (Tamale, 2000).

Women's unity groups are seen as extensions of the political ruling class. As such, they have failed to vigorously advocate for women's issues and challenged the existing status quo; thus their agenda is considered egotistical (Tamale, 2000). Feminist writers on Africa have compared the African woman during the precolonial and postcolonial periods and define the former as a "strong, powerful, activist, independent and socially relevant." In contrast, the postcolonial African woman is depicted as "weak, dependent, powerless, lacks courage and vision" (Nnaemeka, 1998). Apparently, a lot of factors contribute to this perspective of the contemporary African woman; however, that is an area that we would hesitate to discuss, although we hope subsequent chapters in this book will offer some insights.

Education

The type of education provided by the colonial masters and missionaries is blamed for laying a foundation for the masculine leadership practices, which prepared men for civic and administrative positions in government and ignored the women. Mostly, women were denied formal education; the only education offered by the colonialist was meant to prepare them for their roles as wives and mothers (Aidwo, 2010). It was believed that women could not handle intellectual materials; hence the decision to deny them an education (Courtrier and Chepko, 2001). In Zimbabwe as in other colonized states, missionaries and colonial administrators planned to teach women to be proper women (Bryson, 2002) and Christian wives (Allen, 1972); thus gender was an impediment to getting education. The colonial educational policies disadvantaged women to the extent that today, the educational pyramid is wide at the base, with an almost equal representation of girls and boys; but the pyramid sharply narrows at the apex, favoring men (Aidwo, 2010). At independence, only 36 percent of girls were enrolled in school in 1969; 49.8 percent were enrolled in primary school while about only 4.5 percent of girls were enrolled in secondary schools. In 1972, only 16.6 percent of students in post-secondary institutions were women (Sudarkasa, 1986). Moreover, the majority of these women were in the female-dominated areas such as education and nursing, with very few women in law and medicine.

Labor

The imposition of religious practices such as Christianity and Islam denied women their former rights (Njoh & Rigos, 2003). Division of labor, employment, and educational policies by colonialists all excluded women from actively participating in the public life. Instead, the private life was designated as a place for women. Research findings have discounted the assumption that gender inequality existed in African traditional culture. For instance, the Urhobo and Igbo communities of Nigeria had their women in powerful positions (Allen, 1972) and participated in agricultural activities, selling food crops and crafts. Also, the Dahomey communities of Benin were known for having strong market groups that were led by women; they determined prices of their products and even where to sell them. Likewise, the Kikuyu women of Kenya were in charge of agriculture including land, production, and sale of crops. This practice was discontinued through the introduction of capital markets, which were used to disorganize the previously organized economic activities through appointing men to do administrative jobs that were well paying. The relocation of the women into the urban centers denied them a chance to continue with their farming and trade businesses, resulting in dependency on men (Sudarkasa, 1986). Nevertheless, what is also apparent that in the 1950s–1960s, African women constituted 70–80 percent of agricultural laborers (Bryson, 2000).

On the other hand, men still participated in agriculture but in cash crop farming which was introduced by Europeans, while women were left to do food crop farming, provide for their families, and be caretakers of the family property (Bryson, 2002). Bryson points out that as the urban centers grew, so did the food crop business flourish for the female farmers thus increased economic power (Bryson, 2002); but they had to put in more working hours because of lack of modern technological farming methods. The interaction with foreign cultures and the colonialist imposition of foreign cultural practices that subordinated women in African communities marked the beginning of gender inequality, resulting in women's loss of economic and political power (Allen, 1972).

Women in Contemporary Society

Over the years, a number of strides have been made with regard to the roles and status of women in society. First, with the end of colonial rule, African nations embarked on the agenda of building their nations, for the most part, there was the element of inclusion of both men and women. Because a number of women had fought for the freedom in their nations, there was the increased demand by women for representation and restoration of their lost status. Education served as one of the ways through which women could claim some positions in governance; thus more women started getting an education. Another factor that helped increase the participation of women in governance arose from the women's feminist movements that started in Europe having repercussions around the world. Women became increasingly demanding of their rights. Also, the UNHR Act of 1974, with its declaration of the equal rights for all, resulted in nations attempting to adhere to the UN call to provide for equal services for its citizens. Consequently, more women have been able to access and acquire education. There has been an increased entry of women into professional careers that were once considered "male preserves." As signatories of the UN protocols, governments around the world have supported the UN's agenda of removing all forms of discrimination.

Subsequently, a number of nations have established ministries and departments within the government that deal with gender issues; with a focus on increasing the allocation of leadership positions for women. Most prominent in advocating for the improved status of the women are the 2000 Millennium Development Goals (MDGs), which target eradication of poverty, increased access to education for girls and women, and eradication of diseases, all of which afflict more women than men. Both the international communities and the world governments have embarked on a mission to correct the problem that was created by colonial mindsets through eradication of discriminatory policies and practices that marginalized one sector of the population. The education of the girl-child, eradication of disease and other issues that afflict women, and women's increased participation in nation development are at the top of most of the national and international agendas (Njoh & Rigos, 2003).

Politically, African women are becoming more empowered and consistently claiming a share in governance of their institutions. Affirmative action and other empowerment policies are regarded as some of most powerful tools that women could use to achieve equal representation. The 2005 report on women's representation in parliament showed that African women held more political positions in the world compared with their Western counterparts, with Rwanda having the highest number of elected women in politics. As of the year 2009, Rwanda at 56.3 percent was the nation with the highest number of women in parliament in Africa; Comoros had the lowest with 3 percent. These results indicated that only six other nations had at least 30 percent representation

Table 1:Gross enrollment in sub-Saharan Africa region, level and sex in thousands

Year	Primary			Secondary			Tertiary		
	Male	Female	EI	Male	Female	EI	Male	Female	EI
1970	14,421	9,983	69	1,644	806	49	143	36	25
1980	29,228	22,969	79	5,934	3,438	58	438	125	29
1990	35,365	29,213	83	8,536	6,327	74	950	438	46
1997	44,524	36,511	82	11,688	9,327	80	1,408	769	55

Note #1: Adapted from "Women's Education in the Twenty-first Century: Balance and Prospects Dream" by N. Stromquist, 2007 in *Comparative Education: the dialectic of the global & the local.* p. 156. Arnove & Torres, Rowan & Littlefield Publishers.

Table 2: 15+ older estimated adult literacy rates in sub-Saharan Africa 1970–2004

Year	Total %	Female %	Male %
1970	22.6	13.2	32.5
1980a	32.5	22.3	43.2
1980b	40.2	29.2	51.8
1985	45.6	34.9	56.7
1990	47.3	35.6	59.5
1995	56.8	47.3	66.6
2000	60.3	52.0	68.9
2004	61.2	53.3	69.5

Note#2: Adapted from "Education for all in Africa: still a distant dream" by J. Samoff, & B. Carrol. 2007. *Comparative Education: the dialectic of the global & the local.* p. 370. Arnove & Torres, Rowan & Littlefield Publishers.

by women in parliament, and they included South Africa (44.5 percent), Angola (37.3 percent), Mozambique (34.8 percent), Uganda (30.7 percent), Burundi (30.5 percent), and Tanzania (30.4 percent). Generally Africa can be said to be performing poorly in regard to the Affirmative action, which requires at least 30 percent representation of women in parliament. Overall only 15.2 percent of the forty-six nations sampled had met the required percentage. In all, 21.8 percent had less than 10 percent female representation in parliament, while 65.2 percent registered less than 20 percent female representation (Africa Development Indicators Factoids 2011).

Women are more aware of their rights and have participated in various conferences where they demand increased participation in society. Such conferences have included the First Global Conference on Women, held in Mexico City, Mexico (1975), as a result of which 1975–1985 was declared the First UN Decade of Women; the World Conference on Women, held in Nairobi, Kenya (1985); and more recently, the UN-sponsored Fourth World Conference for Women held in 1995 in Beijing, China, (Njoh & Rigos, 2003). Subsequently, there have been notable increases in the participation levels of women in education and other socioeconomic sectors. For the majority of the women, active engagement in the socioeconomic and political structure serves as a powerful medium of redefining themselves and creating their own space (Fox, 2007).

Women in Politics

Underrepresentation of women in politics was a common practice in Africa, especially with the advent of colonialism. Colonial masters brought many changes to Africa that affected the leadership position held by women in precolonial times. Women were sidelined from any leadership roles. Even after independence around the 1960s, a majority of the African countries maintained the political system of their colonial nations and did not seem to realize the system was undermining women's role, clearly because politics was a male preserve. Pankhurst (2002) explains that only when women began to question various forms of discrimination did they finally obtain governments' attention. Women started empowering themselves through small groups, in churches or homes, which ultimately developed into large organization that began to advocate for women's equality. It was through such institutions that women voiced their issues; in the 1980s and early 1990s gender issues gained international attention. The fourth World Conference held in Beijing, China, in 1995 was the highlight of change. The meeting advocated a 30 percent representation of women in all government positions. This was a proposal of the quota and reserve seat system that contributed to increased female representation in national governments.

However, Gouws (2008) states that the idea is criticized as a game of numbers that perpetuates placing in power women who are not qualified for government office. Despite such criticism, the majority of the countries that have increased female representation in their parliament have achieved it through the quota system. For instance, female representation in parliament has increased to the following: Rwanda 48.8 percent; Mozambique 34.8 percent; South Africa 32.8 percent; Burundi, 30.5 percent; United Republic of Tanzania 30.4 percent; Uganda 29.8 percent. Moreover, women have experienced an increase in political representation as shown in the following countries: Namibia 26.9 percent; Tunisia 22.8 percent; Eritrea 22 percent; Senegal 22.0 percent; Ethiopia 21.9 percent. All the countries have female representation above the world average of 15.1 percent. This data backs the statement that Africa has the highest number of female representation in parliament.

Despite the increase in female representation in government positions, women were not state leaders until 2005 when Ellen Johnson-Sirleaf, as Liberian president, became the first woman to be elected as president in Africa. In her interview with Daniel Bergner on the significance of women as state leaders, she stated, "Women are more committed, they work hard, and are more honest; they have less reason to be corrupt," unlike men who have more distraction from their secret lovers and multiple wives due to the polygamy system that exists in Africa. Men therefore, have to meet all the needs of people around them. This attribute makes women great leaders for the office of the president. Conversely, women have been faced with diverse opposition from the government and society due to stern traditions that favor patriarchal systems. Gordon (2007) notes, "Some observers argue that parliaments in Africa are not where real power lies.... Real power is invested in the office of the president" (p. 306), which is still a male preserve. This raises the question as to whether women need to be state leaders to better address gender issues.

Education

Stromquist (2007) has noted that very little progress has been made in terms of equality rights of women, even though such rights are considered to be a tool of empowerment and a top-priority need by world bodies. Research findings indicate that increased access to education as indicated in the 1988–1993 statistics has not translated into equality for women and that "a consistent finding has been that schooling increases women's earnings but does not remove dependency on men" (p. 152). Specifically, developed nations have been closing the gender gap faster than the developing nations. This is quite ironic considering the various commitments by world governments to documents aimed at eradicating the existing inequalities through supporting the education of the girl-child. Among the most notable documents were those signed at the Third World Conference on women in Nairobi (1985), the Fourth World Conference in Beijing (1995); and the Education for All (EFA) 1990 conference in Jomtein, Thailand. The table above indicates the school enrollment level in sub-Saharan Africa by gender from 1970 to 1997.

The Equity Index indicates significant progress has been made, but gender inequality persists, in that the levels of illiteracy projection for 2005 for Africa showed women as having a higher percent (43.3 percent) of illiteracy than men (26.9 percent). In their analysis of education in Africa, Samoff and Carrol (2007) concluded that education for all was still a pipe dream for most African nations as indicated by the UNESCO world education report and World Bank's development report for the years 1970–2004. These reports indicated that women were the most affected by the illiteracy levels in sub-Saharan Africa as they had lower literacy levels when compared with men.

This table indicates that the women's literacy level ranks very low, thus depicting the dire situation of women's education in Africa.

Economy

There is a general consensus among researchers that agriculture plays a key role in economic development in Africa (Gordon, 2007). This huge participation of men and women in the industry is attributed to favorable climatic condition in Africa. However, in contemporary African society, agricultural contribution to the economy has declined over the past decade. According to World Development Indicators (WDI) (2006), the share of agriculture in the Gross Domestic Product in sub-Saharan and North Africa has declined since the 1960s from 46 percent to approximately 19 percent and 10 percent respectively. In addition, the number of people living in rural areas has decreased from 90 percent to approximately 50 percent due to increased urbanization (WDI, 2006). Although both men and women participate in agriculture, women are known to engage in subsistence agriculture while men engage in cash crops. However, this trend has been changed by urbanization and population increase, grounding women in engaging in a rapid increase in cash crop production while men engage in the formal sector, which has higher remuneration and greater job security (African Union, 2004).

To increase their economic income, women started to participate in the informal sector, self-employment, and micro and small-scale enterprises. It has been noted that self-employment constitutes 70 percent of informal employment in the nonagriculture sector. Women's choice of business is affected by factors such as ability to work from home, level of education, available capital and land and the ability to use home labor. Access to financial services has been improved by new financial institutions that focus on providing credit to support women in starting their businesses. Most of the financial organizations, such as the Kenya Women Finance Trust (KWFT), were modeled after the Graham Bank of India. In spite of access to financial services, women are still impeded by limited access to the market, poor infrastructure, and lack of adequate skills to run their business.

Men still dominate the most profitable sectors in the business such as financial services, urban manufacturing, and transportation; leaving women in the less profitable sectors such as wholesale and retail trade. This kind of gendered enterprise ownership puts women at a disadvantage as they do not benefit from their business efforts as much as men do since men own the most profitable sectors. Even when women decide to venture into those enterprises, they typically experience gender inequality and end up leaving the market (Institute of Economic Affairs, 2008).

Challenges Encountered by Women

The disenfranchisement of women's former powerful positions during colonialism denied them culturally defined authority (O'Barr, 1975), and hence made them subordinate to men. Despite the international efforts in acquiring gender equity, the resulting conflict between African cultures and the supposed "Western culture-equity" has slowed the progress toward empowerment. In a study of women in New Guinea, it was quite noticeable that men conveniently used culture to block women's participation in governance; they considered equity a Western idea that went against their culture (Fox, 2007).

The UNESCO, EFA global monitoring report of 2010 revealed that 54 percent of girls worldwide were not in school, often as a result of poverty, cultural practices, early marriages and pregnancy, all circumstances that prevented them from enrolling or forced them to interrupt their education or to drop out entirely. It was reported that almost 12 million girls compared to 7 million boys in Africa were never expected to enroll in schools. Since education is critical to both the development of the individual and of society, lack of education denies women a chance to effectively participate in economic activities and in the governance of their social institutions. Samoff & Carrol (2007) identify "parental attitude, gender differentiated expectations for future income, labor and household responsibilities of women, absence of role models at home and in school, implicit and explicit discouragement for pursuing particular courses of study, parents' educational achievements, family religious and moral prospects and sexual harassment and early pregnancy" (p. 372) as impediments to enrollment in school or causes of higher attrition. Thus, lack of education results in gender inequalities.

Related to the issue of lack of education is poverty, which is caused by restrictive property rights, weak governance, and civil conflicts (McPherson, 2010), most of which have been found to affect women more than men. In some communities, women have not been entitled to own anything. All the family income has been entrusted to the man for him to decide how the money will be spent. In addition, women could attain the power to use land only through their parents or husbands. For instance, it has been found that although women provide 80 percent of agricultural labor, only 5 percent of land is owned by women, a reality that essentially disempowers women (Bryson, 2002).

Other challenges include sexual discrimination and domestic violence; incest and rape are also common. In Kenya, the Gender Monitoring Unit reported that between April 2004 and March 2005, 1,483 women were raped, while 117 children were defiled (Institute of Economic Affairs, 2008, p. 39). Also, the 2003 Kenya Demographic and Health Survey (KDHS) indicated that women experience violence from their husbands with 40 percent and 16 percent of cases being physical and sexual respectively. It is quite evident that "domestic violence has locked up potential and opportunities for women who cannot develop themselves because they are afraid of the husband's attitude and reactions" (Institute of Economic Affairs, 2008, p. 44).

Though apparent gains have been made due to empowerment policies, the role of mother and wife remains a stumbling block for women wishing to compete for leadership positions outside the home. This is fueled by African cultural and traditional practices that believe that home management and "care giving is the responsibility of the mother ... with the assistance of their extended family" (UNECA, Cassirer & Addati, 2007, p. 3), this "extended family" being most likely female individuals as well. Hence, household responsibility is left to the women, with childcare support from the government being either scarce or totally lacking. Given the enormous responsibilities, women are hardly left with time to engage in economically productive activities in the formal and informal sector. In extreme cases, employers will hardly employ women with children as they are perceived as a risk to the institution.

In politics, women are less likely to be appointed to political offices because of the existing stereotypes of a woman's inability to lead. Generally women are viewed as lacking the mantle or confidence and authority to lead when compared to men (Abdela, 2000). Other challenges have involved resistance from men and society when competing for public office or leadership positions (Taiwo, 2010). There is no doubt about the role of women in the socioeconomic development of their communities. Society stands to benefit from the inclusion of women in its social development activities—the merging of the traditional with the modern practices—creating a balance and ensuring equal participation without one party feeling oppressed.

Conclusion

Although research shows that women have never been given due recognition for their role in nationalist or liberation movements (O'Barr, 1975), in the recent past, women have achieved a lot in the socioeconomic and political arenas. Among the notable achievements by African women have been the election of the first African woman, Ellen Johnson, as Liberian president; Winnie Mandela's role in the liberation of South Africa; and, in Kenya, Wangari Maathai's 1990s mobilization of women to protest and protect the environment from a dictator government, an act lauded as one of the most daring in modern Kenya, and efforts that were eventually recognized when she was named the Nobel Peace Prize winner of 2004.

"… Increasing female participation in the formal economy constitutes a viable strategy for promoting national development. Sub-Saharan African countries will therefore do well to craft and implement meaningful plans designed to achieve gender equity in especially crucial sectors of the formal economy" (Njoh & Rigos, 2003, p.108). Women should be cognizant of the empowerment policies, take advantage of those policies, and become more engaged in the decision-making process. As the gender debate continues, the question yet to be answered is whether women are ready to come out and take the leadership mantle. The recently promulgated constitution of Kenya allows for women to vie for 30 percent of representation/allocation of all government positions. However, recent appointments of high court judges and the judicial team members did not reflect this new legislation; specifically, women were blamed for not applying for judicial positions advertised. In view of this, one may be tempted to agree with the notion that the modern woman is not as assertive as the traditional woman; she is weak, dependent, is powerless, and lacks vision or courage (Sofola, 1998).

Improving the status of women through increased participation of women in the formal sector is seen as one way for women to redefine themselves and establish their own space and women's voices (Fox, 2007). Another way is through increased educational opportunities and acquisition of leadership positions, which will enable women to accrue the same benefits as do men—empowerment being among those benefits (Longwe, 2000). Most critical is the need to change society's attitudes to be more accommodating to women and to change the sociopolitical cultures that inhibit women from engaging in community development. Women should not be perceived as competing for men's positions; instead, they should be viewed as their partners in development, not their rivals. In summary, we agree with Aidoo (1998) when she states that "it is not possible to advocate independence for the African continent without also believing that African women must have the best that the environment can offer" (p. 47)

Review Questions

1. Discuss at least four roles of women in African traditional society (i.e., during the precolonial period).

2. Briefly explain the concept of woman-to-woman marriage in African traditional society (precolonial period).

3. Discuss three ways in which women's roles in the precolonial period were impacted by colonialism.

4. What are the two most powerful tools that women could use to achieve equal representation in politics?

5. Explain at least three issues that women face in contemporary society.

6. What are some other challenges faced by women that are discussed in the chapter?

Bibliography

Abdela, L. 2000. "From Palm Tree to Parliament: Training Women for Political Leadership and Public Life." In C. Sweetman, ed., *Women and Leadership.* Oxford, UK: Oxfam GB.

Adeyemi, M. B., and A. A. Adeyinka. 2003. "The Principles and Content of African Traditional Education." *Educational Philosophy and Theory,* 35 (4).

Afisi, Oseni Taiwo. 2010. "Power and Womanhood in Africa: An Introductory Evaluation." *The Journal of Pan African Studies,* 3 (6).

African Union (2004). The Road to Gender Equality in Africa: An Overview. Retrieved from http://www.africa union.org/au summit 2004/gender/THE ROADTO GENDER 2.pdf

Aidoo, A. A. 1998. "The African Woman Today." In O. Nnaemeka, ed. *Sisterhood, Feminisms and Power: From Africa to the Diaspora.* Trenton, NJ: Africa World Press.

Allen, J. V. 1972. "Sitting on a Man:" Colonialism and the Lost Political Institutions of Igbo Women. *Canadian Journal of African Studies,* 6 (2).

Bergner, D. 2010. An uncompromising woman. *The New York Times.* Retrieved from http://www.nytimes.com/2010/10/24/magazine/24sirleaf-t.html?ref=ellenjohnsonsirleaf.

Boserup, E. 1970. *Woman's Role in Economic Development.* New York: St. Martin's.

Brooks, G. 1976. "The Signares of Saint-Louis and Goree: Women Entrepreneurs in the Eighteenth-Century Senegal." In N. J. Hafkin, & E. G. Bay, eds., *Women in Africa: Studies in social and economic change.* Stanford, CA.

Bryson, J. C. 2002. "Women and Agriculture in Sub-Saharan Africa: Implications for Development (an Exploratory Study)." *Journal of Development Studies*.

Cheater, A. P. 1986. "The Role and Position of Women in Pre-colonial and Colonial Zimbabwe." *Zambezia*, 8(2).

Chuku, G. 2005. *Igbo Women and Economic Transformation in Southeastern Nigeria, 1900–1960*. New York & London: Routledge.

Chukukere, G. 1998. "Appraisal of Feminism in the Socio-political Development of Nigeria." In O. Nnaemeka, ed. *Sisterhood, Feminisms and Power: From Africa to the Diaspora*. Trenton, NJ: Africa World Press.

Couturier, L., and S. Chepko. 2001. "Separate World, Separate Lives, Separate Sporting Models." In G. L. Cohen, ed., *Women in Sport: Issues and Controversies*. 2nd ed. Exonhill.

Dejene, Y. (Draft). Promoting women's economic empowerment in Africa. Retrieved from http://www. uneca.org/aec/documents/Yeshiareg Dejene.pdf

Eisenstein, Z. 1999. "Constructing a Theory of Capitalist Patriarchy and Socialist Feminism." *Critical Sociology. 25*(2).

Ekechi, F. K. 1995. "Gender and Economic Power: The Case of Igbo Market Women of Eastern Nigeria." In B. House-Midamba, & F. K. Ekechi, eds., *African Market Women and Economic Power: The Role of Women in African Economic Development*. Westport, CT, London: Greenwood Press.

Falola, T. 1995. "Gender, Business and Space Control: Yoruba Market Women and Power." In B. House-Midamba, & F. K. Ekechi, eds., *African Market Women and Economic Power: The Role of Women in African Economic Development*. Westport, CT, London: Greenwood Press.

Fox, C. 2007. "The Question of Identity from a Comparative Education Perspective." In R. F. Arnove & C. A.Torres, eds. (3rd ed.). *Comparative Education: The Dialectic of the Global and the Local*. Rowman & Littlefield.

Freedman, E. B. 2002. *No Turning Back: The History of Feminism and the Future of Women*. New York: Ballantine Books.

Gordon, A. A. 2007. "Women and Development." In A. A. Gordon & D. L. Gordon, eds. Understanding Contemporary Africa. Boulder, CO: Lynne Rienner Publishers.

Greene, B. 1998. "The Institution of Woman-Marriage in Africa: A Cross-cultural Analysis." *Ethnology*, 37 (4).

Hopkins, A. G. 1973. *An Economic History of West Africa*. New York: Columbia University Press.

Institute of Economic Affairs. 2008. Profile of Women's Socioeconomic Status in Kenya.

Kenya Demographic Health Survey. 2003; Kenya National Bureau of Statistics. 2007. *Basic Report on Well-Being in Kenya*. Nairobi: the Regal Press. Retrieved from http://www.ieakenya.or.ke/documents/ Profiling%20Women%20in%20Kenya.pdf.

Kenyatta, J. (1965). Facing Mount Kenya: The tribal life of the Gikuyu. New York: Vintage Books.

Longwe, S. H. 2000. "Towards Realistic Strategies for Women's Political Empowerment in Africa." In C. Sweetman, ed. *Women and Leadership*. Oxford: Oxfam GB.

Marah, J. K. (2006). The virtues and challenges in traditional african education. The Journal of Pan African Studies,1(4), 15-24

Nnaemeka, O. 1998. "Introduction: Reading the Rainbow." In O. Nnaemeka, ed. *Sisterhood, Feminisms and Power: From Africa to the Diaspora.* Trenton, NJ: Africa World Press.

Njoh, A. J., & P. N. Rigos. 2003. "Female Participation in the Formal Sector and Development in Sub-Saharan Africa." *Journal of Third World Studies*, 20 (2).

O'Barr, J. F. 1975. "Making the Invisible Visible: African Women in Politics and Policy." *African Studies Review*, 18 (3).

Oboler, R. S. 1980. Is the Female Husband a Man? Woman/Woman Marriage among the Nandi of Kenya." *Ethnology* 19 (1).

Ogbomo, O. W. 1995. "Esan Women Traders and Precolonial Economic Power." In B. House-Midamba, & F. K. Ekechi, eds. *African Market Women and Economic Power: The Role of Women in African Economic Development.* Westport, CT, London: Greenwood Press.

Omwami, E. M. 2011. "Relative-change Theory: Examining the Impact of Patriarchy, Paternalism, and Poverty on the Education of Women in Kenya." *Gender and Education,* 23 (1).

Samoff, J., & B. Carrol. 2007. "Education for All in Africa: Still a Distant Dream." In R. F. Arnove & C. A.Torres, eds. (3rd ed.). *Comparative Education: The Dialectic of the Global and the Local.* Rowman & Littlefield.

Sofola, Z. 1998. "Feminism and African Womanhood." In O. Nnaemeka, ed. *Sisterhood, Feminisms and Power: From Africa to the Diaspora.* Trenton, NJ: Africa World Press.

Stromquist, N. P. 2007. "Women's Education in the 21st Century: Balance and Prospects." In, Arnove, R. F. & C. A.Torres, eds. (3rd ed.). *Comparative Education: The Dialectic of the Global and the Local.* Rowman & Littlefield.

Sudarkasa, N. 1986. *The Strength of Our Mothers: African & African American Women & Families. Essays & Speeches.* Trenton, NJ: Africa World Press.

Tamale, S. 2000. "Point of order, Mr. Speaker: African Women Claiming Their Space in Parliament." In C. Sweetman, ed., *Women and Leadership* (8–15). Oxford, UK: Oxfam GB.

World Bank, 2007. Gender and Economic Growth in Kenya (Africa Development Indicators Factoid).

Chapter Eight

The Millennium Development Goals And Agriculture In Rural Sub-Saharan Africa

By Maria Navarro

The Millennium Development Goals

The Millennium Development Goals (MDGs) represent the commitment of world leaders to work together to eliminate extreme poverty around the world. The eight goals, listed below in figure 1, address the many dimensions of poverty, "income poverty, hunger, disease, lack of adequate shelter, and exclusion—while promoting gender equality, education, and environmental sustainability" (UN Millennium Project, 2005a, p. 1). Since the signature of the UN Millennium Declaration in 2000, progress in achieving the MDGs has been irregular, with both impressive successes and devastating failures. The most celebrated success stories report improvements affecting worldwide averages, and tend to be interpreted as if the whole world were advancing together toward a universal elimination of all manifestations of poverty and exclusion.

It is true that since 2000 the rate of child mortality in the world has decreased, and there have been increases in the world's average per capita income, life expectancy, and percentage of people with access to water. It is true that "the number of undernourished people has declined but remains unacceptably high" (Food and Agriculture Organization [FAO], 2010). It is true, too, unfortunately, that there is also a long list of local and regional failure stories with which there has been little or no progress with many of the Millennium Development Goals.

Sub-Saharan Africa and the Millennium Development Goals

Sub-Saharan Africa is one of the epicenters of failure of the Millennium Development Goals (UN Millennium Project, 2005a), as exemplified by Somalia's famine of 2011, one of the worst—if not the worst—humanitarian crises in history. Sub-Saharan Africa has the world's highest prevalence and intensity of multidimensional poverty (see box 2), meaning that in some areas many of the MDGs are failing simultaneously. For example, in Niger, 92.7 percent of the

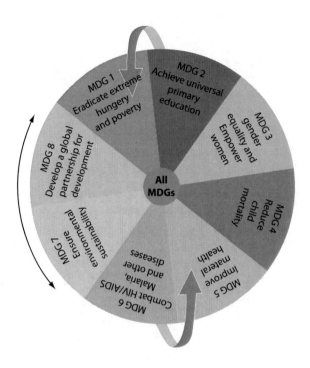

Figure 1. The Millennium development goals

Box 1. Representation of the Millennium Development Goals

The representation of the MDGs in figure 1 symbolizes the following:

1. The fight against poverty is a global, dynamic, and continuous process that can start with any or all goals, on a small or large scale;
2. The fight against poverty can start anywhere, take different directions, and find singular paths;
3. The fight against poverty is multidimensional, and all efforts to achieve the goals are connected at the core, interdependent, and transferable.

---

population is in multidimensional poverty, with an average intensity of deprivation of 69.3 percent, both measures being the highest in the world (United Nations Development Programme [UNDP], 2010). On average, 46 percent of the 2001 population of sub-Saharan Africa lived under extreme poverty ($1.08/day) (UN Millennium Project, 2005a). However, regional averages can conceal important disparities among countries and a wide range of values (Rösling, 2009). The two following examples show that there are clear differences between countries regarding the severity and pervasiveness of poverty.

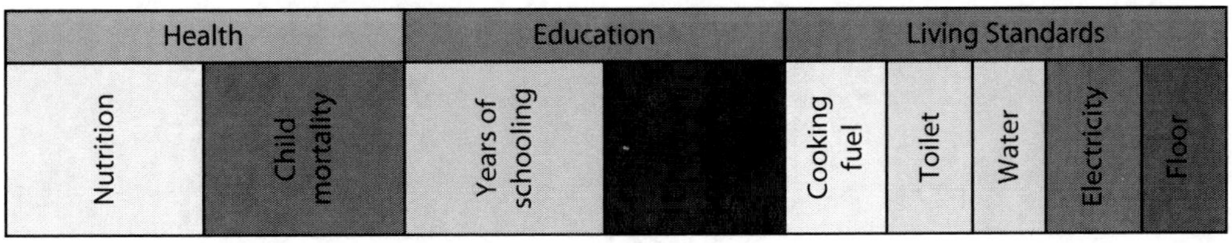

Source: UNDP (2010).

Figure 2. Graphic representation of the Multidimensional Poverty Index (MPI)

> **Box 2. A new measure of poverty: the Multidimensional Poverty Index (MPI)**
>
> The new United Nations Multidimensional Poverty Index (MPI) was developed in response to the need to measure poverty from a multidimensional perspective. The dimensions considered are health, education, and living standards. For each dimension, it measures several deprivations using the following indicators: health (nutrition and child mortality), education (years of schooling, and child enrollment), and living standards (cooking fuel, toilet, water, electricity, floor, and assets). The MPI measures the percentage of people in multidimensionally poor households and the intensity of their deprivation (average number of overlapping deprivations per household) (UNDP, 2010).

1. In South Africa, only 3.1 percent of the population suffer from multidimensional poverty, as opposed to 92.7 percent in Niger (UNDP, 2010);
2. On average, in 2009, sub-Saharan Africa had a mortality rate of children under five of 129.6 (per 1,000), much in contrast with the world's average of 61 (per 1,000). In Mauritius, the mortality rate of children under five is 17 (per 1,000), while in Chad the rate is 209 (per 1,000) (World Bank, 2011).

About three-fourths of the poor in sub-Saharan Africa live in rural areas and depend directly on agriculture for their survival. They are small and landless farmers, wage laborers, and artisanal fishermen (Diao, Hazell, & Thurlow, 2010; International Fund for Agricultural Development [IFAD] 2001; Karekezi, 2002; UN Millennium Project, 2005a). Thus, many of the programs being developed as part of the plans to achieve the Millennium Development Goals in sub-Saharan Africa focus on improving the lives of the small and poor farmers of the region. For these programs to succeed, it is necessary that program personnel engage consistently and regularly in comprehensive needs assessment and strategic planning together with the stakeholders and intended beneficiaries of the program, the farmers. Three very important components of these needs assessments include in-depth analysis of (1) the characteristics of small-scale agriculture in the target area; (2) the factors that affect the lives of project stakeholders; and (3) the role of agricultural development in achieving the Millennium Development Goals.

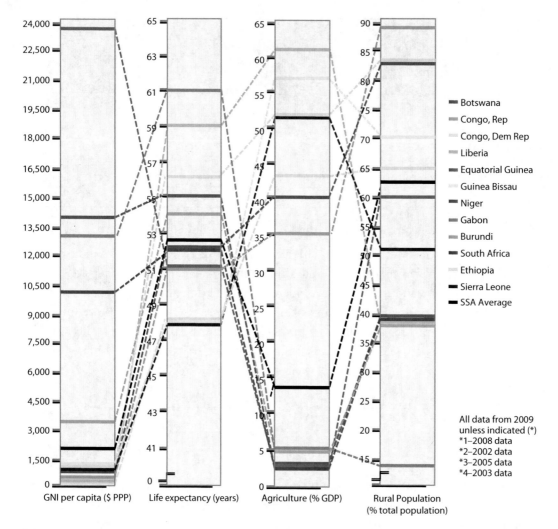

(1) Income per person (GNI per capita, PPP current international $); (2) Life expectancy in years; (3) Agriculture and value-added agriculture (percentage of total GDP); (4) Rural population (percent of total population).

Data source: World Bank, 2011. Figure prepared by Jennifer Johnson.

Figure 3. Comparison between selected countries for four indicators

The size of the cell of each indicator indicates its relative weight. For a household to be multidimensionally poor, it would need to be deprived in at least two to six indicators, depending on the weight of each indicator. For example, if a household was deprived in nutrition and children enrollment, it would be multidimensionally poor. However, if it was deprived in toilet, water, and electricity, it would not yet be considered multidimensionally poor.

Table 1: Criteria used to classify farming systems: climate zones, corresponding ecosystems, and country Examples in sub-Saharan Africa

Climate zones and modified Köppen classification	Ecosystem	Country example[1]
Tropical wet (Af)	Rainforest	Congo, Democratic Republic
Tropical wet and dry (Aw)	Savanna	Nigeria
Tropical dry (BW)	Desert	Namibia
Middle latitude dry (BS)	Steppe	Lesotho
Mediterranean (Csa)	Chaparral	South Africa (Cape Town Region)
Humid Subtropical (Cfa)	Mesotherms (varies)	Mozambique (interior provinces)
Mountain/Highland (H)	Montane	Tanzania
Climate zones: Affected by altitude, latitude, topography, surrounding bodies of water, and currents		

Note 1: The country examples give an example of a country where that climate zone and ecosystem are important. However, it is possible to find more than one climate zone and ecosystem in any given country. For example, South Africa has been listed for the Mediterranean climate and the chaparral ecosystem, but the country has at least four more climate zones (and corresponding ecosystems): tropical dry, middle latitude dry, mountain, and humid subtropical.

Sources: Alfaro-Pelico (2010); Brandt (2010); Brown & Crawford (2009).

Farming Systems in Sub-Sahran Africa

On average, agriculture accounted for 13.1 percent of the Gross Domestic Product (GDP) of sub-Saharan countries in 2009. However, the numbers varied considerably between countries: In some countries (e.g., Central African Republic, Sierra Leone, Ethiopia), agricultural production accounted for more than 50 percent of GDP, while in others (e.g., Botswana, Equatorial Guinea, Gabon), it amounted to less than 5 percent of GDP (World Bank, 2011). There are many indicators that can help in the analysis of agricultural systems in a region. For the purpose of this chapter, we have chosen four indicators to show the similarities and differences between countries that we can find in the region (figure 3). These indicators are (1) income per person (Gross National Income [GNI] per capita, in Purchasing Power Parity [PPP] current international $); (2) life expectancy in years; (3) agriculture and value-added agriculture (percentage of total GDP); (4) rural population (percent of total population).

It is important to note that the values of indicators between countries do not develop similarly or in the same order (e.g., some countries first had health and then wealth; others had first

Table 2 Criteria used to classify farming systems: types of dominant livelihood sources of small-scale agricultural systems in sub-Saharan Africa

Settled farming
• Food staples

• Arid and semiarid regions (greater drought tolerance): millet and sorghum
    • Increased rainfall (semiarid, subhumid, highlands): maize (corn)
    • Humid lowlands: tuberous roots (sweet potatoes, cassava), tubers (potatoes), and plantains
    • River basins: rice
    • Other: bananas, barley, beans, coconut, cowpea, eggplant, green banana, lentils, peanut, pigeon peas, spinach, sweet potatoes, wheat, and horticultural crops

• Cash crops: cashews, citrus, cocoa, cotton, coffee, oil palm, pineapple, rubber, sisal, sugarcane, tea, timber, tobacco, vine
• Tree crops   • Mixed farming (animals and crops)
Nomadic and settled pastoralism, artisanal fishing

• Arid regions: camels
    • Arid, semiarid, sub-humid, and highland: cattle
    • Humid lowlands: small ruminants (goats and sheep—greater tolerance to sleeping sickness) Poultry and some swine
    • Aquaculture
    • Artisanal fishing

Other dominant livelihood sources

• Hunting and gathering
    • On-farm value-added post-harvest processing (i.e., food processing)
    • On-farm, nonfarming activities (arts, crafts, soap making)
    • Off-farm employment, nonagricultural
    • Off-farm employment, agricultural, seasonal migration, remittances

Sources: Dixon, Gulliver, & Gibbon (2001); U.S. Congress, Office of Technology Assessment [USC-OTA] (1988).

wealth and then health; others have health but not wealth; and some have wealth but not health) (Rösling, 2007). Figure 3 illustrates this point: Equatorial Guinea and Burundi have very different incomes per person ($23,810 and $390 respectively), but they have the same life expectancy (51 years); the Democratic Republic of the Congo and Liberia have very similar GNI ($310 and $330 respectively), but very different life expectancy (48 and 59 years respectively) (World Bank, 2011).

Table 3 Criteria used to classify farming systems: natural resources available, water supply, degree of commercialization, implements used for cultivation, farm size, tenure, and organization, and level of technology and external input used

Criteria and description
Natural resources available
• Water availability • Soil types • Land cover
Water supply
• Irrigated farming • Rainfed farming
Degree of commercialization
• Subsistence farming (most crops used for household food) • Partly commercialized farming • Commercialized farming
Implements used for cultivation
• Hoe-farming (most subsistence agriculture uses hoe-farming) • Farming with plows and animal traction • Farming with plows and tractors
Farm size and tenure
• Farm size (small-scale is 0 to 5 Ha) • Tenure (state, communal, customary, individual) (landless)
Level of technology
• Low technology • Moderate technology • High technology

Sources: Dixon et al. (2001); Economic Commission for Africa (ECA, 2004). Kuiseu, Ndlovu, Dike, Kagaruki, Kashaija, Musibono, Ndirika, & Rakotonjanahary (2009).

Similarly, the percentage of people living in rural areas does not determine the percentage of total GDP in agriculture: Equatorial Guinea has 60 percent of the population living in rural areas, and only 3 percent of its GDP comes from agriculture; Sierra Leone has 62 percent of the population in rural areas, and 51 percent of the GDP comes from agriculture (figure 3) (World Bank, 2011).

Table 4: Farming systems in sub-Saharan Africa, grouped by prevalence of poverty in the system

Farming system	% total	Farming system	% total
Limited prevalence of poverty			
Irrigated	2	Cereal-root crop mixed	15
Limited-moderate prevalence of poverty			
Tree crop	6	Root crop	11
Moderate prevalence of poverty			
Rice-tree crop	2	Maize mixed	15
Mixed cereal/livestock	4	Coastal artisanal fishing	3
Urban-based agriculture	3		
Moderate-extensive prevalence of poverty			
Highland temperate mixed	7		
Extensive prevalence of poverty			
Forest based	7	Highland perennial	8
Agro-pastoral millet/sorghum	8	Pastoral	7
Sparse (arid)	1		

Source: Dixon et al. (2001).

Criteria used to classify farming systems in sub-Saharan Africa

There are many different criteria by which one could classify farming systems in sub-Saharan Africa. Tables 1, 2, and 3 summarize some of these criteria. Table 1 provides a list of the seven climate zones found in sub-Saharan Africa, the corresponding ecosystems, and some country examples. Table 2 summarizes the types of dominant livelihood sources of small-scale agricultural systems in sub-Saharan Africa. Table 3 summarizes the types of systems that will result from classification using the following criteria: (1) natural resources available; (2) water supply; (3) degree of commercialization; (4) implements used for cultivation; (5) farm size, tenure, and organization; and (6) level of technology and external input used.

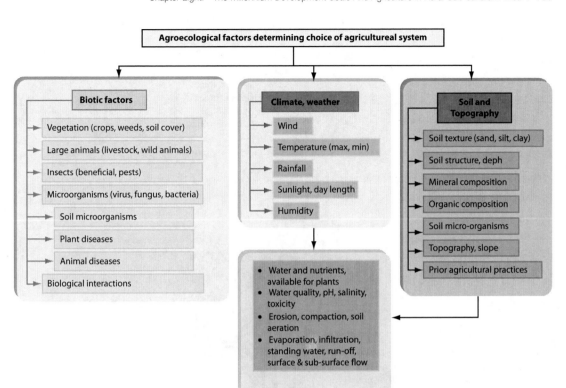

Figure 4. Agroecological factors determining the choice of agricultural system in small-scale, low-external-input agriculture

Farming Systems in Sub-Saharan Africa: Is there a typical farm?

There is not such a thing as a typical farm in sub-Saharan Africa. One can find as much diversity in farming systems as in cultures, languages, climates, systems, organizations, tenure systems, crops or animals. Using some of the criteria summarized in tables 1, 2, and 3, Dixon et al. (2001) described fifteen types of farming systems in sub-Saharan Africa. Table 4 lists these farming systems and gives an approximation of the population they represent as a percentage of the total.

Small-Scale Agriculture in Sub-Saharan Africa

In sub-Saharan Africa, small-scale farmers (about 96 percent of all farmers) are responsible for about 90 percent of total agricultural production. These small-scale farmers have less than 5 hectares of land, and about two-thirds of them have less than one hectare (Spencer, 2002). Some of the common characteristics of most small-scale agricultural systems include (1) low external

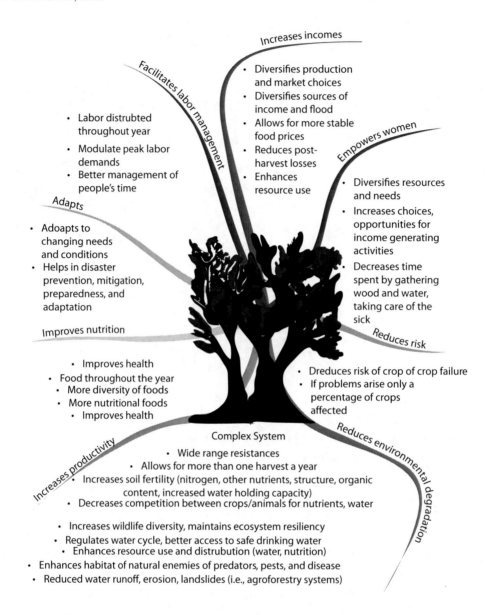

Facilitates labor management

Increases incomes

Empowers women

Adapts

Reduces risk

Improves nutrition

Increases productivity

Reduces environmental degradation

- Labor distrubted throughout year
- Modulate peak labor demands
- Better management of people's time

- Diversifies production and market choices
- Diversifies sources of income and flood
- Allows for more stable food prices
- Reduces post-harvest losses
- Enhances resource use

- Diversifies resources and needs
- Increases choices, opportunities for income generating activities
- Decreases time spent by gathering wood and water, taking care of the sick

- Adoapts to changing needs and conditions
- Helps in disaster prevention, mitigation, preparedness, and adaptation

- Dreduces risk of crop of crop failure
- If problems arise only a percentage of crops affected

- Improves health
- Food throughout the year
- More diversity of foods
- More nutritional foods
- Improves health

Complex System
- Wide range resistances
- Allows for more than one harvest a year
- Increases soil fertility (nitrogen, other nutrients, structure, organic content, increased water holding capacity)
- Decreases competition between crops/animals for nutrients, water

- Increases wildlife diversity, maintains ecosystem resiliency
- Regulates water cycle, better access to safe drinking water
- Enhances resource use and distrubution (water, nutrition)
- Enhances habitat of natural enemies of predators, pests, and disease
- Reduced water runoff, erosion, landslides (i.e., agroforestry systems)

Figure 5. Diversity of small-scale, low-external-input agricultural systems

input; (2) low risk; (3) dependency on agroecological factors; (4) complexity and diversity; (5) divided labor; and (6) land tenure.

Low External Input

The small-scale (0 to 5 Ha) corn (maize) farms in the high and mid-altitude savannas of Zimbabwe, Kenya, and Zambia have much lower yields than the large-scale (80 Ha or more) farms in the same area (1.5 Ton/Ha vs. 5 to 6 Ton/Ha respectively). Yet the difference in yield is not the result of inefficiency of the farmers. On the contrary, small-scale farmers may be more efficient than large-scale farmers and use their resources well, but they are very poor and have no avenues to secure external inputs for their land (purchased fertilizers, seeds, and pesticides; off-farm water for irrigation, wage laborers, etc.). In addition, they have often been relegated to degraded lands, and have little access to roads, markets, and services, including extension services (Spencer, 2002).

Thus, poor and small-scale farmers generally have low currency costs and use very few off-farm inputs, relying primarily on indigenous knowledge and on-farm, and accessible, resources, including large quantities of "family" labor (USC-OTA, 1988). For example, they may use on-farm animal and green manure to fertilize their land rather than purchase fertilizers; spend high amounts of time hoeing, hand sowing and harvesting rather than using a plow, a tractor, or other machines requiring fuel; reuse their own seeds from each year's harvest rather than purchase seeds of improved varieties; manage weeds by hand pulling, moving soil, mulching, and carefully crafting crop rotations and combinations of crops, rather than purchase and use synthetic herbicides. Though these systems are often called *low-input agricultural systems*, they should not be called *low input* given the extensive knowledge and the familial, on-farm, and local resources that they use. It is more appropriate to call them *low-external-input agricultural systems* (Norman, Janke, Freyenberger, Schurle, & Kok, 1997).

Enhancing the knowledge, information, resources, and appropriate technology available to small-scale farmers could be an avenue to expand their opportunities, strengthen their systems, and increase their yields, and, in turn, pave a better path toward achieving the Millennium Development Goals. There is, however, disagreement on what should be considered appropriate technology, how this change should happen, and what needs to be done to avoid possible negative consequences. Some of the possible negative consequences often discussed include (1) pollution (soil, water, air) and human health problems due to overuse and misuse of fertilizers and pesticides; (2) lowering of the water table due to irrigation overuse; (3) decreased crop diversity and its associated problems, including increased risk of crop failure, higher crop susceptibility to pests and diseases, and reduction of nutritional quality of food available to rural people; (4) exploitation and consequent degradation of marginal lands not suited for agriculture; (5) farmers being forced into a cycle of cash dependency, indebtedness and economic distress; (6) growing gap between rich and poor, and marginalization and displacement of farmers who cannot afford inputs or cannot adapt to change in market patterns; (7) unemployment of agricultural wage laborers replaced by technology (herbicides, machinery, etc.); and (8) loss of indigenous knowledge and genetic resources (Navarro, 2006). All of these concerns need to be addressed to assure positive changes in rural sub-Saharan Africa.

Low Risk

Poor farmers are usually very conservative. In fact, farmers who depend on a harvest to be able to eat cannot "experiment" with their farms because crop failure could mean death for them or other members of their family. This does not mean they do not like, accept or understand innovation; it just means they favor strategies that minimize uncertainty and ensure stability, even at the expense of potentially large but uncertain benefits. Agricultural development efforts and innovations that consider and address farmers' risk aversion are more likely to be adopted by small-farmers and succeed.

Dependency on Agroecological Factors

Small-scale, low-external-input agriculture is highly dependent on local knowledge, culture, and agroecological factors. Figure 4 summarizes the main agroecological factors that determine the choice of agricultural system in small-scale, low-external-input agriculture.

Complexity and Diversity

One notable characteristic of small-scale, low-external-input agricultural systems is that they are often highly diversified, dynamic, and quite complex. Figure 5 summarizes the advantages bestowed by the complexity and diversity of these systems. Development efforts that value and build upon the diversity and complexity of agricultural systems are more likely to succeed.

Divided Labor

Labor and responsibilities are often divided by gender and age. Women are in charge of many "invisible" tasks necessary for the family's survival. For example, women are responsible for providing fuel and water for their family, which frequently takes them more than four hours per day. Women also care for their children, healthy or sick, which reduces their opportunity to participate in remunerated work, often reserved for men (Watkins, 2006).

Both women and men are active participants in agriculture-related labor. Both share the work of seeding and harvesting. Men are usually responsible for clearing and preparing the land, while women do most of the weeding, transplanting, and managing of the crops (ECA, 2004). Women do almost all of the food processing. However, women's contribution tends to receive much less recognition, they rarely have control over resources and income, and they have fewer decision-making opportunities than men. Men have more access to land, and women have more hurdles to overcome than men to access credit, agricultural inputs, services, knowledge, appropriate technology, farmer organizations, and extension education (FAO Women and Population Division, n.d.).

Increasing women's access to extension education and services would bring many benefits to women, and to agriculture in general. Some areas to consider that would lead to significant benefits include the following:

1. Enhancing women's access to information and knowledge about agriculture and agricultural innovations;
2. Facilitating women's access to credit and agricultural inputs (fertilizers, seeds, tools, water, land);
3. Helping extension educators and researchers understand and focus on women's needs;
4. Improving research efforts to address issues faced by women;
5. Supporting the development of appropriate technology for small-scale agriculture;
6. Increasing women's access to markets;
7. Increasing women's access to community organizations and representation;
8. Enhancing women's relationships with providers of other services (health, education, water for irrigation, clean drinking water and sanitation);
9. Increasing—even if only indirectly—women's participation in governance and decision making.

Land Tenure

Land tenure, sometimes referred to as ownership, differs significantly among countries. For example, in South Africa, only 1.4 percent of rural families living on less than $1 per person per day own land, while in Ivory Coast, 63 percent of rural families living on less than $1 per person per day own land (Banerjee & Duflo, 2007). As a general rule, land is unequally distributed between men and women, with men having more rights to land than women. Lacking land tenure, many small-scale women farmers are denied credit. In some regions, they may also be denied membership in water user associations, which might preclude them from gaining access to water (Watkins, 2006). Land is also often unequally distributed across races, classes, and ethnicities. In South Africa, white farmers have an average farm size of 1,570 Ha each, while blacks own on average less than 2 Ha each (ECA, 2004).

Poor farmers usually own small parcels of less than 5 Ha of marginal and poor land. This greatly affects their food and social security, and affords them few resources and opportunities to purchase productive inputs, access credit, or improve their land. Assurance to permanent land tenure also affects environmental sustainability: It influences decisions made regarding land use (crops, diversity of crops, grazing, etc.), and long-term investment in the land (i.e., conservation measures, planting of perennials and trees, etc.). In a 2004 document, the Economic Commission for Africa indicated that the most stable form of food security for the

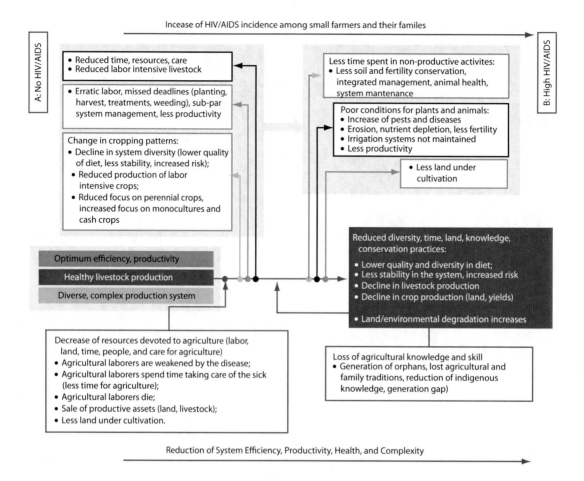

Source: Association for International Agriculture and Rural Development [AIARD], (2003).

Figure 6. **The losses in small-scale agriculture from HIV/AIDS**

poor was more control over natural resources, including land tenure, and argued that this could not be achieved without some form of land redistribution (ECA, 2004).

Factors Affecting Rural Life in Sub-Saharan Africa

i. *The Poverty Trap*

More than half of the rural poor depend directly on agriculture for their survival. Though they produce most of the food available in the region, they often have less food security than the urban poor. Among the rural poor, some are poorer than others. In sub-Saharan Africa, social inequality is ubiquitous and often observed among gender, classes, races, and ethnic groups

(Brockerhoff & Hewett, 2000; ECA, 2004). Moradi and Baten (2005) found that there was more social inequality where there was a monoculture of cash crops than under a diversified system.

The poor are usually deprived in more than one of the health, education, and standard of living dimensions of poverty (see box 2). Caught, they feel forced to make choices that will dig them even deeper into poverty. For example, poor rural families may have to send their children (particularly girls) to gather fuel, food, and water rather than to school, a choice that may trap another generation in poverty. Sometimes, poor people are not even aware of the negative consequences of their decisions. For example, deprived communities cut forest trees for fuel and money; then they cultivate annual crops on the bare slopes left after deforestation without the knowledge, time, energy, or resources to build terraces and protect the soil against erosion. Such actions contribute to accelerated degradation of the environment that further reduces their ability to produce food and puts at them at risk of plain flooding and mud slides.

Many models of development programs and institutions have successfully helped the rural poor escape the poverty trap. One example of a short-term program is to give poor people access to microloans to start productive activities that will help generate income. Examples of items acquired with money from microloans include fabric and thread for a weaving and embroidery business; a cell phone to become a village phone operator; materials necessary to open a coconut kiosk; a dairy cow; and a flock of chickens. Microloans for the poor as we know them today were first established by Muhammad Yunus through the Grameen Bank. The main differences between these microloans and the status quo loans were that the microloans were too small for banks to even consider giving (an average of $69 in Bangladesh in 2004); they were given to people who usually had no collateral (mostly women, who would have been unable to get any

---

Box 3. Recommendations of the UN Millennium Project Task Force on halving hunger (UN Millennium Project, 2005b)

Global level
1. "Move from political commitment to action"

National level
2. "Reform policies and create an enabling environment"

Community level
3. "Increase the agricultural productivity of food-insecure farmers"
4. "Improve nutrition for the chronically hungry and vulnerable"
5. "Reduce the vulnerability of the acutely hungry through productive safety nets"
6. "Increase incomes and make markets work for the poor"
7. "Restore and conserve the natural resources essential for food security"

Source: UN Millennium Project (2005b)

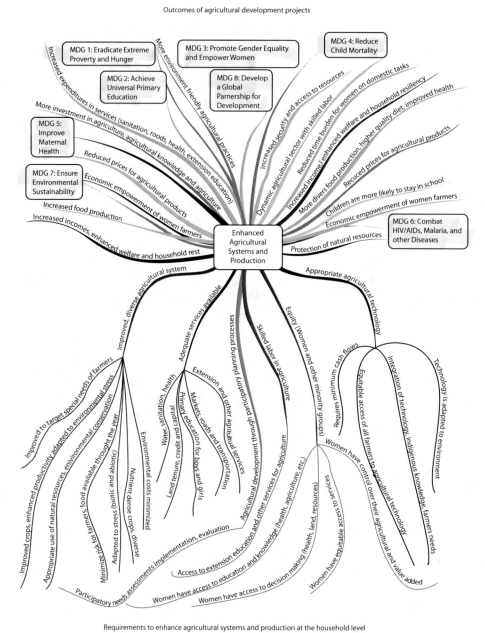

Outcomes of agricultural development projects

Requirements to enhance agricultural systems and production at the household level

Source: World Bank and International Food Policy Research Institute, (n.d.)

Figure 7. Summary of how improvements in small-scale agriculture can support efforts to achieve the Millennium Development Goals in sub-Saharan Africa.

credit from traditional banks); and they were given through a group-lending model (Grameen Foundation, n.d.; Sengupta & Aubuchon, 2008). For the first time, the poor, including women, were able to apply for and receive a loan. This was a hugely significant first step out of poverty and onto the road toward building a successful life.

ii. Violent Conflicts

Violent conflict represents another deadly trap faced by the rural poor: Persistent poverty feeds conflicts, and conflicts give rise to poverty. Analyzing the types, length, frequency, intensity, causes, and consequences of conflict is essential for successful planning and implementation of rural and agricultural development efforts. There are large-scale and small-scale; short-term and long-term; political, ethnic, and religious conflicts. There are wars between countries, uprisings against governments (ranging from low-intensity and small-scale to large-scale and intense civil wars), and guerrilla warfare. There are conflicts involving diamonds, oil, and rubber. In most cases, there is disagreement regarding whether the resources are the cause of the conflict or simply what sustains the conflict. Finally, there are conflicts over natural resources that usually go unreported and unnoticed by the international community. They happen in rural areas and occur over cattle and grazing land among pastoralists, over fertile agricultural land among farmers, or over watering holes. Such conflicts, often decades or even centuries long, have always existed, but population pressure and land degradation has intensified their frequency and intensity in recent years and they are greatly affecting the outcomes of agricultural development efforts (Bujra, 2002).

It is obvious that people affected by conflict may suffer from death, fear, violence, hunger, poverty, health problems, displacement, and abandonment, both during and years after the conflict. However, few people fully appreciate the spectrum of other "silent" effects of violent conflict. From an agricultural development perspective, conflict can cause direct, indirect, immediate, and long-term harm to agriculture. Some examples are (1) burning of annual crops, perennials, and trees; (2) destruction or damage to infrastructure such as water reservoirs, wells, or irrigation systems; (3) environmental degradation (e.g., smoke; deforestation and consequent soil erosion; pollution of water resources); (4) abandonment of lands and consequent abandonment of strategies to protect the soil against erosion; (5) destruction of carefully designed and maintained agricultural diversity and complexity; (6) loss of agricultural indigenous knowledge due to abandonment of agricultural practices, death of knowledge bearers, or displacement of people to areas unknown to them; (7) unsustainable agricultural practices employed by displaced people in their new "homes" because they lack the necessary knowledge to adapt to a new environment; (8) desperate and unsustainable agricultural practices at the brink of starvation; (9) failure to invest in long-term stewardship of the land because recurrence of conflict has taught farmers to plan only for annual results, and immediate harvest; and (10) rendering land unusable due to the risk of landmines. Any and all of these are very important factors to take into account when planning for agricultural development.

iii. Environmental Degradation and Natural Disasters

Poverty is both a consequence and a cause of environmental degradation in Africa. According to the United Nations Environment Programme [UNEP] (1999), about 65 percent of the agricultural land had been affected by soil degradation from 1950 to late 1998; deforestation had affected 39 million Ha (an area the size of Zimbabwe) of tropical forest during the 1980s; biodiversity is declining; and the number of countries subject to water scarcity and water pollution is growing (UNEP, 1999). Environmental degradation accentuates the risk to natural disasters (which in turn increase poverty, which contributes to environmental degradation). Poor people in marginal areas, without infrastructure and institutional services, in the poorest countries, are the ones in greatest danger of natural disasters, and have less ability to prevent, prepare, receive early warning, protect, cope, and recover (Balcu, 2010).

Agriculture is highly dependent on agroecological factors, which include climate, weather, and water availability. These factors may all be highly favorable, resulting in an abundant, profitable crop or completely unfavorable, bringing total disaster. The impacts of natural disasters on rural life and small-scale agriculture can be direct or indirect, tangible or intangible, and include (1) death and diseases of people and livestock; (2) direct economic losses (i.e., damage or loss of crops); (3) indirect economic losses or loss of potential production (i.e., inability to plant because the land is flooded; reduced productivity because of soil erosion, compaction, or depletion of fertility); (4) damage to perennial crops, productive trees, forests, machinery, and buildings; (5) intangible impacts such as fear of future disasters, fear of investing in agriculture, anxiety, and emotional problems; (6) loss of work and employment; (7) increased soil and water salinity; (8) reduced access to transportation (i.e., roads damaged by a hurricane or flood), and reduced access to market and services; (9) displacement of people (Sivakumar, n.d.).

Poverty and natural disasters seem to be in a self-perpetuating, destructive cycle. To address the needs of the poor in sub-Saharan Africa, there needs to be more investment in preventing disasters rather than responding to them (Sivakumar, n.d.).

iv. Climate Change

The Intergovernmental Panel on Climate Change (IPCC) predicted that many changes will occur in Africa due to climate change, including a temperature increase (most accentuated in the dry regions) and a decrease in rainfall (except for eastern Africa, where an increase in precipitation is expected). These changes are likely to have a negative effect on most agricultural production, by reducing areas suitable for agriculture, decreasing rainfall and irrigation water at times and places where crops and people most need this water, and shortening the growing seasons and reducing production potentials (Eriksen, O'Brien & Rosentrater, 2008). In addition, Burke, Miguel, Satyanath, Dykema, and Lobell (2009) analyzed historical data of civil wars in sub-Saharan Africa and predicted that an additional secondary consequence of rising temperatures could be an important increase in the occurrence of civil wars, 50 percent in the next twenty years. The possible threat of climate change is considered to be worse in sub-Saharan Africa because of the high percentage of households that, with no capacity for adaptation, depend on agriculture for their survival and are already one harvest away from starvation. In addition, existing strategies are insufficient to cope with the expected effects of climate change, and the region lacks the technological, institutional, and financial capacity to cope or adapt to the impacts of climate change (Eriksen et al., 2008).

v. Health

Rural people have limited access to safe drinking water, one of the key determinants of their health. Everyone benefits from clean drinking water because they do not contract water-associated diseases. Women benefit more because (1) they do not have to walk for hours to supply water for their families, or take care of family members who contract water-associated diseases; (2) they have time to finish other responsibilities; and (3) they may be able to engage in remunerated activities thanks to all the time saved. Any health problem is magnified for poor rural people because they do not have proper access to health services and medicine, and their bodies are weakened by malnutrition. Key health problems in many rural areas are HIV/AIDS, tuberculosis, malaria, and women's health concerns, including childbirth-related death. HIV/AIDS particularly affects small-scale agriculture. Figure 6 summarizes the losses in small-scale agriculture from HIV/AIDS.

The Role of Agricultural Development in Achieving the Millennium Development Goals

Many believe that agricultural development can have a key role in Africa's escape from poverty because (1) it has a demonstrated potential for growth; (2) it is the only sector that can influence growth in a significant manner at the country level; (3) it can work in parallel with other sectors; (4) it directly addresses poverty reduction by allowing for greater participation of the poor in the growth process and creating employment for poor workers; (5) it benefits and raises the incomes of a high proportion of the population; and (6) managed appropriately, it can help reduce the risk of environmental degradation (Diao et al., 2010; see also World Bank, 2008).

However, there is also some uncertainty about agriculture's potential to drive Africa's growth because of (1) agriculture's meager results to date; (2) the poor performance to date of agricultural extension services and other rural development organizations; and (3) the increasing land and environmental degradation, as well as the deterioration of conditions due to climate change (Diao et al., 2010). All these reasons, both from proponents and skeptics, need to be taken into account when planning programs of agricultural development to help achieve the MDGs.

The most common strategies of small-scale farmers to escape poverty include increasing production (by increasing inputs and yields, or increasing farm size), diversifying (higher agricultural output value or off-farm income), or migrating to urban areas. Some strategies have good results in some systems, but do not work in others (Dixon et al., 2001). Similarly, agricultural development efforts can take as many routes and have as many consequences as there are systems, people, and situations. Thus, for agricultural development to have a positive role in achieving the Millennium Development Goals, it needs to be tailored specifically to each situation, with the intended beneficiaries, with a multidisciplinary perspective, and keeping both short-term and long-term goals in mind.

In 2002, the UN Secretary General commissioned the UN Millennium Project to develop a worldwide action plan to achieve the Millennium Development Goals. One of the project's task forces, the Task Force on Halving Hunger, focused primarily on agriculture and nutrition, and called for simultaneous action at three levels: global, national, and community. They presented their plan in the report: *Halving Hunger: It can be done* (UN Millennium Project, 2005b). Their recommendations are listed in box 3.

Recommendations 3 and 7 are of special interest for discussion in this chapter. Recommendation 3, "increase the agricultural productivity of food-insecure farmers," stressed the importance of (1) controlling soil erosion and improving soil health and fertility; (2) improving methods for water conservation, collection, management, and use; (3) giving the poor access to improved varieties of trees, crops, and animal breeds adapted to marginal conditions; (4) increasing choices for the poor to allow for diverse and value-added systems; and (5) updating extension services so they can better address the needs of small farmers (UN Millennium Project, 2005b). Recommendation 7, "restore and conserve the natural resources essential for food security," addressed similar issues, including (1) restoring and improving natural resources; (2) securing tenure, access, and management rights of rangelands, forests, and fisheries; (3) developing "green enterprises;" and (4) paying the rural poor for their environmental services (UN Millennium Project, 2005b).

Figure 7 concludes the chapter with a graphic representation of how improvements in small-scale agriculture can support efforts to achieve the Millennium Development Goals in sub-Saharan Africa.

Review Questions

1. List the Millennium Development Goals.

2. Detail the criteria used to classify farming systems in sub-Saharan Africa.

3. Describe major characteristics of small-scale agriculture in sub-Saharan Africa.

4. Analyze the factors that affect rural life in sub-Saharan Africa.

5. Explain how improvements in small-scale agriculture can support efforts to achieve the Millennium Development Goals in sub-Saharan Africa.

Practical Work

In-class discussion: Discuss how you would assess the needs and plan for an agricultural development project in a country of your choice. What would your project look like? How would you evaluate it? What could be some negative consequences of your project? What would you do to minimize these negative consequences?

Take-home written assignment: Choose a Millennium Development Goal, and write a two-page essay with a minimum of three references explaining how agriculture can support efforts to achieve that goal in a country of your choice.

Bibliography

Alfaro-Pelico, R. I. (2010). *Africa and Climate Change: Impacts, Policies and Stance Ahead of Cancún (ARI)*. Real Instituto Elcano. Retrieved from http://www.realinstitutoelcano.org/.

Association for International Agriculture and Rural Development [AIARD]. (2003)*. *The Agriculture, Nutrition, and HIV/AIDS Connections in Developing Countries*. Retrieved from http://www.aiard.org/communications/HIV-AIDS_Connection.pdf.

Balcu, C. (2010). Environmental Influence on Natural and Anthropogenic Disasters. *Revista Academiei Fortelor Terestre*, 15 (3):383–387.

Banerjee, A. V., & E. Duflo. (2007). The Economic Lives of the Poor. *Journal of Economic Perspectives*, 21 (1), 141–167. doi: 10.1257/jep.21.1.141.

Brandt, R. R. (2010). Climate Types. In *Encyclopedia of Geography*. Retrieved from http://www.sage-ereference.com/view/geography/n178.xml.

Brockerhoff, M., and P. Hewett. (2000). Inequality of Child Mortality among Ethnic Groups in Sub-Saharan Africa. *Bulletin of the World Health Organization*, 78 (1):30–41.

Brown, O., and A. Crawford (2009)*. *Climate Change and Security in Africa*. International Institute for Sustainable Development. Retrieved from http://www.iisd.org/pdf/2009/climate_change_security_africa.pdf.

Bujra, A. (2002). *African Conflicts: Their Causes and Their Political and Social Environment*. DPMF Occasional Paper, No 4. Development Policy Management Forum (DPMF), United Nations Economic Commission for Africa (UNECA), Ethiopia. Retrieved from http://www.dpmf.org/Publications/Occassional%20Papers/occasionalpaper4.pdf.

Burke, M. B., E. E. Miguel, S. S. Satyanath, J. A. Dykema, and D. B. Lobell. (2009). Warming Increases the Risk of Civil War in Africa. *Proceedings of the National Academy of Sciences of the United States of America*, 106 (49), 20670–20674. doi:10.1073/pnas.0907998106.

Diao, X., P. Hazell, and J. Thurlow. (2010). The Role of Agriculture in African Development. *World Development*, 39 (10), 1375–1383. doi:10.1016/j.worlddev.2009.06.011.

Dixon, J., A. Gulliver, and D. Gibbon. (2001). *Farming Systems and Poverty: Improving Farmers' Livelihoods in a Changing World*. Rome and Washington, DC: FAO and World Bank.

Economic Commission for Africa [ECA]. (2004). *Land Tenure Systems and Their Impacts on Food Security and Sustainable Development in Africa*. Addis Ababa, Ethiopia: Economic Commission for Africa. Retrieved from http://www.uneca.org/eca_resources/publications/sdd/land_tenure_systems.pdf.

Eriksen, S., K. O'Brien, and L. Rosentrater. (2008). *Climate Change in Eastern and Southern Africa: Impacts, Vulnerability and Adaptation*. GECHS Report 2008:2. Oslo: Global Environmental Change and Human Security. Retrieved from http://startinternational.org/library/archive/files/cc_impacts_eafr_univoslo_2008_b4331455b2.pdf.

International Fund for Agricultural Development [IFAD]. (2001). *Rural Poverty Report 2001—The challenge of ending rural poverty*. Retrieved from http://www.ifad.org/poverty/.

Food and Agriculture Organization [FAO]. (2010)*. *The State of Food Insecurity in the World: Addressing Food Insecurity in Protracted Crises*. Rome, Italy: Food and Agriculture Organization. Retrieved from http://www.fao.org/docrep/013/i1683e/i1683e.pdf.

Food and Agriculture Organization [FAO] Women and Population Division (n.d.) Towards Sustainable Food Security: Women and Sustainable Food Security. *SD dimensions*. Sustainable Development Department, FAO Women and Population Division. Retrieved from http://www.fao.org/sd/fsdirect/fbdirect/FSP001.htm.

Grameen Foundation. (2011). Grameen Foundation Home Page. Retrieved from http://www.grameen-foundation.org/.

Karekezi, S. (2002). Poverty and Energy in Africa–A brief Review. *Energy Policy, 30*(11–12), 915–919. doi:10.1016/S0301-4215(02)00047-2.

Kuiseu, J., Ndlovu, L., M. Dike, L. Kagaruki, I. Kashaija, D. Musibono, V. Ndirika & X. Rakotonjanahary. (2009). Chapter 2: Typology and Evolution of Production, Distribution and Consumption Systems. In B. D. McIntyre, H. R. Herren, J. Wakhungu & R. T. Watson, eds., *Agriculture at a Crossroads. International Assessment of Agricultural Knowledge, Science and Technology for Development IAASTD: Sub-Saharan Africa (SSA) Report*. Island Press, Washington, DC.

Moradi, A., and J. Baten. (2005). Inequality in Sub-Saharan Africa: New Data and New Insights from Anthropometric Estimates. World Development, 33(8), 1233–1265. doi:10.1016/j.worlddev.2005.04.010.

Navarro, M. (2006)*. How Can Agricultural and Extension Educators Contribute to a Successful New Green Revolution? *The Journal of Agricultural Education and Extension, 12*(2):83–94. doi:10.1080/13892240600861559.

Norman, D., R. Janke, Freyenberger, B. Schurle, and H. Kok. (1997). *Defining and implementing sustainable agriculture*. Kansas Sustainable Agriculture Series, Paper #1; Manhattan, KS: Kansas Agricultural Experiment Station. Retrieved from http://www.kansassustainableag.org/lIBRARY/ksas1.htm.

Rösling, H. (2007). *Hans Rösling's New Insights on Poverty*. TED Talks. Retrieved from http://www.ted.com/talks/lang/eng/hans_rosling_reveals_new_insights_on_poverty.html.

Rösling, H. (2009). *Hans Rösling: Let My Dataset Change Your Mindset*. TED Talks. Retrieved from http://www.ted.com/talks/lang/eng/hans_rosling_at_state.html.

Sengupta, R., and C. P. Aubuchon. (2008). The Microfinance Revolution: An overview. *The Federal Reserve Bank of St Louis Review,* 90 (1): 9–30.

Sivakumar, M. V. K. (n.d.) *Natural Disasters and Their Mitigation for Sustainable Agricultural Development.* World Meteorological Organization. Geneva, Switzerland. Retrieved from http://www.wamis.org/agm/pubs/agm10/agm10_15.pdf.

Spencer, D. (2002). Sub-Saharan Africa. In *Sustainable Food Security for All by 2020: Proceedings of an International Conference,* September 4–6, 2001, Bonn, Germany. International Food Research Policy Institute [IFPRI], Washington, DC. Retrieved from http://www.ifpri.org/sites/default/files/publications/2020conpro.pdf.

U.S. Congress, Office of Technology Assessment [USC-OTA]. (1988*). Enhancing Agriculture in Africa: A Role for U.S. Development Assistance,* OTA-F-356. Washington, DC: U.S. Government Printing Office. Retrieved from http://www.fas.org/ota/reports/8814.pdf.

United Nations Development Programme [UNDP]. (2010)*. *Human Development Report 2010. The Real Wealth of Nations: Pathways to Human Development.* Retrieved from http://www.beta.undp.org/content/dam/undp/library/corporate/HDR/HDR_2010_EN_Complete_reprint-1.pdf.

United Nations Environment Programme [UNEP] (1999). *Global Environment Outlook 2000. Overview GEO-2000.* Division of Environmental Information, Assessment and Early Warning. Nairobi, Kenya: http://www.unep.org/geo2000/ov-e/ov-e.pdf.

UN Millennium Project. (2005a)*. *Investing in Development: A Practical Plan to Achieve the Millennium Development Goals. Overview.* Retrieved from http://www.unmillenniumproject.org/documents/overviewEngLowRes.pdf.

UN Millennium Project. (2005b)*. *Halving Hunger: It Can Be Done.* Task Force on Hunger. Retrieved from http://www.unmillenniumproject.org/documents/Hunger-lowres-complete.pdf.

Watkins, K. (2006)*. *Human Development Report 2006: Beyond Scarcity: Power, Poverty and the Global Water Crisis.* Published for the United Nations Development Program. Basingstoke, NY: Palgrave Macmillan. Retrieved from http://hdr.undp.org/en/media/HDR06-complete.pdf.

World Bank. (2008)*. *World Development Report 2008: Agriculture for Development.* Washington, DC: World Bank. Retrieved from http://siteresources.worldbank.org/INTWDR2008/Resources/WDR_00_book.pdf.

World Bank. (2011). *World Bank Data.* Retrieved from http://data.worldbank.org/.

World Bank and International Food Policy Research Institute. (n.d.)* *Agriculture and Achieving the Millennium Development Goals. REPORT No. 32729-GLB.* Washington, DC: World Bank. Retrieved from http://siteresources.worldbank.org/INTARD/Resources/Ag_MDGs_Complete.pdf.

* Additional references.

Chapter Nine

The Quest For Development: Regional Integration In Africa

By Mwita Chacha

Introduction

Africa's record of economic development is dismal. Despite its vast amounts of natural resources, most sub-Saharan states have yet to attain levels of economic growth comparable to other regions that were at the same level in the 1960s. Table 1 below provides per capita GDP statistics for Nigeria and South Korea between the years 1960 and 2009.

Despite having comparable per capita GDP figures in the 1960s, Nigeria and South Korea have taken divergent paths toward socioeconomic development. Nigeria's statistics epitomize other states in sub-Saharan Africa that, despite having had so much promise following independence in the 1960s, have continued to lag behind economically. While various reasons, including poor governance, corruption, and conflict, have previously been proposed to explain Africa's underdevelopment, this chapter focuses on the experience of regional integration in Africa. Regional integration in Africa not only predates attempts at economic integration on other continents, but also the emergence of the modern state system in Africa. Despite its promise, however, the mismanagement of regional integration has contributed to Africa's underdevelopment. The next section provides a brief overview of theories of regional integration and economic development. Various regional integration arrangements in Africa and their performance are then presented. A discussion of reasons for these arrangements' varied performance follows this presentation and then leads to the chapter's conclusion.

Regional Integration and Economic Development: Theoretical Perspectives

Political scientists and economists have developed various theoretical explanations for regional integration in both developed and developing states. Political scientists have tended to focus on explaining reasons for integration and motivations for deepening cooperation while economists have examined factors that influence integration in the first place without necessarily discussing

Table 1: Per capita GDP for Nigeria and South Korea

Year	Nigeria	South Korea
1960	92.9	156
1965	117	106
1970	222	279
1975	434	608
1980	862	1670
1985	334	2370
1990	293	6150
1995	254	11500
2000	368	11300
2005	797	17600
2009	1090	17100

Source: World Bank. Figures in current US $

the evolution of regional integration. Regardless of these minor differences, both economists and political scientists theoretically discuss and empirically show how regional integration affects economic development. Hypotheses raised by these two academic fields have influenced policymakers in sub-Saharan African states and in multilateral institutions, such as the United Nations Economic Commission for Africa, to push for economic integration on the continent.

The main impetus for regional integration is increased trade. Regional integration entails the coordination of economic, social, and political policies among a group of states. Haas (1958) defines integration as the process "whereby political actors in several, distinct national settings are persuaded to shift their loyalties, expectations, and political activities toward a new center, whose institutions process or demand jurisdiction over the preexisting national states." In most instances, regional integration commences with trade policy coordination involving the reduction and eventual elimination of trade tariffs and other barriers to trade. In one early theoretical explanation of regional integration, economist Jacob Viner (1950) contends that regional trade liberalization is premised on increasing the level of trade among the states that partake to lower or eliminate their trade tariffs. By lowering or eliminating tariffs within a regional context, states are able to create a wider preferential market for their producers. With a wider market, producers are able to reap more benefits from trade that can be used to expand and enhance production in the future. In later works among political scientists, regional trade liberalization is shown to increase the level of trade for both developed and developing states. Goldstein, Rivers, and Tomz (2007) find that regional integration increases trade for both developed and developing states. These benefits could explain the proliferation of regional integration arrangements mainly among developing states since the end of the Second World War (Mansfield and Reinhardt, 2003).

Regional integration as a means of coordinating economic policies has also been shown to increase foreign direct investments. Schiff and Winters (1998) show this impact of regional integration by noting how a government signing on to regional trade agreements usually signals its commitment to sound economic policies that improve the state's standing as a favorable investment destination. Schiff and Winters (1998) write, "FDI from outside the bloc may increase as foreigners seek to exploit new investment opportunities and to use one member as a platform for serving the whole bloc." Additionally, through economic policy coordination, regional integration enhances economic efficiency that can contribute to economic growth. Through coordinating monetary policies, states are able to reduce market uncertainties for traders and other economic actors within the regional arrangement and enhance fiscal policy discipline that can aid in attracting foreign investments necessary for job creation (Cohen, 1997). However, not all states in these regional integration arrangements in Africa have witnessed increases in FDI inflows.

These variations among RIAs and among member-states of RIAs on the benefits of economic integration point to yet another discrepancy among RIAs in Africa: their level of economic integration depth. Theories of European integration contend that the benefits of economic integration can influence the deepening of cooperation. Liberal intergovernmentalism argues that economic groups lobbying governments to pursue economic cooperation because of the perceived economic benefits these groups expect from integration fuel the process of integration (Moravcsik, 1998). However, economic lobbying in African states is not as robust as that among European Union member-states. Indeed, governments rarely take into consideration the preferences of business groups when making policies of regional integration. A good example is the Tanzanian government's exit from COMESA despite multiple business groups that were benefiting from COMESA membership lobbying against this move.

From this brief theoretical overview, two patterns can be observed. First, the effect of RIA membership in increasing trade and investment varies among African RIAs. Second, there is a discrepancy in the depth of cooperation among RIAs in Africa. While depth of cooperation is not a guarantor of economic development, understanding factors that have affected the deepening of African RIAs can shed some light on why some have been able to increase trade and investment, the raison d'être of regional integration, while others have not. The next section briefly discusses some RIAs in sub-Saharan Africa to provide a glimpse of regional integration on the continent.

Assessing Regional Integration Arrangements in Africa

Most regional blocs in sub-Saharan Africa have followed the economic integration trajectory described above. While some of these RIAs have included joint-development projects in their integration endeavors, the main impetus has been integration of markets for the purpose of increasing trade and investment, and in the process spurring economic growth. This section discussed the Common Market for Eastern and Southern Africa (COMESA), the East African Community, the Economic Community of West African States (ECOWAS), Economic and Monetary Community of Central African States (CEMAC), and the Southern African Development Community. These five have been selected as they encompass a majority of sub-Saharan African states and are also some of the more active RIAs on the continent. While there are close to twenty RIAs in Africa, the narratives of these five are representative of the path of regional integration on the continent.

The Common Market for Eastern and Southern Africa is the successor organization of the Preferential Trading Area for eastern and southern Africa (PTA). According to the COMESA Web site, PTA was formed "to take advantage of a larger market size, to share the region's common heritage and destiny, and to allow greater social and economic cooperation, with the ultimate objective being to create an economic community." In 1994, PTA members signed a new treaty creating the Common Market for Eastern and Southern Africa (COMESA). The goal of this new establishment was to build upon the achievements of PTA by promoting economic development through further liberalization of intra-regional trade.

Because the PTA had already put into place mechanisms to reduce tariffs among member-states, COMESA set out to establish a free trade area that was finally realized on October 31, 2000. Only ten members of COMESA acceded into the free trade area while the rest maintain some level of preferential tariffs on intra-COMESA trade. The next goal for COMESA is the establishment of a customs union with a common external tariff. Its membership, as of 2010, included Burundi, Comoros, Democratic Republic of the Congo, Djibouti, Egypt, Eritrea, Ethiopia, Kenya, Libya, Madagascar, Malawi, Mauritius, Rwanda, Sudan, Seychelles, Swaziland, Uganda, Zambia, and Zimbabwe.

The East African Community is the youngest bloc and the smallest bloc analyzed in this study, although economic cooperation in this region dates back before decolonization. The EAC as of 2000 comprised Kenya, Uganda, and Tanzania. However, by the end of 2007, Burundi and Rwanda had acceded to the EAC. The history of the EAC dates back to pre-independence under British rule whereby a customs union between Kenya and Uganda was established in 1917. The first major agreement for integration after decolonization was signed in 1967, establishing the original East African Community. This bloc, however, lasted only ten years and was disbanded in 1977, mainly due to political differences among the leaders of the three member-states. Negotiations for a revival of the East African Community began in 1984, culminating in the establishment of the East African Cooperation in 1993. The aim of the Cooperation was to facilitate the revival of the East African Community, which was realized on November 30, 1999. The revived East African Community is unique in the sense that it seeks to liberalize trade among the member-states, while also pushing for eventual political unification. The EAC sought to create a customs union, which came into existence on July 1, 2004. In 2010, a common market was launched. The five member-states are now discussing future plans to include the formation of a monetary union.

The Economic Community of West African States was established in 1975. As of 2010, its members included Benin, Burkina Faso, Cape Verde, Ivory Coast, Gambia, Ghana, Guinea, Guinea-Bissau, Liberia, Mali, Mauritania, Niger, Nigeria, Senegal, Sierra Leone, and Togo. ECOWAS seeks to promote cooperation among member-states through policy coordination in the fields of trade, monetary affairs, infrastructure, and regional politics.

ECOWAS experienced a long period of stagnation of economic integration in the 1980s due to various factors, including civil conflicts in its member-states. In 1993, a new treaty that sought to revitalize integration efforts was negotiated and ratified. A program of tariff reduction was established in that year while new institutions to manage ECOWAS integration were put in place. The goal since revitalization efforts of the mid-1990s has been trade liberalization through the establishment of a free trade area and culminating in the establishment of a common currency.

The Economic and Monetary Community of Central African States is one of the oldest regional integration arrangements in Africa having been established in 1964. Along with the West African Economic and Monetary Union, CEMAC member-states use the CFA Franc that was initially pegged to the French Franc but is now pegged to the Euro. While its level of economic integration was high due in part to its colonial past, cooperation among CEMAC members declined in the 1970s and 1980s. It was not until 1993 that CEMAC revitalized its economic integration. In 1994, CEMAC established a free trade area along with putting in place a common external tariff. Interestingly, the CFA Franc continued to be the currency of CEMAC states despite the decline in economic integration. Its members as of 2010 include Cameroon, Central African Republic, Chad, Republic of Congo, Gabon, and Equatorial Guinea.

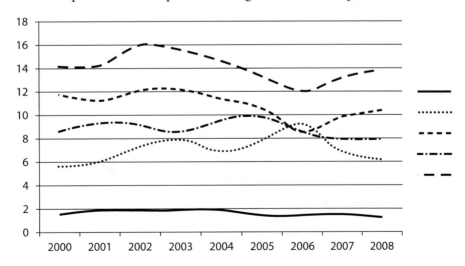

Source: IMF Direction of Trade Statistics, UN Regional Integration Knowledge System

Chart 1: Intra-RIA trade share (2000–2008)

Table 2: Levels of economic integration attained

RIA	Level of integration at founding	Level of integration in 2010
COMESA	Preferential Trade Area	Incomplete Free Trade Area
EAC	Incomplete Customs Union	Customs Union
ECOWAS	No market integration	Preferential Trade Area
CEMAC	Customs Union with Single Currency	Free Trade Area with Single Currency
SADC	Preferential Trade Area	Free Trade Area

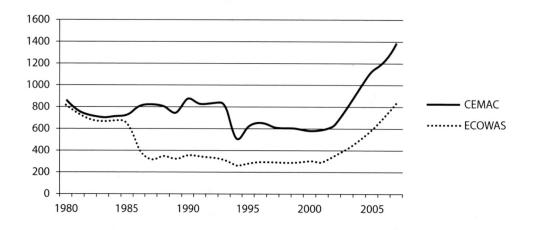

Source: World Bank. Figures in current US $

Chart 2: RIA per capita GDP for CEMAC and ECOWAS

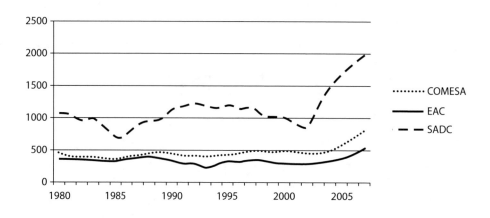

Source: World Bank. Figures in current US $

Chart 3: RIA per capita GDP for COMESA, EAC, and SADC

The Southern African Development Community is the successor organization of the Southern African Development Coordination Conference, SADCC. The SADCC was founded in 1980 to foster regional development through policy coordination in socioeconomic areas and reduce the member-states' dependence on apartheid South Africa. In 1992, the SADCC was transformed into the Southern African Development Community, SADC. The SADC seeks to widen areas of cooperation among the member-states to include political and security issues. The 1990s also witnessed the end of apartheid and the entry of South Africa to SADC. The area of trade integration has also been included with a trade protocol calling for the establishment of a free trade area by the year 2008. Member-states, as of 2010, included Angola, Botswana, Congo-Kinshasa, Lesotho, Malawi, Mauritius, Mozambique, Namibia, Seychelles, South Africa, Swaziland, Tanzania, Zambia, and Zimbabwe.

Performance of African RIAs: Some Descriptive Statistics

This section provides some statistics for the aforementioned five RIAs to gauge their progress and performance over time. First, since these are trade-liberalizing ventures, examining how important the regional market is to the RIA is crucial. Through regional integration, markets are expected to be easily accessible to traders, thus increasing the level of trade conducted between member-states of a particular RIA. Chart 1 graphs intra-RIA trade share as a percentage of total trade of the five RIAs discussed above. Notice the variation in the share of intra-RIA trade between the five RIAs.

As chart 1 shows, there is a great variation in the dependence of regional markets among the five RIAs in Africa. Whereas SADC has continuously maintained its RIA trade share above 12 percent despite being a burgeoning free trade area, CEMAC has not been able to increase its intra-RIA trade share beyond 2 percent. Indeed, other RIAs depicted in chart 1, such as COMESA and ECOWAS, have recently been witnessing a decline in their respective shares of intra-RIA trade. According to the UN Economic Commission for Africa, intra-RIA trade among African RIAs remains low on average despite grandiose plans to establish integration arrangements similar to the European Union.

To better evaluate these trade statistics, one should also observe the levels of economic integration attained by these five RIAs. Table 2 provides a summary of the attainment of economic integration depth. A comparison of integration depth at the time of their founding and in 2010 is provided.

From these statistics, one can observe that some RIAs have existed for over two decades, yet they have attained only shallow levels of economic integration. ECOWAS, for instance, was established in 1975 with goals of emulating the European integration process. However, by 2010, it had only attained the shallowest of economic integration levels. Moreover, other RIAs, such as CEMAC, have managed to deepen economic integration but have failed to match such extensive commitment with increased regional trade as noted in chart 1. What can explain these variations in the depth of economic integration?

Since RIAs are established to facilitate economic development, another way of gauging their success is to examine trends in per capita gross domestic product. Since per capita GDP is one way of measuring economic development, RIAs would be expected to positively affect this statistic. Charts 2 and 3 portray RIA per capita GDP for the five RIAs being discussed.

While the five RIAs have witnessed a rise in per capita GDP, this increase seems insignificant when compared to other regions. In chart 2, per capita GDP for ECOWAS declined in the early 1980s and remained stagnant till the early 2000s. The recent rise in the past few years has brought back per capital GDP to its 1980s levels. In chart 3, EAC and COMESA have witnessed only a slight rise in per capita GDP since their respective years of establishment. Indeed, the trends that chart 2 and chart 3 depict echo the statistics displayed in table 1 on comparing per capita GDP for Nigeria and South Korea. What can explain this discrepancy between Nigeria and South Korea? Why have African RIAs witnessed a slow rise in per capita GDP?

Various explanations have been offered to explain Africa's slow levels of economic development. The varied record of the performance of African RIAs can shed some light on explaining economic development in Africa. The next section discusses several reasons why some RIAs in Africa have not been successful at facilitating economic development for its member-states. Specifically, the management of these RIAs can help explain why some RIAs are more successful than others.

The Management of RIAs and Economic Development in Africa

a) Overlapping Memberships among African RIAs

Commitment of member-states is crucial for the success of regional integration arrangements. For African states, attaining the goals and objectives they set out for their RIAs requires them to demonstrate loyalty to their respective RIAs. Commitment or loyalty to an RIA "results in the modification of domestic institutions, making them compatible across members" (Feng and Genna, 2005). This compatibility of domestic institutions ensures that member-states of a particular RIA advance their economic integration agenda by making and adhering to similar trade and economic policies that facilitate liberalization. However, wavering actions of states that impinge on their ability to harmonize and/or coordinate their policies to be in line with those of other members of an RIA can have a negative impact on the success of regional integration. One such action that has received attention from policy practitioners of regional integration is pursuing and maintaining membership in multiple RIAs.

Overlapping memberships is one of the main characteristics of regional integration in sub-Saharan Africa. For instance, Feng and Genna (2005) observe that African RIAs have attained only limited goals when compared to RIAs in Asia and the Americas due to many African states continuing to pursue memberships in multiple RIAs. Sally (2006), in a general assessment of the effects of overlapping membership, asserts that the different regional blocs a state belongs to may "have different tariff schedules, rules of origin, and implementation periods." Due to these differences, many problems may arise for the nation involved and for the progress of integration in the bloc or blocs concerned. Jakobeit, Hartzenberg, and Charalambides (2005) in their policy report on overlaps in regional trade blocs in sub-Saharan Africa capture the effects of this phenomenon. They write that overlap in membership increases the strain on the regional bloc and member-states still at a burgeoning state of integration; they also contend that such overlap increases legal uncertainty especially when different trade arrangements apply to trade between two countries. These uncertainties "not only undermine the implementation of the agreements that aim to establish rules-based dispensations, but it also adds considerably to transaction costs and duplication in both regional trade and trade with outside partners" (Jakobeit, et al., 2005, p. 22). Others have also observed the commitment problems that result from overlapping memberships among African RIAs that increase the costs of intra-RIA trade and limit the realization of RIA goals and objectives (Draper et al., 2007; Bienen, 2010).

Among the five RIAs discussed above, the shallowness of economic integration among some of these RIAs may be attributed to overlapping memberships. For instance, all but one member of ECOWAS is currently pursuing membership in another RIA with similar trade liberalization goals. This high level of overlapping memberships among ECOWAS members has been cited as a reason for its slow progress over the years (Asante, 1990). It has also been observed that there is a high level of overlapping memberships in COMESA, EAC, and SADC that has not only resulted in conflicting objectives but has also limited success in attaining deeper economic liberalization levels (Jakobeit, Hartzenberg & Charalambides, 2005). These conflicting objectives affect traders and business persons in COMESA states who have to deal with different trade rules of each of the RIA their respective state is party to, resulting in slow trade (Charalambides, 2005).

The problem of overlapping memberships in eastern and southern Africa has recently received much attention from member-states of COMESA, EAC, and SADC. In 2008, heads of governments of member-states of these three RIAs formally began negotiations to create a tripartite free trade area encompassing the three RIAs in order to mitigate the adverse effects of overlapping memberships (EAC, 2008). Through such an initiative, we could expect African RIAs to limit the adverse effects that overlapping memberships have had on intra-African trade and the success of regional integration arrangements on the continent.

b) Institutional Deficiencies of African RIAs

While the choice of pursuing multiple memberships is solely in the hands of state governments, institutional mechanisms within RIAs can influence the interests of states through their policy recommendations. Once founded, RIAs usually establish secretariats with the purpose of monitoring and enforcing agreements that states have reached regarding regional integration. For example, the European Union has the Commission that has served this institutional role of managing the integration process of the European Union. The Commission is in a position of influencing member-states of the EU through its recommendations on various issues pertaining to the integration process. Indeed, this role of the Commission and of other institutions of the European Union has been extensively theorized by neo-functionalist literature that argues that the process of European integration has been driven to a large extent by the institutions' participating governments created to manage the integration process.

Institutions ensure that governments adhere to the rules and objectives of RIAs. Since it would be inefficient for states to monitor the behavior of other states in the RIA to ensure they do not renege on their commitments, states establishing an RIA would transfer these enforcement and monitoring capabilities to a neutral arbiter in the form of an RIA secretariat. The secretariat is expected to have the powers of advising governments on integration matters with the purpose of ensuring that the RIA realizes its goals of economic and trade liberalization. A secretariat ensures that governments of member-states adhere to treaties of the RIA that seek to, for instance, liberalize trade. The secretariat is expected to be in a position of identifying states that do not adhere to these treaties and recommend to other member-states what course of action should be taken so as to punish the violating state and ensure future compliance. This has been how the Commission of the European Union has operated and ensured that even powerful states such as France and Italy adhere to the treaties and obligations that come with EU membership.

The case with African RIAs, however, is different from the EU experience. While it might be harsh to compare the EU and African RIAs as they both have faced very different circumstances, RIA institutions of African RIAs are relatively weak. CEMAC, COMESA, EAC, ECOWAS, and SADC have secretariats tasked with the management of regional integration of these RIAs. Yet, the impact of these secretariats as managers of regional integration is limited. In his examination of institutional similarities between three RIAs in Africa, including COMESA and ECOWAS, Ntumba (1993) notes the weaknesses in the main supranational bodies of these RIAs, the secretariats and the tribunals adjudicating the RIAs' treaties. Ntumba (1993) argues that a "strong institutional mechanism … can act as a locomotive or leavening agent of the [integration] process." However, the institutions within COMESA and ECOWAS are "handicapped by severe institutional weaknesses." Both secretariats of COMESA and ECOWAS do not have any real decision-making powers as their independent influence has been constrained by the ever-present hand of governments of member-states that dominate all decision making within these RIAs. As Ntumba (1993, p. 314) acknowledges, "In an institutional environment so heavily penetrated by intergovernmentalism, the secretariats are incapable of acting as the engine of regional integration and unable to safeguard the integrity of their respective treaties" similar to the commission of the EU.

In negotiating regional integration treaties, states craft agreements in a manner to ensure that their interests are served. Part of these interests might include limiting the powers given to secretariats. Yet limiting secretariats' capabilities might ensure that treaty obligations are not adhered to fully and to the letter. RIA institutions have the potential of ensuring compliance from states on these treaty obligations that can serve to increase intra-RIA trade, the inflow of foreign investments, and generally facilitate an economic environment that encourages business activity. For African RIAs to increase the likelihood of success and spur economic growth for their member-states, there is need for facilitating better institutions to manage integration matters.

c) Regional Leadership

While not a panacea, regional integration arrangements that involve economically powerful states tend to be more successful at spurring economic activity in the region necessary for economic development. European integration has centered around Germany, Europe's economic hegemon, while MERCOSUR has benefited from South America's economic powerhouse, Brazil. This economically powerful state in the RIA serves as the main market for other RIA members, provides financial support to member-states that are less well off in order to enable them to meet their RIA obligations, serves as the lead state by coordinating RIA activities among member-states, and generally promotes the economic integration agenda. At the global economic and financial level, the United States has been given this economic leadership role (Krasner, 1976; Gilpin, 1987). At the regional level, Switky (2000, p. 28) points out that "a regional hegemon may be necessary for the rise and maintenance of regional trading blocs."

The idea of a regional hegemon implies that a single state acts as the main driver of deepening integration and ensuring that the process is not derailed. A regional leader would be the state, which seeks integration and serves as the main promoter of further integration within the bloc. Mattli (1999, p. 42) gives the main attributes of the regional leader that "serves as a focal point in the coordination of rules, regulations, and policies; it may also help to ease tensions that arise from the inequitable distribution of gains from integration." Mattli goes on to argue that the lack of such a leader may make coordination of integration efforts difficult. Greico (1997, p. 173) takes this argument a step farther, positing that "we should observe regionalism developing more fully in those areas of the world in which there is a local hegemon able to create and maintain regional economic institutions, and we should observe regionalism advancing at a less pronounced pace in those areas where local hegemonic leadership is less visible."

The regional hegemonic explanation has been applied in various cases of regional integration. Webber (2001), using the approach Mattli (1999) puts forward as stated above, argues in his analysis of why regional integration had failed to mature in Asia, especially with ASEAN and APEC, that one of the reasons for the failure of these blocs was the lack of a regional hegemon. On the successful side, Mattli (1999, p. 100–104) examines the European integration process, identifying Germany as the nation that played the regional leader role, especially in the mid-1970s. Mattli identifies Germany's economic might, which translated into political influence with Europe. "Germany has been the key policy initiator and institutional agenda setter in a wide range of issue areas." This would include Germany's being the member-state that initiated the European Monetary System, the precursor to the European Monetary Union. Furthermore, Germany has eased distributional tensions with the EU by acting as "regional paymaster" (Mattli, 1999, p. 101). Mattli points out that Germany is the largest net contributor to the EU budget, having supported several funds with the EU that deepen and widen the integration process. Germany has also been promoting greater transparency, accountability, and human and social rights (Mattli, 1999, p. 105). Germany has thus played a crucial role in the success of the European integration process. Aside from South Africa within SADC, African RIAs lack such regional hegemons to spur economic activity and advance integration within the region.

Of the five RIAs discussed in this chapter, only SADC might qualify as an RIA with a regional hegemon with the potential for influencing integration. While SADC has not made great strides in deepening integration or spurring economic development among its member-states, it is better placed at utilizing South African capital and financial support to encourage economic activity in the region. Although Nigeria is the more powerful state economically in ECOWAS, its internal wrangles have diminished its capabilities as a regional hegemon. Instead of being in a position to influence and guide the integration process of ECOWAS fully, Nigeria has over the years been forced to deal with its own civil wars and those of its neighbors. Indeed, it might be argued that ECOWAS, with the help of Nigeria, has been more successful as a regional security arrangement, but not an economic integration venture. There is no decisive economic hegemon within CEMAC to serve as the regional leader while in the EAC, although Kenya has been touted as the economic powerhouse of the region, its influence has not been significant enough to spur regional economic development.

There is no clear solution to the lack of regional leadership in many of Africa's RIAs as states are free to establish and join any RIA. However, the presence of an anchor state economically increases the likelihood that such an RIA might serve as an engine for economic development for participating states. It would therefore be prudent for states to form RIAs with economically powerful states on the continent such as SADC with South Africa. Other economic powerhouses on the continent, such as Nigeria, Ghana, Kenya, and Egypt, might in time be able to serve this regional leadership function and facilitate successful regional integration on the continent. Smaller RIAs, however, such as the Economic Community of Great Lakes Countries involving Burundi, Democratic Republic of the Congo, and Rwanda (CEPGL), or the large and extremely diverse Economic Community of Sahel-Saharan States (CEN-SAD), are not in a position of having an economic hegemon as a member to serve as the main promoter of regional integration. Indeed, since member-states of RIAs such as these are already involved in other relatively more successful RIAs, they are better off focusing on the more successful RIA in order to have a better chance at using regional integration as an engine for economic development.

Conclusion: Regional Integration for Economic Growth

In her book *Dead Aid*, Dambisa Moyo criticizes foreign aid as a failed attempt at spurring economic growth in Africa despite fifty years or so of its disbursement. Moyo notes how foreign aid has encouraged corrupt leadership and poor economic policies that have failed to raise populations of Africans out of poverty. Her alternative path toward economic growth for African states hinges on trade and other paths of raising capital necessary to promote economic growth. Moyo notes the potential of regional integration arrangements in increasing intra-African trade and in the process facilitating economic growth. She also notes such arrangements serving as blocs for raising capital through issuing bonds in world markets. Regional integration has a potential that remains untapped in Africa.

This chapter has sought to provide an overview of the state of regional integration in Africa as a source of economic development and reasons why regional integration arrangements have not facilitated economic growth. The chapter has discussed five RIAs on the continent, CEMAC, COMESA, EAC, ECOWAS, and SADC, and has provided some descriptive statistics comparing their economic performance. The performance of these RIAs is crucial for promoting economic development. The chapter then focused on three main reasons that could explain the economic performance of these RIAs. These reasons, overlapping memberships, institutional deficiencies, and regional leadership, can shed light on why some African RIAs have not made major strides in deepening economic integration or, more important, in spurring economic growth among their constituent member-states.

Policy practitioners and scholars have cited several reasons why many African states remain poor. Some of these reasons, such as corruption, poor planning and governance, and poor infrastructure, are also useful in explaining why regional integration has yet to bring sustainable economic growth to African states. Responsible and accountable governments can ensure that regional trade agreements are adhered to while also enhancing coordination in infrastructure and other development projects within a regional setting. While the three reasons identified in this chapter are important when examining RIAs as units, factors affecting governance are equally important and should not be disregarded as explanations for unsuccessful RIAs and economic underdevelopment in Africa.

Regional integration is not the universal remedy for economic underdevelopment in Africa. However, if well managed in a manner that limits overlapping memberships, ensures better RIA institutional mechanisms, and is supported by economically powerful member-states, regional integration can contribute positively to Africa's quest for sustainable economic development.

Review Questions

1. How is regional integration expected to increase economic growth?

2. Discuss the three factors that have impeded regional integration in Africa.

3. What is the role of a regional hegemon in a regional integration arrangement? What characteristics should a regional hegemon have? What are some regional hegemons in Africa and how effective have they been in sustaining regional integration?

4. What is one remedy for the problem of overlapping memberships in Africa?

5. Explain how institutional deficiencies have affected RIAs in Africa. How can these institutions be improved to facilitate economic growth?

6. In your own assessment, what are the prospects of regional integration in Africa?

Bibliography

Bienen, D. 2010. The Tripartite Free Trade Area and Its Implications for COMESA, the EAC and SADC. *Trade and Development Discussion paper* no. 01/2010.

Charalambides, N. 2005. The Private Sectors Perspective, Priorities and Role in Regional Integration and Implications for Regional Trade Arrangements.

Cohen, B. J. 1997. The Political Economy of Currency Unions. In Edward D. Mansfield & Helen V. Milner, eds., *The Political Economy of Regionalism*. New York: Columbia University Press.

Draper, P., D. Halleson and P. Alves. 2007. SACU, Regional Integration and the Overlap Issue in Southern Africa. *Technical report Trade Policy Report*.

East African Community. 2008. Final Communique of the Joint COMESA-EAC-SADC Heads of State and Government Tripartite Summit. URL: <http://www.eac.int/services/reports/>.

Feng, Y. and G. M. Genna. 2005. "Measuring Regional Integration." *Claremont Regional Integration Workshop with Particular Reference to Asia*. Vol. 25. Claremont.

Gilpin, R. 1987. *The Political Economy of International Relations*. Princeton, NJ: Princeton University Press.

Goldstein, J. L., D. Rivers, and M. Tomz. 2007. "Institutions in International Relations: Understanding the Effects of the GATT and the WTO on World Trade." *International Organization* 61 (01).

Greico, J. 1997. "Systemic Sources of Variation in Regional Institutionalization in Western Europe, East Asia, and the Americas." In Edward D. Mansfield & Helen V. Milner, eds. *The Political Economy of Regionalism*, (pp. 164–187). New York: Columbia University Press.

Haas, E. B. 1958. *The Uniting of Europe: Political, Social and Economical Forces, 1950–57*. Stanford, CA: Stanford University Press.

Jakobeit, C., T. Hartzenberg, and N. Charalambides. 2005. Overlapping Membership in COMESA, EAC, SACU and SADC. *Trade Policy Options for the Region and for EPA Negotiations,*

GTZ: Eschborn: Retrieved from: http://tanzania.fesinternational.De/infoservice/docs/overlapping-membership-incomesa-eac-sacu-andsadc.

Krasner, S. D. 1976. "State Power and the Structure of International Trade." *World Politics.* 28.

Mansfield, E. D. and E. Reinhardt. 2003. "Multilateral Determinants of Regionalism: The effects of GATT/WTO on the Formation of Preferential Trading Arrangements." *International Organization* 57 (04), 829–862.

Mattli, W. 1999. *The Logic of Regional Integration: Europe and Beyond.* Cambridge University Press.

Moravcsik, A. 1998. *The Choice for Europe: Social Purpose and State Power from Messina to Maastricht.* Cornell University Press.

Moyo, Dambisa. 2009. *Dead Aid: Why Aid Is Not Working and How There Is Another Way for Africa.* New York: Farrar, Straus and Giroux.

Ntumha, L. L. 1993. "Institutional Similarities and Differences: ECOWAS, ECCAS, and PTA." In R´eal Lavergne, ed., *Regional Integration and Cooperation in West Africa* (pp. 303–320), Trenton, NJ: Africa World Press.

Nyirabu, M. 2004. "Appraising Regional Integration in Southern Africa." *African Security Review* 13 (1).

Rivoli, Pietra. 2005. *The Travels of a T-Shirt in the Global Economy.* New York: John Wiley & Sons.

Sachs, Jeffrey D. 2005. *The End of Poverty: Economic Possibilities for Our Time.* New York: Penguin Books.

Sally, R. 2006. "Free Trade Agreements and the Prospects for Regional Integration in East Asia." *Asian Economic Policy Review* 1 (2).

Schiff, M., and L. A. Winters. 1998. "Regional Integration as Diplomacy." *The World Bank Economic Review* 12 (2).

Switky, B. 2000. "The Importance of Trading Blocs: Theoretical Foundations." In Bart Kerremans & Bob Switky, eds. *The Political Importance of Regional Trading Blocs.* Burlington, VT: Ashgate Publishing Company.

Viner, J. 1950. "The Customs Union Issue." *Technical Report.* New York: Carnegie Endowment for International Peace.

Webber, D. 2001. "Two Funerals and a Wedding? The Ups and Downs of Regionalism in East Asia and Asia-Pacific after the Asian Crisis." *The Pacific Review.* 14:3.

Chapter Ten

Africa, Health Care Systems, And The Hiv/Aids Pandemic

By Ibigbolade S. Aderibigbe and Simon Mutembo

Introduction

The African continent has witnessed a variety of problems in relation to its health care system. Indeed, the crisis associated with the health care sector in Africa is not limited to a section of the continent. It is a continent-wide phenomenon. This situation prompted the World Health Organization in 1978 to declare the campaign to achieve "Health for all by the year 2000" (Abubakar, 2006:269). Unfortunately, this campaign failed to meet the desired goal, in spite of the human and financial commitments of bodies such as the G8 countries, New Partnership for Africa Development (NEPAD), UNICEF, and the UADP.

Indeed, based on available statistics, there is evidence of acute degeneration of health care systems in all parts of Africa. A number of factors have been identified as responsible for this situation, one that has substantially impacted the human, social, and economic development of the continent, particularly the sub-Saharan region. While the continent is still battling with the health delivery crisis occasioned by the prevalence of infant mortality, malaria, and tuberculosis, among many other challenges, the advent of HIV/AIDS has further compounded the African situation. Currently, sub-Saharan Africa is estimated to account for 70 percent of the 24.5 million people affected with HIV/AIDS worldwide (Plaskovic & Stern, 2002:210). The pandemic nature of HIV/AIDS has, in addition to other major diseases, constituted grave challenges to the fragile and inadequate health care systems in Africa. Consequently, the continent is subjected to a health crisis with far-reaching implications for its developmental dynamics.

As a consequence of this situation, this chapter attempts a discourse on the health care systems in Africa with focus on the pandemic nature of HIV/AIDS and its implications for the health sector and ultimately the totality of human development on the continent. To achieve this objective, the chapter explores the following issues:

(i)   forms of health care systems in Africa
(ii) current status of African health systems and their attendant crises

(iii) HIV/AIDS in Africa, origin and nature
(iv) HIV/AIDS and African health systems and development

Forms of Health Care Systems in Africa

As in other dynamics of life in Africa, there are two identifiable forms of health systems in Africa—the traditional and the modern (Western). The traditional health care system incorporates the age-old method(s) of diagnosing, preventing, and curing illnesses or diseases. It is the practice of the holistic art of medicine, which is grounded in religious sensibilities. The modern or Western health care system is generally referred to as the orthodox practice of medicine, a byproduct of the establishment of health facilities by first, the missionaries, and later, by colonial governments in different parts of Africa.

Traditional Health Care System Background

The traditional health system is defined by the World Health Organization as follows:

> The sum total of all knowledge and practices whether explicable or not used in diagnosing, prevention and elimination of physical, mental and social imbalance and relying exclusively on practical experience and observation handed down from generation whether verbally or in writing (W.H.O. 1976:3–4).

However, it is important to point out that the African traditional health system is based on the people's concept of medicine, which is a core part of the African traditional religious belief. Indeed, African belief in medicine along with magic constitutes the fifth segment of the major belief in the hieratical structure of African traditional religion as propagated by Bolaji Idowu (1996:63). Thus, African medicine is inextricably intertwined with religion. This is aptly demonstrated by the roles played by rituals, divinities, taboos, offerings, sacrifices, and the supernatural in African medical practices. In fact, the professional medicine man, for example, in Yoruba land, sees his profession squarely in the realm of religion.

A number of characteristics uniquely designate the African medicine man as a health care provider. For instance, Parrinder describes the activities of the African medicine man thus:

> The medicine man is a kind of scientist in that he seeks to discover and use laws of the universe, not only of inanimate nature but also spiritual forces. He believes that there are powers, hidden secrets that can be tapped, laws which may be set in motion by the knowledgeable in order to meet various ailments (Parrinder, 1969:120).

Shishioma in the same vein describes the African medicine man as follows:

> A consultant specialist in traditional worldview. He can explain the complexities in the world and provide solutions to problems arising from it which borders on human life. In a nutshell, his work is to make people whole (Shishma, 2004:121).

For Dopamu, the art of the African medicine man is holistic. This is so because, according to him, the African medicine man "does not concern himself only with the treatment of diseases but he also understands the nature and etiology of diseases or illnesses before embarking on treatment" (Dopamu, 2004:4).

The holistic nature of the African traditional health care system hinges on the fundamental belief that the art of prevention and cure of diseases or illnesses is not just physiological but also spiritual. This again results from the belief that more often than not, the illnesses originate from nonhuman or physical sources. In reflecting this dynamic, the belief and practice of medicine in Africa is at two levels—the simple and the complex. The simple practice of medicine is associated with less physically recognizable and treatable ailments. Such ailments include, for example, piles, headache, cough, fever, whitlow, diarrhea, gonorrhea, and so on. This category of ailments can actually be treated by nonmedical practitioners who can prescribe a collection of known common herbs available to any member of the community.

The complex practice of medicine involves the treatment of very serious ailments or health conditions believed to have originated from non-normal causations. Consequently, they are conceived to involve an unhealthy state of body and mind of the victim. Such ailments can only be diagnosed and treated by the professional traditional medical practitioner. Both the diagnosis and treatment usually consist of spiritual and physical therapeutic consultations and treatments steeped in divination, appeasement through offerings and sacrifices, and application of herbal prescriptions.

In sum, the African traditional health care system aptly confirms Taylor's postulation, "A man's well-being consists only when he maintains a harmonious relationship with the cosmic totality" (Taylor, 1963:67).

Thus to the African, when there is a disruption or disturbance of this harmony or relationship at any level, diseases or illnesses can result. Africans further believe that this malfunction could be at the spiritual, moral, or social level. Thus, sometimes the physiological manifestation of an ailment is only a symptom of a deeper moral or mystical problem (Dopamu, 1977:394).

Based on the aforementioned African notions of causes and treatments of different forms of human health malfunctions, the African traditional health care system can be concisely described as "the traditional art and science of the prevention and cure of diseases. It is the use of natural/supernatural substances to prevent, treat, and cure diseases. It can also mean medicament used internally and externally" (Dopamu 1979:4).

Current Status

In contemporary African societies, traditional health care systems have witnessed substantial changes in conformity with evolving social, cultural, religious and other developmental influences and realities, particularly modern or orthodox medicine. Consequently, new trends in processes, methods and personalities in traditional health care systems are rapidly developing. Perhaps, the greatest and most observable changing dynamic is the movement toward de-emphasizing the spiritual and metaphysical components of traditional medicine. This is largely premised on the fallout of the strong influence of the Western orthodox medical practice. The "new-generation" traditional medical practitioners are attempting to imbibe the "philosophy" of the Western orthodox practice, which places almost exclusive premium on the physiological and technical diagnosis and medication for ailments (Aderibigbe, 2006:376).

It is important to state here, however, that in spite of the development described above, the traditional practice of medicine in its original form, which combines the physiological and metaphysical process, the traditional method and practitioners still abound. Indeed, this form of health care system continues to enjoy a large return of clients, due in part to its accessibility, affordability, and clients' faith in its effectiveness, and also in part because of the inadequate resources, unpleasant personalities, and high costs of the modern health care system.

Currently, the most developed branch of the traditional health care system is herbal medicine. This is quite understandably so because in all parts of Africa, herbs are in great supply and have immense potentialities as sources of new drugs. Consequently, the "new generation" African traditional medical practitioners have taken full advantage of this potential to revolutionize health care delivery in the treatment of a large range of ailments, particularly those that Western orthodox medicine seems not to have cures for. For example, in southwestern Nigeria, the herbal branch of traditional health practice, sometimes called alternative medicine, has expanded into a large and highly organized commercial enterprise. One of the most prominent and successful faces of this form of health care delivery is the Yem-Kem International Center for Alternative Therapy. The organization was founded by Akintunde Ayeni, who built his practice on the experience of his father who was a traditional herbalist. Indeed, Akintunde's herbal center has become an expansive international organization with a herbal research and production center, equipped with modern facilities. The center's products, well over thirty in number, are now available in either capsule or tonic form. They are packaged or bottled at standards comparable to orthodox Western ones. Also the products are marketed in Nigeria, other parts of Africa, Britain, and the United States (Aderibigbe, 2006:376).

A number of advantages are associated with the current development in the African traditional health care system, particularly with regard to the crisis facing the Western orthodox (modern) health care system in different parts of Africa.

First, developing herbal and other medicines based on primarily African resources, should reduce the dependency of research and production of drugs on foreign pharmaceutical organizations. This should make the drugs in particular, and health care in general more affordable to the largely poor communities of rural areas of Africa. These generic drugs and medications should enhance the treatment of many common ailments in most African communities.

Second, the increasing available traditional health care practitioners, who are specialists in herbal research, production, and prescription, can be trained in line with modern preventive strategies of health care. Such training in hygiene, general modern health concepts, health education and environmental sanitation, should not only improve [the] health care system generally, but [should] also raise its standard and effectiveness. The functionality of this exercise has been effectively demonstrated in some African countries, such as Zimbabwe, Zaire, Angola, Ghana, Mali, Nigeria, Tanzania and Ethiopia. Indeed, in the case of Nigeria, thousands of traditional birth attendants (TBAs) have been trained and deployed as providers of [a] primary healthcare system in different parts of the country (Ransome-Kuti et al., eds., 1991:95–96).

Third, the cultural context in which the traditional health care system is provided has instituted the confidence of Africans in the system as "home grown." This has distinguished it from the Western orthodox system, which is regarded as an imposition from Europe, and is consequently subsumed in European industrial culture alien to the African indigenous heritage and values. Indeed, much suspicion has been drawn to the motives of the West, particularly against its history of imperialist tendencies (Abubakar, 2006:279).

Fourth, and most important, the African traditional health care system does not depend on herbal medicine alone. Other treatment techniques include therapeutic fasting and dieting, hydrotherapy, radiant heat therapy, legery and bone setting, psychiatry and preventive medicine. A conscious and sustainable development of all these branches with the herbal branch is bound to provide an improved, accessible, and affordable health care system devoid of the usual dysfunction of the modern health care system, being currently witnessed, due to a complete lack of or merely inadequate infrastructures both in human and mechanical resources. In addition, if the process, method, and personnel of the traditional health care system are aligned with the communal living and kinsmanship guaranteed by the extended-family system, which is the hallmark of the African social culture, the African traditional health care system will not only have a lot to offer in the health care arena, but it will also become immensely important and relevant in the contemporary context of African communities.

Western (Modern) Health Care System in Africa

The origin and development of a Western (modern) health system in Africa are traceable to the efforts of different organizations, groups, governments, and private individuals at different stages and decades. However, the pioneering work of establishing health care delivery in most parts of Africa was undertaken by various Christian missionaries. From the very beginning of missionary activities in Africa, particularly in sub-Saharan Africa, health care work became a central focus. This is attributable to a number of reasons:

1. The early missionaries identified with the medical welfare of the "native" based on their own experiences with physical and mental health deprivations on the continent.
2. The missionaries established health care services in order to ensure social development in conformity with the Christian philosophy of promoting the dignity of the individual as a creation of God.
3. Health care delivery was regarded as a charitable Christian engagement used as a strategy for community and faith outreach and practical ingredients of evangelism (Todd, 1962:124–125).

Consequently, in the late nineteenth and early twentieth centuries, different missionary groups in Africa established health care facilities.

Christian Missionaries and Social Services—the Colonial Period

Within the confines of initiation, provision, and development of basic social services in Africa, alongside spiritual engagements, the various Christian missionaries made significant contributions to the African continent. A brief exposition of these efforts would suffice here. In the first instance, in the annals of the history of the continent, the greatest contribution of the missionaries, inclusive of African church workers, was the announcement of the good news of Jesus Christ, which heralded in a wonderful transformation in people's lives. The fear that hitherto kept many in bondage suddenly disappeared, paving the way for a new life of joy and freedom for the people. The missionaries thus became the pathfinders to a happy and new way of community spiritual living.

Linguistically, in the area of language, the missionaries played a significant role in assisting the Africans, particularly, in the area of writing. Before 1878, only very few African languages south of the Sahara had an alphabet and a means of writing. The early missionaries attempted to introduce an orthography with letters to meet the needs of each local language. This made it possible for each of the tribes to keep written records for the first time in their history. The church not only introduced the means for writings; it also, through its missionaries, provided both the reading and writing materials. As a matter of fact, without the church establishing schools, the development of the continent might have been significantly delayed many, many years because the colonial government would not have been able to establish all the schools built by the missionaries from 1804 through 1914. Some such institutions strategically established were the famous Fourah Bay College in Sierra-Leone; the Castle School in Cape Coast, Ghana; Loyola College in Nigeria; Alexander High School in Monrovia, the capital of Liberia; Maseno Secondary School in Kenya, to mention but few among many others scattered around the African continent. Therefore, the educational system of Africa owes a great debt to the various mission churches for the great services rendered.

In the areas of health, the missionaries were usually the ones to establish in any new places hospitals, and maternity centers. Through their efforts, new treatment was given to ancient diseases. Some of the hospitals built by the Roman Catholic Church in Nigeria still exist. These include St. Mary Catholic Hospital and Eye Centre located in Eleta in Ibadan, the Oluyoro Catholic Hospital located in Yemetu Town of Ibadan, and the Sacred Heart Hospital, Abeokuta, in Ogun State. Many others are located in different parts of Nigeria. In the area of food production and mechanized farming, many early missionaries and African church workers helped greatly in imparting new knowledge of farming. As a result of new crops being produced and better production methods being taught, the quantity and quality of food production increased rapidly. In addition to instruction about the Gospel and agricultural techniques, the early church missionaries also provided converts with technical, practical instruction in tailoring, carpentry, and blacksmithing. All such instruction contributed to the enhancement of converts' standard of living.

In summary, Protestant and Catholic missions clearly pioneered a Western (modern) health care system in most parts of Africa. This was done decades before colonial governments began to build health facilities. Indeed, a century later, a Christian-based health care system accounted for 25 percent to 50 percent of all health care services in most African nations (Good, 1992:1). It is instructive to note that the various missionary organizations played important roles in medical training and education. Consequently, there were provisions for training nurses and paramedical personnel. Some of these individuals were actually trained in Europe. For instance, many first-generation doctors were Western educated. Through these media, the missionaries actually laid the groundwork for the wide distribution and acceptance of the modern health care system.

In the late nineteenth century, various colonial governments in Africa began to be involved in the provision of health care services. For example, in Nigeria, the British colonial government began the provision of formal health care delivery in the 1870s. It began to build hospitals and clinics in Lagos and Calabar. However, unlike the missionary health care services that were extended to the "natives," the colonial services initially were exclusively for the Europeans. Later, African employees were allowed access to the health facilities. On this basis, colonial hospitals and clinics actually moved their facilities to accommodate the locations of the Europeans and their employees. Thus, the hospital in Jos was established in 1912 to provide health services for the employers and employees of the tin-mining industry.

The extension of health services to the general African population effectively began after World War II in response to nationalist agitations. In Nigeria, the British colonial government announced a ten-year health development plan in 1946. In consequence of this, the University of Ibadan was established in 1948. The institution included a faculty of medicine and the University Hospital. Thereafter, nursing and pharmacy schools were established. By 1960, when Nigeria became independent, there were sixty-five government nursing and midwifery schools.

Also, the 1946 health plan established a Ministry of Health, which coordinated all health services provided in the country. It also allocated funds for hospitals and clinics. However, as in all other parts of Africa, Nigeria's colonial government hospitals and clinics were concentrated in major cities to the negligence of the rural areas where the vast majority of the population resided.

As various African nations began to gain independence beginning in the late 1950s, the national governments began to play an important role in establishing a modern health care system. They commenced building on and also complementing the pioneering efforts of the Christian missionaries and colonial governments. Again, to illustrate using the Nigerian example, governmental involvement in a health care system occurs at the three levels of government, these being federal, state and local. In addition, privately owned health care facilities have complemented government initiatives, alongside still-existing faith-based ones.

Nigeria became independent in 1960. By 1979, the country had 562 general hospitals. These were supplemented by 16 maternity and pediatric hospitals. In addition, there were 11 armed forces hospitals, 6 teaching hospitals, and 3 prison hospitals. These facilities represented 44,600 beds. Apart from these hospitals, there were an estimated 600 general health centers, 2,740 general clinics, and 930 maternity homes. By 1985, the numbers of health facilities owned by the three tiers of government in Nigeria had substantially increased. The federal government owned about 84 health facilities (13 percent). Some 3,023 (47 percent) were owned by various state governments. The various local governments owned 6,331 (11 percent). Private establishments complemented these with about 1,436 (14 percent). However, just as in the case of the colonial government, the distribution of the health facilities was lopsided, both in geographical and population divisions. There were more facilities in the southern geographical locations and in cities, thereby placing the northern and rural areas of the country at a disadvantage. This could be said to be the pattern of appropriation of health facilities in most African countries.

Current Status of the Health Care System in Africa

The current status of the health care system in Africa can be discerned from a number of factors. These are ultimately located, from our perspective, in three major areas. The first relates to the problems associated with the health sector on the continent. The second borders on the effects of Africa's development problems related to its health care system. The third has to do with the nature and composition of the present state of health facilities in Africa.

Problems of Health Sector

Some of the problems facing the health care system in many African countries are traceable to specific issues. The first of such problems stems essentially from the disposition of many African governments and their agencies toward health issues. Even when these governments or agencies have struggled to effect economic and health sector reforms, the efforts have not been as successful as they were intended or designed to be. Indeed, the envisaged improvements have not been achieved. Rather, the health sector has witnessed large-scale degeneration. The World Health report, credited to its director general, Dr. Go Harlan Brundtlard, confirmed this ugly situation:

> The impact of the failures in the health system was observed to be most severe on the poor everywhere, who are driven deeper into poverty by lack of firmed protection against ill-health. And in trying to buy health from their own pockets, they pay and become poorer (CBS, 2003:84-85).

Second, most African governments fall short of having the political will and commitment necessary to ensure the success of the health sector. This is because in these countries, poor management becomes the bane of the sector. This situation was complicated by the acceptance and implementation of the Structural Adjustment Program (SAP) at the insistance of the World Bank and International Monetary Fund (IMF). The outcome of this exercise was that these African countries monetized and commercialized health services to meet SAP conditionalities as provided by the World Bank and IMF. This situation provoked high inflation and worsened the poverty status of most Africans. As a result, they were deprived access to even the most basic health care services (Diop et al., 1986).

Third, and in consequence of the two aforementioned problems, African countries became heavily dependent on foreign aid/assistance. For instance, by 1990, African countries had assistance of more than $1.2 billion. This was not different from the situation in the 1980s, when the breakdown of the assistance was 32 percent from bilateral donors, another 32 percent from multilateral agencies, and 6 percent from nongovernmental agencies. In terms of individual African countries, Uganda, for example, had 87 percent of funds for its health development coming from foreign sources between 1988 and 1989. For Mali, 63 percent of its health spending in 1990 was foreign sourced. The same was true of Lesotho, with 80 percent of its Ministry of Health total budget coming from foreign sources (World Bank, 1995, p. 152).

The implication of all this overdependence on foreign donors was that the donors were in a powerful position, dictating and determining not only how the receiving government was to invest or spend the money, but also stipulating the conditionality that all purchases must be made in the donor country. Apart from these stipulations, such assistances have become significantly reduced due to lack of interest or inability of many donor nations to continue the practice due to prevailing economic realities in their own countries.

Developmental Problems

Another problem facing the African health sector is traceable to the effects of general developmental problems faced by African countries. Because of declining foreign assistance, these countries are in a great predicament as to finding a source of funds for national development in general, including development and maintenance of the health sector. This has landed most, if not all, African governments in an economic crisis of huge proportion. Matters are compounded by many African countries' trade and purchasing powers being very limited. Also, in postcolonial Africa, the share of Africa's export in world trade has always been on the decline. Indeed, it has been estimated that the continent will be $2.6 billion poorer every year due to decline in its export values (Ndukwe, 2002, p. 7).

In an attempt to assist African countries to cope with their staggering economic crises, the World Bank and IMF instigated moves to directly manage Africa's monetary affairs. Consequently, several of these countries were forced to adopt the Structural Adjustment Program (SAP). The implementation of the program in many of the countries began in the 1980s. Unfortunately, the program has not only led to a decline in African GDP from 30 percent to 40 percent, but in addition, it has actually compounded the problems associated with the pace of development in all sectors of life for the African people. The IMF conditionality of government stoppage of participation in economic and social development by withdrawal of public funding of social services has stiffened if not practically terminated any meaningful development, beneficial to the majority of the African population. Particularly in the health sector, people who are already abjectly poor, and living on less than one dollar per day, have to pay charges in hospitals, dispensaries, and clinics. These services were provided free by governments under pre-IMF conditions of SAP. In consequence, the majority of Africans are denied access to even the most basic and essential health services because they cannot afford the costs.

One other developmental problem facing the African health sector is the brain drain phenomenon. Though this syndrome cuts across African professionals, the health sector has suffered most. There has been unprecedented "migration" of health experts from various African countries to Britain, Canada, and the United States. Most of these experts are doctors and nurses. Statistics show, for instance, that there are, today well over 21,000 Nigerian doctors in the United States alone. In 2001, Britain also recruited 2,114 nurses from South Africa, 473 from Zimbabwe, and 195 from Ghana. In addition, it is estimated that at least 50 percent of doctors who trained in Ghana have emigrated to the West. Also more than 90 percent of all graduates of medical schools in Sierra Leone leave the country for destinations abroad (CBS, 2003, p. 85). Invariably, the African continent is not only deprived of expert medical manpower, but it also incurs the loss of the monetary investment in having trained the migrated experts and the cost of replacing them.

Nature and Composition of the Present State

Against the scenario presented above, the nature and composition of the health care system in Africa are in extreme jeopardy. This is vividly reflected in the inability of health facilities and services in most African countries to cope with various common but pandemic diseases both at the preventive and curative levels. Consequently, today, millions of Africans die from easily preventable illnesses. These include malaria, diarrhea, and measles. For example, it is estimated

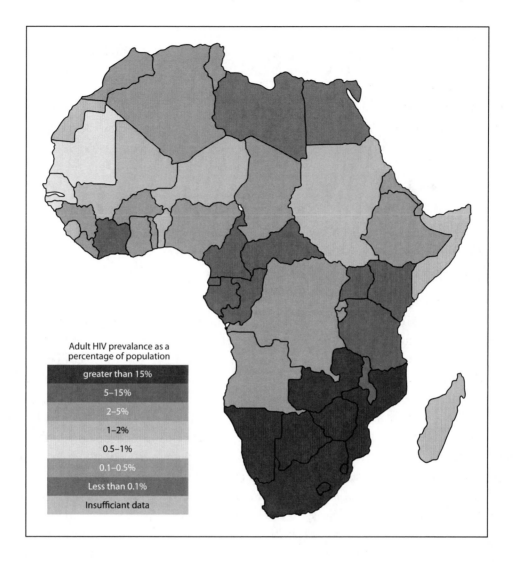

Source: UNAIDS 2007

Figure 1: Map showing the prevalence of HIV in Africa by country

that 80 percent of 110 million cases of malaria worldwide occur in sub-Saharan Africa. In addition, an estimated 20–50 percent of all patients who visit health facilities in Africa, suffer from malaria. However, statistics also show that only about 8–25 percent of those who have malaria actually go to health facilities (WB, 1995, p. 19). Another area where health care facilities and services in most African countries have not been able to cope is infant mortality. This has been vividly demonstrated by statistics from the World Bank (2002) that show an increase in infant mortality in sub-Saharan Africa from 11.5 per 1000 live births in 1980 to 159 in 1999. Also, the same source of statistics indicates that maternity mortality was also on the rise, totaling 700 per 100,000 live births.

Abubakar (2006) clearly indicates that these figures are not absolute and that they vary from one African country to the other. For example, while the mortality rates of infants under five years old in countries such as Mali, Angola, and Mozambique are estimated to be about 200 per 100,000, in Botswana and Zimbabwe they are about 1000 per 100,000. This trend is equally noticeable in maternal mortality in these countries. The challenges faced by various health care systems in different African countries became more grievous with the advent of HIV/AIDS. The disease has become not just a major threat to the health care system on the continent, but in addition, its pandemic nature has transformed it into a multidimensional scourge on the social, economic, and political systems affecting the vast majority of Africans living in almost all parts of the continent.

HIV/AIDS in Africa—Origin and Spread

Before 1980, HIV/AIDS was not yet characterized and was probably not causing any health problems in the human population. Jonathan Mann postulates that the current epidemic of HIV started in the mid- to late 1970s and that by 1980, HIV had spread to at least five continents (North America, South America, Europe, Africa, and Australia). During this period of silence, spread was unchecked by awareness or any preventive action, and approximately 100,000–300,000 persons may have been infected (J. M. Mann, 1989). The origin of HIV has been an issue of debate from the time the virus was discovered. Several explanations ranging from a promiscuous flight attendant to a suspect vaccine program have been offered. Counter arguments have also been presented from different parts of the globe.

Though it is now broadly acclaimed that HIV originated in Africa, the first cases of AIDS were identified in the USA in the early 1980s among gay men in New York and California who suddenly began developing rare opportunistic infections and a rare cancer known as Kaposi's sarcoma (K. B. Hymes et al., 1982:589). At this stage, there was no name for the new disease. It was, however, obvious that all the afflicted gay men were suffering from the same syndrome. The term AIDS (Acquired Immune Deficiency Syndrome) was developed and first properly defined by the CDC in September 1982 (MMWR Weekly, 1982:523). In 1983, the French at the Pasteure Institute reported that they had isolated a virus that might be the cause of HIV (F. Barre-Sinoussi, 1983).

At this time, doctors working in Zambia and the Democratic Republic of the Congo, then known as Zaire, had noticed the reemergence of Kaposi's sarcoma, which had been rare in this region during the preceding years (A. C. Bayley, 1984:126; R. Coker, 1986). Researchers from the USA who had visited Africa reported having seen a number of AIDS cases in Kigali Rwanda and Kinshasa, Zaire. This led to joint research by Zairean (Congolese) doctors, American and European researchers under a project called SIDA (J. Mann, et. al., 1986). By 1986, scientists had accumulated enough evidence to form an overview of AIDS in Africa. The conclusions were made from the reports of the "slim disease" in the late 1970s in Uganda in the early 1980s and of the outbreak of cryptococcal meningitis, an opportunistic disease in Zaire (Congo) in the late 1970s and the early 1980s (D. Serwadda, 1985:850). Although AIDS is said to have been present in the 1970s in Africa, there is no convincing explanation as to why there was a sudden, rapid, and wide transmission of the virus in Africa, the USA, and Haiti during the 1980s and the following years.

Epidemiologists have also conducted studies on blood specimens collected in the 1950s in order to be able to explain the origins of HIV. The earliest retrospective diagnosis of HIV-1 infection was made from a serum specimen collected in 1959 in Kinshasa. HIV type 1 virus has also been isolated in the chimpanzee in Central Africa. HIV-2, a second type of HIV rarely found outside western Africa, is found in sooty mangabeys. The exact circumstances of cross-species transmission in Central Africa are uncertain, but opportunities for human exposure to simian viruses through hunting and related activities are abundant. Over time, the virus presumably adapted to the human host and began to spread from person to person (Kevin M. Decock, 2011).

Since its discovery thirty years ago, HIV/AIDS has affected the African continent more than any other part of the world. It has been recognized that the HIV pandemic is no longer just a health problem but affects the social and the economic framework of the African continent. However, since 2003 after the launch of the WHO-led Three by Five Initiative, there has been an improvement in the implementation HIV treatment and prevention programs in Africa (WHO, 2010). With the improvements in the care and treatment, the median HIV prevalence among adults aged between 15 and 49 years has declined from 5.8 percent in 2001 to 5.0 percent in 2009 (WHO, Regional Office for Africa, 2010:11). Sub-Saharan Africa has remained the epicenter of HIV, and an estimated 22.5 million adults and children are living with HIV/AIDS. This figure represents 68 percent of the global 33.3 million people living with HIV/AIDS, although only about 12 percent of the global population lives in sub-Saharan Africa (WHO, Regional Office for Africa, 2010:12). The number of people living with HIV has also increased, although the rate of people being newly infected in 2009 is 25 percent lower than the peak value experienced in the 1990s (WHO, Regional Office for Africa, 2010:12). The number of people living with HIV has been increasing because the people on highly active antiretroviral treatment are living longer.

Africa is a vast continent with different social and physical environments, and therefore the HIV prevalence varies across the continent. In Somalia and Senegal, the HIV prevalence is under 1 percent of the adult population, whereas in Namibia, Zambia, and Zimbabwe, 10–15 percent of adults are infected with HIV; in South Africa, the HIV prevalence is 17.8 percent. In the other southern African countries, the national adult HIV prevalence rate now exceeds 20 percent. These countries are Botswana (24.8 percent), Lesotho (23.6 percent), and Swaziland (25.9 percent) (UNAIDS, 2010). West Africa is less affected by HIV and AIDS, but some countries are experiencing rising HIV prevalence rates. In Cameroon, HIV prevalence is now estimated at 5.3 percent; in Gabon, it stands at 5.2 percent. In Nigeria, the HIV prevalence is low (3.6 percent) compared to the rest of Africa. However, because of its large population (it is the most populous country in sub-Saharan Africa), this equates to around 3.3 million people living with AIDS (UNAIDS, 2010).

Prevalence Factors

A lot of African researchers in various parts of the continent had conducted studies to understand and identify the main drivers of the epidemic. Although the virus is thought to have originated in Central Africa, the prevalence of HIV is highest in the southern part of Africa with South Africa alone accounting for one-sixth of the world's population of people living with HIV (Kevin M. Decock, 2011:1045). The reasons for the high prevalence of HIV and the geographical distribution are not very clear, but biological, social, and economic factors have been postulated to explain this distribution.

Studies in Africa frequently report that counseling and testing are associated with reduced risk behaviors and lower rates of seroconversion among HIV serodiscordant couples (M. P. Thomas, 2001:1397). However, despite the knowledge of HIV being universal in most parts of Africa, the enormous majority of the population does not know its HIV status. For example, in Zambia, one of the nations most affected by HIV, only 20 percent of the population has undergone counseling and testing and knows its HIV status (CSO, 2007:191).

It is believed and generally accepted that risky sexual behavior is one of the major reasons why the prevalence of HIV is high. However, Larry Sawers and Eileen Stillwaggon argue that by almost all measures of risky sexual behavior, the African continent is not any different from other regions around the world (Sawers, L., S 2011:202). Multiple concurrent partners have been accepted as one high-risk behavior that plays a significant role in the transmission of HIV AIDS. Concurrence has been demonstrated to be unusually high especially in sub-Saharan Africa; hence the association with the high HIV prevalence (Halperin and Ebstein, 2004:4). Multiple concurrent relationships can increase the risk of HIV transmission, especially in a set-ting where the use of condoms is low. Although it is not feasible to measure the use of condoms, data from most of the DHH surveys show that condom use is very low in most parts of Africa. Anna Foss and colleagues conducted a systematic review of studies on the use of condoms in sub-Saharan Africa and Asia and found out that most people generally use condoms in casual and commercial sex but do not use condoms in their intimate/marital relationships. The concurrence theory is supported by cultural and socioeconomic factors on the continent. It is believed that men are biologically programmed to have sex with more than one woman and can therefore be justified to have concubines or to be polygamous. Also, the mobility of the population, especially with a high number of men migrating to the urban areas and to areas that provide a source of livelihood, has led to a high level of prostitution and concurrence as women seek economic survival from the working men who are away from their wives.

In the developed nations, the rate of heterosexual HIV transmission is very low. In the African region, the major mode of HIV acquisition is through heterosexual means. Field research has found substantial evidence of a high prevalence of sexually transmitted diseases in Africa and has also demonstrated that the presence of sexually transmitted infections increases the chances of transmitting HIV and holds as one of the reasons for the very high prevalence of HIV in Africa (L. Sawers, E. Stillwaggon, and T. Hertz, 2008:488). Yet another reason proposed as one of the reasons for the endemicity of HIV in Africa is the low circumcision rate among the majority of the tribes in Africa. Male circumcision practices vary throughout Africa. Countries in West Africa, where male circumcision is common, have HIV prevalence levels well below those of countries in eastern and southern Africa despite the presence of other risk factors. In countries of southern and eastern Africa with the highest HIV prevalence, male circumcision rates are generally under 20 percent (WHO, 2006).

Apart from the biological factors, the role of social factors has been recognized as one of the main risks for the transmission of HIV. Gender inequality in the African setting has a major influence on the high HIV prevalence among women and children on the continent. It is important to understand that in the African culture, the man is the decision maker, and, in most of the religions practiced in Africa, the man is viewed as the head of the family. This has translated into female oppression by reducing women's income, assets, and power, which makes it very difficult for them to negotiate for safe sex and encourages them to engage in transactional sex. Jewkes has shown how women with a certain level of education can negotiate for the use of a condom while the least uneducated cannot (R. K. Jewkes, 2003:125).

It is important to mention here that the poor nations have a bigger share of HIV and other infectious diseases. Larry Sawers and colleagues explain that poor countries are less likely to provide safe medical care and effective infection control procedures as compared to higher-income countries. They further say that poverty may push some people into risky behavior. Even the affluent in a poor country are surrounded by sick people and thus are more likely to become ill than in the developed world. Although inadequate, this is a probable explanation for the role of poverty in the high HIV prevalence in Africa (Sawers, Larry, and Eileen Stillwaggon, 2010:201).

Fallouts of Prevalence

In 2009, around 1.3 million people died from AIDS in sub-Saharan Africa, and 1.8 million people became infected with HIV. Since the beginning of the epidemic, 14.8 million children have lost one or both parents to HIV/AIDS (UNAIDS, 2010). The social and economic consequences of the AIDS epidemic are widely felt, not only in the health sector but also in education, industry, agriculture, transport, human resources, and the economy in general. The AIDS epidemic in sub-Saharan Africa continues to devastate communities, rolling back decades of development progress (Avert, 2011). Most of the people affected are in the productive age group and from the population segment on which the economy of Africa depends for its recovery.

The AIDS epidemic has diminished production and food security in most parts of Africa. For example, in Malawi where food shortages have had a devastating effect, it has been recognized that HIV and AIDS have diminished the country's agricultural output. It was calculated in 2006 that by 2020, Malawi's agricultural workforce will be 14 percent smaller than it would have been without HIV and AIDS; in other countries, such as Mozambique, Botswana, Namibia, and Zimbabwe, the reduction is likely to be over 20 percent (UNAIDS, 2006). At the household level, the number of street children orphaned by HIV has increased, and each family has taken on one or more dependents. In Botswana, it is estimated that, on average, every income earner is likely to acquire one additional dependent over the next ten years due to the AIDS epidemic (UNAIDS, 2006). As the parents become ill, children take on the responsibility of fending for themselves, making it difficult for them to access quality health care, education, and nutrition. Therefore, fewer children are receiving education, and this has a cyclic effect on the prevention of HIV.

Health Care System Challenges and Responses

The impact of HIV/AIDS on the health care system has been severe, with the cost of running hospitals and providing antiretroviral drugs being beyond the economic capability of most countries, if not all the African nations. The issue of sustaining the cost of the antiretroviral treatment program has arisen frequently at international fora. No one seems to have the answer to how to sustain the number of people under treatment should the external donors decide to stop funding the HIV programs in Africa. It is not only the cost of the health care that is astronomical in the regions afflicted by HIV, but there is also a shortage of available health workers because so many have themselves been affected by HIV. Therefore, Africa is faced with the challenge of having to provide health care, antiretroviral treatment, and support to a growing population with HIV while also needing to reduce the number of new infections by empowering the community to control the spread of the disease. As if this were not enough of a challenge, the continent must also cope with the impact of millions of AIDS deaths on millions of survivors, many of whom are now orphans.

The fight against HIV has encountered a number of challenges at both the domestic and international level. The late response and inadequate response by African leaders and global leaders is probably one of the factors contributing to the epidemic. Stigma at the individual level, community, and institutional level is still a big challenge in the prevention and treatment of HIV thirty years after the virus was discovered. In most countries, political, community, and church leaders have acted as role models to fight stigma and misconceptions. For instance, Zambia's former president Kenneth Kaunda has played a leading role in HIV prevention, and President Yoweri Museveni of Uganda provided the stimulus to all the African countries to rise to the challenge. Community engagement, especially of the community leaders, has helped to address misconceptions such as the belief of misguided traditional healers that a person with HIV can be cured by having sexual intercourse with a virgin.

Another challenge in the fight against HIV has been the overdependence on international donors. At the global fund replenishment meeting, pledges from the donors were $13 billion below the estimated budget. No government in Africa made a commitment to fund the difference domestically for its country (Avert, 2010).

African nations, their agencies, nongovernmental organizations alongside many global organizations, have offered a variety of responses to the challenges of the HIV/AIDS pandemic on the continent. For example, in the realization of the failures of the ABC strategy, which was the mainstay of the HIV prevention in the earlier days, African countries have moved to implement a combination of behavioral and biomedical strategies in the control of HIV. The strategies aim at addressing the identified drivers of the epidemic. Most of the African countries and governments have demonstrated political leadership in the fight against HIV. Notable among these is Uganda, which has been able to reduce the HIV prevalence. In most countries such as Zambia, Zimbabwe, and Uganda, the prevalence has stabilized because of the provision of antiretroviral treatment and the reduction in the number of new infections.

Also, African countries are signatories to many global commitments related to AIS, among them the "three ones" principle that provides for the framework for the AIDS response. The governments in countries with the highest HIV prevalence by an act of parliament have formed National AIDS Coordinating Authorities with a broad-based multisectoral mandate. The international community has provided leadership in research and provided technical and financial resources for the fight against the scourge. Developed countries have increased funding for the fight against AIDS in Africa in recent years, perhaps most significantly through the Global Fund and PEPFAR. The Global Fund was started in 2001 to coordinate international funding and by the end of 2008 had approved grants totaling US $7.2 billion to help fight AIDS, TB and malaria in 137 countries (The Global Fund. 2009). However the funding from these organizations has been leveled off, providing a further challenge and a call for commitment among the African leaders.

Several behavioral change programs have been implemented at the community level and at the same time there have been a lot of biomedical interventions such as the scale up of male circumcision, prevention of mother-to-child transmission of HIV/AIDS, and universal access to highly active antiretroviral treatment. According to the UNAIDS global report on the epidemic, the ten countries in the region that account for 80 percent of the AIDS cases have been able to reduce the HIV incidence by as much as 25 percent. AIDS-related deaths among people living with HIV/AIDS have also been reduced as much as 72 percent in some countries (Calverton 2010). Most of the countries have been able to increase the access to highly active antiretroviral treatment; hence the number of people living with HIV has been increasing.

This chapter will be incomplete if the role of the African traditional healer in the treatment and prevention of HIV is not recognized. The field of African medicine is vast, diverse, complex, mysterious, and difficult to document. It is mostly based on oral evidence; very little is written down or published. As early as 1990, the World Health Organization had recognized the role of traditional healers in the control of HIV and recommended that traditional healers should be included in the national responses to HIV (UNAIDS: Best Practices Collection, 2006). Since the vast majority of the African population lives in the rural areas and those that live in the urban areas cannot afford the cost of Western medical care, traditional healers are consulted more often than is documented. Additionally, traditional healers are members of the community who provide health care that is culturally acceptable. In most of the countries, traditional healers have representation on national AIDS commissions. Traditional healers have been able to collaborate with national governments and NGOs, and they have affected policy formulation and played a role in counseling and treatment. They have been key players in addressing both the bad practices that may fuel the spread of HIV and the myths surrounding the epidemic. In the early 1990s, the Ministry of Health in Uganda launched an initiative called Traditional and Modern Health together against AIDS (THETA). The aim of this initiative was to foster collaboration between traditional healers and biomedical health providers in the area of treatment for HIV and sexually transmitted diseases (UNAIDS Best Practices Collection, 2000). In Zambia, Malawi, Botswana, Mozambique, and South Africa, selected traditional healers have trained as trainers of trainers for other traditional healers. A number of traditional healers have incorporated new prevention messages in the traditional consulting rooms and have given talks at antenatal clinics (UNAIDS best practices, 2000).

The response in most African countries has shown high-level leadership, the willingness for public policy to be based on scientific evidence, and the acceptance that HIV is sexually transmitted and therefore has social characteristics that must be countered by a multispectral response.

Review Questions

1. Trace and discuss the historical paths of health care systems in Africa, beginning with the traditional forms.

2. What were the main characteristics of traditional health care delivery in Africa?

3. Trace and account for the origin and development of the modern (Western) health care system in Africa.

4. What challenges currently face health care systems in different African countries?

5. HIV/AIDS is currently the most dreadful disease in Africa. Discuss its origin and endemic nature in different parts of Africa.

6. What are the challenges confronting African health care systems and other developments resulting from the pandemic nature of HIV/AIDS?

7. What forms and strategies do you envisage as practical responses to the scourge of HIV/AIDS in Africa?

Bibliography

Aderibigbe, G., and D. Aiyegboyin. 1995. *Religion, Medicine and Healing.* Ilesa: Jola Publishers.

Ake, Claude. 1981. *A Political Economy of Africa.* New York: Longman.

Alfred, E. O., et al., eds. 1986. *The Arts and Civilization of Black and African People.* Lagos: CBAAC.

Anna, F. C. W, V. Peter, B. S. Vickerman. 2003. "Are People Using Condoms? Current Evidence from Sub-Saharan Africa and Asia." www.hivresearchtools.lshtm.ac.uk.

Barre-Sinoussi, F., J-C. Chermann, F. Rey, M. T. Nugeyre, S. Chamaret, J. Gruest, C. Dauguet, Axler-Blin, C., A. C. Bayley. 1984. "Aggressive Kaposi's Sarcoma in Zambia, 1983." *The Lancet* 1.

Brun-Vezinet, F., C. Rouzioux, W. Rozenbaum, and L. Montagnier. (1983). "Isolation of a T-Lymphotropic Retrovirus from a Patient at Risk for Acquired Immune Deficiency Syndrome (AIDS)." Science, May 20.

Central Statistical Office (CSO), Ministry of Health (MOH), Tropical Diseases Research Centre (TDRC), University of Zambia, and Macro International Inc. 2009. Zambia Demographic and Health Survey 2007. Calverton, MD: CSO and Macro International Inc.

Coker, R., and P. B. Wood. 1986. "Changing Patterns of Kaposi's Sarcoma in N. E. Zaire." *Trans R Soc Trop Med Hyg.* 80 (6).

Dopamu, P. Ade. 2001. "Scientific Basis of African Magic and Medicine: The Yoruba Experience." *African Science and Religion in Dialogue.* Ilorin.

Dopamu, P. Ade. 1997. "Yoruba Magic and Medicine and Their Relevance for Today." *Journal of the Nigerian Association for the Study of Religions.* 4. 4.Ilorin: NASR.

Hymes, K. B., J. B. Greene, A. Marcus, et al. 1981. "Kaposi's Sarcoma in Homosexual Men: A Report of Eight Cases." *Lancet* 2.

De Cock, Kevin M., Harold W. Jaffe, and James W. Curran. 2011. "Reflections on 30 years of AIDS. Emerging Infectious Diseases." www.cdc.gov/eid. Vol. 17, No. 6.

Jewkes, R. K., J. B. Levin, L. A. Penn-Kekana. 2003. "Gender Inequalities, Intimate Partner Violence and HIV Preventive Practices: Findings of a South African Cross-sectional Study." *Social Science & Medicine.* 56 (1):1.

Lawal, Nike, ed. 2001. *Yoruba Life and Culture.* St. Cloud, MN: St. Cloud State University.

Mann, J. M. 1989. AIDS: "A Worldwide Pandemic." In *Current Topics in AIDS.* Vol. 2. Edited by M. S. Gottlieb, D. J. Jeffries, D. Mildvan, et al. John Wiley & Sons.

Mann, J., B. Kapita, R. Colebunders, et al. 1986. "Natural History of Human Immunodeficiency Virus Infection in Zaire." *The Lancet,* 2.

Monekosso, G. L. 1994. *"Forward" in Better Health in Africa: Experiences and Lessons Learned.* Washington, DC: World Bank.

Mosby, C. V. 1992. *Mosby Medical Encyclopedia*, rev. ed. New York: Plume.

MMWR Weekly. 1982. "Current Trends Update on Acquired Immune Deficiency Syndrome (AIDS)-United States," September 24, 31(37);507–508, 513–514.

Nicholson, Mark. 1985. "Aids: The African Connections" New African. References

Parrinder, G. 1969. *Religion in Africa.* New York: Penguin.

Ransome-Kuti, O., et al., eds. 1991. *Strengthening Primary Healthcare at the Local Government Level: The Nigerian Experience.* Lagos: Academic Press.

Sawers, Larry, and Eileen Stillwaggon. 2010. "Understanding the African Anomaly: Poverty Endemic Disease and HIV." *Development and Change.* 41(2).

Sawers. L., E. Stillwaggon. T. Hertz. 2008. "Cofactor Infections and HIV Epidemics in Developing Countries: Implications for Treatment." *AIDS Care.* Vol. 20, No. 4.

Serwadda, D., R. D. Mugerwa, N. K. Sewankambo, et al. 1985 "Slim Disease: A New Disease in Uganda and Its Association with HTLV-III Infection," *The Lancet.*

Tamuno, T. N., and J. A. Atanda, eds. 1989. *Nigeria since Independence: The First 25 Years.* Ibadan: Heinemann Education Books.

Taylor, J. V. 1963. *The Primal Vision.* London: SCM Press.

Thomas, M. P. 2001. "Voluntary Counseling and Testing for Couples: A High-Leverage Intervention for HIV/AIDS Prevention in Sub-Saharan Africa." *Social Science & Medicine.*

Todd, J. M. 1962. *African Missions: A Historical Study of the Society of African Missions.* London: Burns and Oates.

Tucker, Nelly. 1999. "AIDS Denial Ravages Africa." *The Detroit Free Press.*

UNAIDS. 2006. *Report on the Global AIDS Epidemic.* Chapter 4: "The Impact of AIDS on People and Societies."

UNAIDS. 2010. Report on the Global AIDS Epidemic.

Vaughan, Megan. 1993. *Curing Their Ills: Colonial Power and African Illness.* Stanford, CA: Stanford University Press.

World Bank. 1995. *Better Health in Africa: Experience and Lesson Learned.* Washington, DC: World Bank.

World Health Organization (WHO). 1976. African Traditional Medicine: African Technical Report Series. Geneva. WHO.

WHO, UNAIDS, and UNICE. Towards Universal Access: Scaling up Priority HIV/AIDS Interventions in the Health Sector. Progress Report 2010. (http://www.who.int/hiv/pub/2010progressreport/en, accessed 4th October, 2011).

WHO, Regional Office for Africa. Progress towards Achieving Universal Access to Priority Health Sector Interventions. 2011 update.

WHO. 2006. Demand for Male Circumcision Rises in a Bid to Control HIV. Bulletin of the World Health Organisation. Vol. 84 (7) http://www.who.int/bulletin/volumes/84/7/news10706/en/.

Chapter Eleven

Introduction To African Literature

By Tayo Ogunlewe

Introduction

It may be instructive to begin with some obvious questions. Is there such a thing as African literature or should it be African literatures? Is African literature a monolithic term? How homogenous are the literary works (both oral and written) from eastern Africa and northern Africa or those from western and southern Africa? Is African literature only those works of imaginative literature composed or written by Africans in Africa, or does it include works by Africans in the Diaspora? What about literary works by foreigners (non-Africans) but which have Africa as their setting or depict an African worldview or consciousness? What if an African writes a play, poem, or a novel with a non-African setting, characters, or consciousness?

The questions are unending; we could go on and on, for there can be no cut-and-dried definition of the term "African literature." However, for the purpose of this essay we shall define African literature as works of imaginative literature written by Africans, that has African characters and setting and depicts an African worldview or consciousness. Virtually all the indigenous African cultures had thriving traditions of oral literature before the coming of the Europeans, and it must be stressed that imaginative literature written in the colonial languages—English, French, Portuguese, and Arabic—is a relatively recent phenomenon when compared with African oral literature.

In order to have a full picture of African literature, it is important to understand that there were oral literary traditions. Unfortunately, however, it seems most modern (contemporary) African writers are hardly aware of the traditions that have shaped their art. In the words of S. E. Ogude, "In a sense African Literature is as old as the African people" (1), literature in this context being the expression of a people's consciousness in a social situation.

The Expression of People's Consciousness

This consciousness or awareness of the various forces that influence the growth, development, and ordering of society was once only heard but can now, in addition, be read, as the literature of the people of Africa. Literature, at this point of historical development, is not simply a reflection of a people's awareness, but the collective experience of a people, expressed collectively. Romanus Egudu's definition of modern African literature as an "artistic study of the African predicament from the colonial era, through the attainment of political independence to the post-independence era in contrast to traditional literature" (9) is a good starting point in our exploration of African literature. The African in literature dates back to, at least, the fifteenth century BC. However, European writers in such publications as Mandeville's *Travels*, Hakluyt's *Principal Navigations* (1859) and *The History and Description of Africa* (1600) had nothing but gloomy pictures of Africa and the African to paint. But these publications are now shrouded in the darks halls of history.

It was the character of Man Friday in *Robinson Crusoe* by Daniel Defoe that was used to identify the African, for a long time. Others such as Joyce Cary in *Mister Johnson*, Joseph Conrad in *Heart of Darkness*, and Elspeth Huxley in *The Walled City* unfortunately further painted a negative picture of Africa for the world to see (or rather, read). It was against this distorted background that writers of African origin who had benefited from Western education began to write in an attempt to correct the worrying and negative impression of Africa that the likes of Defoe and Conrad had painted for the world to see.

Chinua Achebe's *Things Fall Apart* (1958) was written partly in response to the perceived distortion of Africa by Joyce Cary's *Mister Johnson*. Achebe's 1958 effort triggered a spirit of literary nationalism that became an important force in the nationalist struggle to liberate Africa from European colonialism, for with the publication of *Things Fall Apart*, Africa had the classic book that would serve as a point of reference and comparison for future writing and writers who are African. Achebe was one of the earliest African writers to make his mark on the world's literary consciousness, and coincidentally he started writing when independence was already in view. In such a situation, it was possible to look back with impartiality and even detachment at the history of colonialism and try to assess its effects without the escapist romantic-literary writings of the same period. Although the South African novelist Peter Abraham had published before Achebe, for example, *Dark Testament* (1942), *Song of the City* (1945), *Mine Boy* (1946), *Path of Thunder* (1948), *Wild Conquest* (1950), *Return to Goli* (1953), and *A Wreath for Udomo* (1956), just as Amos Tutuola, Achebe's fellow Nigerian, had done with *The Palmwine Drunkard* (1952), it was Achebe's effort that started the redemption of the African image from the damage that the Carys and the Conrads had done over the centuries.

Things Fall Apart remains a seminal novel in African literature for two reasons. The first is the domestication of the English language to tell the African story. Related to this is the second reason, the frequent use of Igbo words directly in the middle of an English sentence.

These two reasons are a major contribution to the problem of "what language to use for African Literature?" which is a continuing debate in African literary discourse. Other prominent names in West African literature include another Nigerian, Wole Soyinka, who is the first African writer to win the Noble Prize for Literature (1986); Ayi Kwei Armah, the Ghanaian novelist; Femi Osofisan, probably Africa's most prolific dramatist; Efua Sutherland; Ama Ata Aidoo; Akachi Adimora Ezeigbo; Ben Okri; Cyprian Ekwensi; Christopher Okigbo; Galdys; Casely-Hayford; Chimamanda Ngozi Adichie; Sefi Atta; and Buchi Emecheta and others.

In Francophone Africa, where the policy of assimilation by the French colonial masters almost obliterated the indigenous cultures, emerged the concept of Negritude, especially in their poetry. With Leopold Sedar Senghor, who later became the first president of independent Senegal, in the forefront the pioneers of African literature in the French language inaugurated the movement of reestablishing the African consciousness in their alienated countrymen. Notable African writers of French expression include the Guinean Camara Laye, a novelist whose *African Child* (1955), *A Dream of Africa* (1967), and *The Radiance of the King* (1970) delineate his experiences in Europe in the course of studying and his vision for Africa; Sembene Ousmane, the Senegalese author of the celebrated novel *God's Bits of Wood Mariam Ba*, as well as the Cameroonians Mongo Beti (*Mission to Kala* and *The Poor Christ of Bomba*, among others), and Ferdinard Oyono who wrote *Houseboy*, and *The Old Man and The Medal*, among other works. From Lusophone Africa has come Agostinho Neto, a poet from Angola, who later became president of his country at independence.

No serious introduction to African literature can omit the contributions of the Ugandan poet Okot P'Bitek who wrote the largely popular *Song of Lawino*, (1966) and later *Song of Ocol* in 1970. Other East African writers include Taban lo Liyong, Ngugi wa Thiong'o, Yusuf Lule, Robert Serumaga, David Rubadiri, David Maillu, and Ngugi wa Miiri, among others. The literary scene in East Africa continues to churn out quality literary artists; but how did it all begin? First of all, it should be emphasized that written literature in English started much later in eastern Africa than in western or southern Africa, but the oral tradition, in the words of Arne Zettersten, "had a life of its own and a long history" (2). Just as the establishment of a university college in Ibadan by the British colonial government in 1948 marked a watershed in the development of West African literature in English, the establishment of similar colleges at Makerere in Uganda (1949), Nairobi, Kenya (1961), and Dare-es-salam, Tanzania (1961) proved to be of great importance for literary activity in East Africa.

Ngugi Wa Thiong'o, the Kenyan writer, is the most visible novelist from East Africa and one of the most dominant writers in African literature with such titles as *Weep Not Child* (1964), *The River Between* (1965), and *A Grain of Wheat* (1967). He has also published plays such as *The Trial of Dedan Kimathi* and *I Will Marry When I Want*, which he coauthored with Ngugi Wa Miiri. His most recent novel is *Wizard of Crow* (2008). In 1977, Ngugi had published the controversial *Petals of Blood*, an analysis of the conflict between African and Western civilizations. Ngugi has also experimented with language; his 1982 novel, *Devil on the Cross*, was initially written in his native Gikuyu language.

From southern Africa have come excellent writers such as Athol Fugard, Dennis Brutus, Doris Lessing, Peter Abraham, and Mazisi Kunene, among other notable names. Contemporary southern African literature is, however, thriving and is at par with any other world literature. It has even produced Nobel laureates in Literature such as Nadimer Godimer (1991) and John M. Coetzee (2003). Southern African literature in its oral form has a long history of development, unlike its written counterparts. But just as in other parts of Africa, colonization did irreparable damage to oral literary traditions. In the words of Mazisi Kunene, the famous South African poet, "The conquest of the African people led to frantic attempts by both missionaries and administrators to climate traditional African values except where they furthered the interests of the conquerors. Inevitably this led to the destruction of the very institutions that had acted as a creative force (1970:9). Whether in West Africa or East Africa, North or southern Africa, the reason and motives for this strategy differed, but the results remained the same—to obliterate African traditions and customs. The effect was to deprive African literature of some of its vital components; for example, African oral literature required communal participation, which is not a vital feature of Western or colonialist literature. And the vast ignorance and usual arrogance of the colonialists meant that in defining African literature, they relegated it to the lowest level of expression.

Literature of the northern part of the African continent has a very different history. The historical experiences of the North African people have brought them into contact with diverse cultures and ethnicities, but so has every other African ethnic nationality. However, the literature from the region unlike that of the other regions is not limited to French, English, and Portuguese, for the influence of Islam, as the dominant religion in the subregion, has also foisted the Arabic language on the populace such that the majority of their literary works are first derived in Arabic before translation to other official (colonialist) languages such as English or French or Spanish.

Even though some North African writers borrow from the indigenous Berber language and the imported Spanish, and fewer still write in English, the bulk of creative artistry, when not in Arabic, is in French. This is so because, except for some parts of Egypt, none of the other North African states have the vivid colonial experiences with the British that have so strongly influenced East and West Africa. Therefore, the North African writer is obliged to confront the question of language very early in his career. Common themes prevalent in North African literature include the legacy of colonization, the horrors of the anticolonial struggle, the role of women, the role of the elite class, the ills of postcolonial societies of the region, patriarchy, religion, and the dangers of Islamist fundamentalism. Notable among North African writers are Naguib Mahfouz, a Nobel Prize winner for Literature (1988) from Egypt, Tayeb Saleh from Sudan, the Somalian Nurudin Farah, the Egyptian dramatist Tawfik Al-Hakim, the Algerian Assia Djebah, the Moroccan Driss Chraibi, the Algerian Kateb Yacine, and even Albert Camus and Edward Said, among others. Contemporary North African literature in French came after, and followed the modern Arabic literary writing as earlier suggested. Kateb Yacine's *Nedjma*

(1956) is usually considered the first significant novel, but Driss Chraibi's *The Simple Past* was published two years earlier in 1954.

Finally, there is a powerful ideological factor responsible for African unity and which would have given birth to the term "African literature." Behind the violent initiation into the industrial age, there was not only an expansionist policy of exploitation and conquest by the various colonial masters but also an assumption that the old African ways were primitive and superstitious and that Africa's cultures were markedly inferior to those cultures that colonized the continent. In order to counter and modify that image, as early as the eighteenth century, but especially in the nineteenth and twentieth centuries, certain African thinkers, who had lived in the West and had received a Western education, challenged that primitive image and insisted on the value of their own culture. This agitation in written form gives rise to African literature as we know it today.

African literature today has produced excellent dramatists, poets, novelists, essayists, critics, and theorists, and it has contributed its fair share of Nobel laureates and others internationally acclaimed writers. New trends are manifest, which shows that African literature bears witness to the African condition, but this condition is a particular historical specification of global influences and human nature; more important, it establishes that African literature offers an unusually good case through which to examine cultural construction as a process that is simultaneously global and local.

Review Questions:

1. It is a challenge defining African literature. What are some of the questions to consider in providing a definition of African literature?

2. In spite of this challenge, how is African literature defined in this chapter?

3. Considering the early works by Europeans about Africa and Africans as well as the works of early African literary pioneers, how is literature a reflection of the collective experience of a people, expressed collectively?

4. What concept emerged out of Francophone Africa due to the policy of assimilation by the French almost obliterating the indigenous cultures? What is your understanding of this concept?

5. Chinua Achebe's 1958 novel, *Things Fall Apart*, was said to have triggered a spirit of literary nationalism that became an important force in the nationalist struggle to liberate Africa from European colonialism. Identify some other prominent West African writers.

6. Written literature began earlier in West African than in East Africa. Who are some of the prominent East African writers?

7. Who are the two winners of the Nobel Prize for Literature from the southern African region?

8. North Africa has also produced a Nobel Prize winner in Naguib Mahfouz who won in 1988. Who are some other prominent North African writers?

Selected Bibliography

Achebe, Chinua. 1975. *Morning Yet on Creation Day*. London: Anchor Press.

Achebe, Chinua. 1958. *Things Fall Apart*. London: Heinemann.

Defoe, Daniel. 1719. *The Life and Strange Surprising Adventures of Robinson Crusoe of York*. London: Mariner Books.

Equiano, Olaudah. 1789. The Interesting Narrative of the Life of Olaudah Equiano, or Gustavus Vassa, the African. Written by Himself.

Grégoire, Henri-Baptiste. 1818. An Inquiry Concerning the Intellectual and Moral Faculties of the Negroes, Paris, 1808. Translated into English by D. B. Warden Brooklyn (1810).

http://www.bbc.co.uk/african literature, 2011.

http://en.wiipedia.org/wiki/Africanliterature.

Kunene, Mazisi. 1979. Zulu Poems. London: Andre Deutsch.

Malt-Douglas, Fedwa, 2009. "Arabic Literature." Microsoft Encarta.

Nasidi, Yakubu. 2001. Beyond the Experience of Limits (Theory, Criticism and Power in African Literature) Ibadan: Caltop Publications.

Nazareth, Peter. 1974. An African View of Literature, London.

Ogbe, N.G. 1997. Essentials of Literature Enugu.

Ogude, S. E. 1983. Genius in Bondage: A Study of the Origins of African Literature in English Ile-Ife: Ife University Press.

Ogunlewe, Adetayo Olurotimi. 2004. "Recent Trends in the Nigerian Novel" (Unpublished PhD Thesis) University of Ibadan.

Soyinka, Wole. 1976. *Myth, Literature and the African World*. Cambridge.

Zettersten, Arne. 1983. *East African Literature: An Anthology*. London: Longman.

Chapter Twelve

Notes On African Drama And Theatre

By Freda Scott Giles

What Is African Theatre?

One chapter in a text could not begin to address all theatrical expression in all of Africa. At least eight hundred languages are spoken in over fifty nations. The climates and terrains are as diverse as the cultures. No theatre course could ever touch on the dramatic expressions of so many peoples. We can select only a handful of playwrights and theatre makers to discuss. We can only begin to explore the richness and variety of types of dramas. When the continent is studied, it is usually divided into two large parts, Northern Africa and sub-Saharan Africa, and then subdivided further. Though northern, southern, eastern and western Africa will be briefly addressed, this chapter will primarily focus on sub-Saharan Africa and on representative writers from Anglophone nations, as texts that address these theatres are more readily available in the United States.

In the preface to his book, *Modern African Drama*, Dr. Biodun Jeyifo describes a theatrical performance by a Yoruba **Alarinjo** troupe in what is now Nigeria. The Yoruba are one of three major ethnic groups (and many smaller groups) who live in Nigeria, and the Alarinjo theatre is a professional theatre with a history that dates back to Europe's medieval period. In 1826, the Alarinjo troupe was hired to perform for a group of British explorers led by Hugh Clapperton. Since he did not understand the conventions of the theatre, and did not know how to interpret the masks and pantomime that were used, Clapperton totally misinterpreted the performance. Clapperton could only understand theatre in terms of what he knew in England. Dr. Jeyifo makes us understand that we must know something of the culture and history of the people making the theatre, in order to appreciate it on its own terms. In the back of his book, Dr. Jeyifo has included a timeline that encapsulates the history of African theatre. The timeline notes that in 1930, the British Drama League sponsored a conference on "Native African Drama," producing a formal declaration at that end that "there is no indigenous African drama" (638). It seems the West has been slow to acknowledge the existence of African drama and theatre. However, dramatic expression thrived in precolonial Africa and remained distinct while incorporating

European modes of drama during the colonial period. During the present postcolonial period, dramatic expression ranges from the traditional to the cutting-edge contemporary. But can we find a general definition of African theatre?

Mimesis and Methexis

African performing traditions are based in a culture of community. In an African performance, everyone is expected to participate. The following description of a storyteller at work expresses the importance of this participation:

> Quality, significance, and manner of narration are the aesthetic qualities sought in the literary arts of epic and lyric poetry and storytelling. Pleasure and entertainment are equally important. The words, symbols, and images used by a storyteller are just as important as his delivery. Also, the extent to which a storyteller can hold the attention of the audience—and so generate audience participation—enhances the quality of the tale. Audience participation is usually best effected through songs sung by both the storyteller and the audience that bear on the theme, mood, and moral of the tale (129).

The traditional storyteller, who is most times also the community historian, is popularly described by the term "griot." The griot/storyteller is a major factor in an oral tradition where knowledge and culture are passed down through human libraries. In the above example, the storyteller has a great story, but the way the story is told is equally significant. The storyteller performs, but the audience is part of the performance. The storyteller can improvise, and the audience can be encouraged to participate through call and response, singing, movement. Sometimes the performer and the audience trade places. Sometimes they are all performing together. This is "methexis"—there is room for improvisation, spontaneity, and audience participation. The texture of the performance is equally as important as the spoken text. This style is different from the Western performance tradition, characterized by the word "mimesis," a word that denotes "imitation." In traditional Western-style theatre, a character is "imitated" by an actor for an audience. The actor acts and the audience watches and listens, responding with laughter, tears, applause. Breaking the "fourth wall" and interacting with the audience is something special. Not so with methexis.

Another example of methexis may be found in the many festivals that abound throughout sub-Saharan Africa. During the Yoruba Egungun Festival, for example, the ancestor is represented by a dancer enveloped from head to toe in colorful, flowing cloth. The Egungun dances through the village. His mask is an invitation to the ancestor to move among the living. In Yoruba cosmology, time and space are shared among the unborn, the living, and the dead. The dancer becomes the ancestor. Dancers and drummers interact with one another, and spectators may spontaneously join the ancestor in dance.

So, what has that to do with African drama and theatre? In a typical performance, the audience will be incorporated in some way, or will find a way to be incorporated. There is a text, but there is room for improvisation. It may not be unusual for the actors to break the convention of the fourth wall and communicate with the audience, even though portraying a character. There is seldom a performance that does not include rhythm and music. Most contemporary African plays, though they have **syncretized** African and Western performance styles, will have some elements of methexis.

The dance, the oldest form of performance, is where it all began. There are various theories on how theatre came into being, but the most popular one is that it began in the rituals that people created to celebrate and affirm their relationships with their environment, one another, and the cosmos. Methexis also takes into consideration the use of rhythm as an underpinning of performance. Traditional performance often includes the use of the mask, and nearly invariably includes the use of the drum. John Picton discusses the complex relationships of the mask to the wearer and the performance in an essay entitled "What's in a Mask." There are numerous interpretations of that word, and its use in describing traditional performance can be confusing. Picton explores the meanings of the mask and masquerade as words, as ideas, as metaphors, and as artifacts. The mask is not a persona to hide behind, as it is in the West; it is an outward expression of attitudes, beliefs, and values.

As an educator, Femi Euba explains in "Forms of Black Drama," any discussion of African and African Diaspora theatrical expression should be segmented into three basic historical divisions: **precolonial, colonial, and postcolonial**. The issues of slavery and colonialism cannot be overlooked; knowledge of this history is essential to appreciation of artistic production during the colonial and postcolonial periods. During the colonial period, Western dramatic conventions were introduced, particularly through the education systems that were imposed. The looser the colonial tie, the stronger the preservation of indigenous culture, though all colonial powers went to great lengths to alienate the colonized from their traditions, the most extreme case being that of eastern and southern Africa. Euba outlines the development of five major dramaturgical categories of black drama: **ritual, political, historical, humanistic (dealing with personal conflicts),** and **satiric.** As he further explains, these categories are neither definitive nor mutually exclusive. They may overlap with one another and with other categories, such as **feminist/womanist**. This is one way of classifying African drama and theatre that can encompass both Western and non-Western structural paradigms.

Wole Soyinka, the first African author to win the Nobel Prize for Literature, in an essay entitled, "Theatre in African Traditional Cultures: Survival Patterns," explains how, by either taking artistic expression underground or combining Western with African forms (creating new forms) through syncretism, African tradition was able to resurface as colonialism receded. Using this thesis, Soyinka outlines the development of Yoruba Opera, Concert Party, and the folk opera tradition.

Though he lived only long enough to see the earliest manifestations of African independence, Franz Fanon's (1925–1961) writings have influenced every generation of writers and theorists on colonialism and postcolonialism since he published *Black Skin/White Masks* in 1952. His best-known work is *The Wretched of the Earth*, published in 1961. In "On National Culture," Fanon examines the tensions, ambiguities, and dilemmas the postcolonial artist must face in attempting to communicate across the ranges of cultural alienation, hybridization, and assimilation that have transpired in accordance with the amount of contact with the colonial power. At first, the artist seeks to prove, through critical affirmation that s/he is capable of skillfully handling the tools of the colonial power. Then, in attempting to express nationalism, s/he attempts to return fully to the roots, through valorization of the indigenous culture. The question of what language to speak in becomes an issue. In speaking of these dilemmas as applied to African American culture, James Weldon Johnson described the "double audience." The black artist is often forced to choose between whether to speak to the colonial culture or his own, as each is operating under an often disparate and incompatible set of assumptions about what the art should communicate. In trying to reach both, he may be unsuccessful in reaching either. Fanon solves this dilemma by delineating a third phase for the artist to reach. He calls this "the fighting phase." The artist accepts the new reality of being a product of a multiplicity of cultural influences, finding his/her own voice of truthful expression of the needs and aspiration of his/her people within that new reality. All of the writers you will be reading have had to think through these issues in some way. All have found their own voices while working through multiple languages and modes of performance.

Chinua Achebe, author of *Things Fall Apart*, the first novel by an African to reach success in the West, stated this about African literature:

> Traditional texts on dramaturgy often discuss the idea of "universality"—the idea that any worthy work of art speaks a truth that transcends issues of time and place. Unfortunately, that idea used to be attached solely to European or European-based cultures and aesthetic values. For many reasons, in our postcolonial, postmodern era, this idea has expanded greatly. The works you will explore when you read or witness African drama and theatre show that the truth of human experience is transcendent in a much broader sense.

Below are brief descriptions of some well-known African playwrights and a few of their works, as well as further information on some areas of contemporary sub-Saharan African drama.

Wole Soyinka: Ogun meets Dionysus

Akinwande Oluwole Soyinka, born in Nigeria in 1934, is the best-known African playwright in the United States. His body of work earned him the Nobel Prize for Literature in 1986, making him the first African author to achieve that distinction. His personal history and his works, whether directly addressing Nigeria or not, are integrally tied to the history of his nation, and of Africa. Though he was from a Christian family, Soyinka grew up well acquainted with traditional Yoruba culture. He chronicled his early years in a memoir, *Ake: the Years of Childhood* (1981). In 1954, he entered the University of Leeds (England), eventually earning a master's degree. By the time he left Leeds for London, Soyinka had begun his career as a playwright. In 1960, the year his nation attained independence, Soyinka returned to Nigeria. In honor of Nigeria's independence, he mounted one of his first major works, the complex and dense *A Dance of the Forests*. He wrote for Nigerian radio and television, as well as theatre, and taught at the universities of Ife and Lagos. He also visited England for an extended period.

Nigeria's postindependence years were scarred by continuous turmoil among the 250 or so ethnic groups pressed into a nation by the British, exacerbated by religious tensions between the primarily Muslim north and the primarily Christian south. Soyinka's outspoken political views resulted in his arrest and trial. His acquittal was not the end of his troubles. In 1966, a military coup overturned the civilian government, but that did little to ease tensions and mistrust among the major ethnic groups, the Hausa in the north, the Igbo in the southeast, and the Yoruba in the southwest. Coup followed coup, and in 1967, civil war ensued. By now, Soyinka was a well-known and prolific writer, unstinting in his defense of human rights. The Biafra War was a brutal and bloody conflict in which the Igbo people sought to secede and form their own nation. Soyinka's efforts to broker a peace resulted in his being imprisoned again and placed in solitary confinement for nearly two years. The war ended in 1970, and Soyinka was released. His account of his imprisonment, *The Man Died*, was published in 1972. *The Swamp Dwellers*, *The Lion and the Jewel*, *The Strong Breed*, *The Trials of Brother Jero*, *Kongi's Harvest* (later made into a film in Nigeria, in which Soyinka appeared), and *Madmen and Specialists* were the major theatre works produced by 1972.

In discussing *The Strong Breed*, Awam Amkpa in his book, *Theatre and Postcolonial Desires*, describes Soyinka's dramaturgy as "his resort to tradition to argue for change; his use of the English language to subvert Western, rational, epistemologies by breaking down the barriers between past and present, the spiritual and the material; and his recourse to Yoruba particularisms to articulate universalist postcolonial desires" (21–22).

These ideas certainly play out in both *The Strong Breed* and *Death and the King's Horseman*, the play often described as Soyinka's masterpiece. Ampka categorizes both *The Strong Breed* and *Death and the King's Horseman* as among Soyinka's "metaphysical dramas." These plays have also been called "**Yoruba tragedy**." He groups Soyinka's plays into three broad categories, the other two being topical political street theatre skits and political satire.

In 1973, *The Bacchae of Euripides* was produced at the National Theatre in London. From 1973–75, Soyinka taught in Cambridge, England, and in Ghana. In 1975, he returned to Nigeria to take a post as professor of comparative literature at the University of Ife, where he would later head the theatre department and form a theatre company. His play entitled *Death and the King's Horseman* was first produced at Ife in 1976. Another major work, a Yoruba opera based on Brecht's *Threepenny Opera*, entitled *Opera Wonyosi* (1977), also premiered there. Civilian government briefly returned to Nigeria in 1979, but the government was weak, and corrupt; a series of military governments again followed, starting in 1983. The worst of the military dictators, Sani Abacha, ruled from 1993 to 1998. Abacha accused Soyinka of treason, forcing him into exile in 1996. Soyinka had seen *The Beatification of Area Boy* premiere in Leeds and gain publication in 1995, the same year that Abacha had had Ken Saro-Wiwa, one of the nation's most popular authors, and an outspoken advocate for his people, the Ogoni (subject to particular oppression because their lands were rich in oil), executed on trumped-up charges. *Area Boy* directly alludes to these and other criminal acts under the Abacha regime. Earlier plays, *Requiem for a Futurologist* (1983), *A Play of Giants* (1984), *A Scourge of Hyacinths* (1991), *From Zia, with Love* (1992), along with another volume of memoirs, and several volumes of essays and poetry, attacked oppression all over Africa. Soyinka spent most of his exile in the United States, teaching at Emory University in Atlanta. In 1998, Abacha died suddenly under mysterious circumstances. Civilian government returned in 1999. Since then, Soyinka's playwriting appears to have tapered off. After *Area Boy*, there are only two more produced plays: *King Baabu*, a satire in the manner of Alfred Jarry's *Ubu Roi* that is thought to be directed in large part against Robert Mugabe, president of Zimbabwe, and *Etiki Revu Wetin*.

So, where do Ogun and Dionysus fit in? Students of Western drama have learned that the classical Greek god that represents tragedy is Dionysus. Dionysus gave humans the gift of wine that has the power to alter consciousness. He represents the creative urge, manifested in the arts and in the rites of fertility. The dithyrambic hymns to Dionysus that told of his passion and sufferings are identified as the wellsprings of tragic drama. As the first actor, Thespis, stepped out of the dithyrambic chorus and sang as Dionysus, rather than about Dionysus, the first step was taken toward the creation of tragic drama. In his own poetics, *Myth, Literature, and the African World* (1976), Soyinka identifies the Yoruba deity, Ogun, as the representation of tragedy in Yoruba cosmology. Ogun is the god of iron, creator of implements, patron of artisans and artists. He is the god of the poet. He is also the god of war, the unleasher of the forces and implements of war. It was Ogun who, when the universe was shattered, was first to act, to leap into the abyss between humans and the gods and attempt to bridge the void. Tragedy abides within this abyss. It is this abyss that Elesin is to help his king to cross in *Death and the King's Horseman*. Soyinka has created a Yoruba tragedy, complete with its songs, dances, and poetry, integral and inseparable from the drama that shows a world on the cusp of change, fearful of freefall into the abyss. In his introduction to the play, Soyinka is adamant that culture clash is not the root of the tragedy but rather the inciting incident. This is to be thought about when analyzing Elesin as a tragic hero. While reading the play, take special note of the use of the **proverbs** that season the play throughout. Proverbs are integral to African culture, and are much more than poetic or metaphoric embellishment. They are vital forms of communication and teaching. Where and when they are expressed is important.

Femi Osofisan

In *Contemporary Nigerian Theatre,* Olu Obafemi groups Wole Soyinka, John Pepper Clark, Ola Rotimi and Zulu Sofola in the "first generation" of Nigerian playwrights. It is they who linked the "literary drama … to the popular drama of their predecessors, as they are both inspired by oral traditional performance. The major difference … is the consciously individualist, metaphysical and tragic visions of the literary dramatists." Femi Osofisan, Bode Sowande, Kole Omotoso and Tess Onwueme, Obafemi explains, belong to the "second generation." Though they have been influenced by the first generation, "they move beyond these influences to design a revolutionary aesthetic based on a conviction of the power of art to function as an instrument of social transformation" (11). This is an apt and succinct appraisal.

Femi Osofisan (1946–) studied French at Ibadan University, conducting his graduate studies at the universities of Dakar and Paris. He earned his PhD at Ibadan, where he eventually joined the faculty. He is a playwright, novelist, critic, and journalist, one of the founders of the highly reputable newspaper, the Nigerian edition of the *Guardian.* When you read about Osofisan, you will invariably be told that his writing is heavily influenced by the ideas of the German director, playwright, and theorist, Bertolt Brecht (1898–1956). One of the most influential theatre theorists of the twentieth century, Brecht attacked what he described as "culinary theatre," the theatre of illusion (**representational**) that satisfies an audience but does not stimulate social consciousness. Brecht developed a theatre that challenged the audience through **alienation**, that is, never letting the audience get sucked into the illusion of reality. Songs would be interpolated that might not be directly connected to the action at hand; there would be titles and signs that would explain the scene, to avoid keeping the audience in suspense; the production elements, such as the lighting instruments, would be fully exposed to the audience. The plays would entertain, but the audience would constantly be stimulated to engage in a dialectic interrogation of contradictions and class struggle in society. Brecht is still a strong influence on political theatre.

Brecht's Marxist/materialist critical frame was compatible with Osofisan's. Brecht's **epic theatre** was also compatible with a theatre Osofisan already knew, a traditional popular theatre where no fourth wall exists, where actor and audience communicate with each other, and where music and dance are incorporated in order to instruct as well as entertain. Osofisan descibes his approach to drama as incorporating Western, Asian, and indigenous African forms; he enjoys playing with form, and form and content walk hand in hand in his plays. As Awam Amkpa, in *Theatre and Postcolonial Desires,* explains, Osofisan uses popular theatre and Yoruba folklore, as well as language, as "a resource for shaping a counter-European and anticolonial esthetic [sic]…"(56), enabling him to conduct a "surreptitious insurrection" by making it possible for him to express politically subversive messages in a hostile and repressive political environment. After Soyinka, Osofisan is most published in the West.

In reading Osofisan's plays, particularly *Esu and the Vagabond Minstrels* and *Once Upon Four Robbers,* there are a few things to note about the Yoruba orishas, or deities, represented, particularly Esu. There is an extensive pantheon, but all are manifestations of Olodumare, God. Esu (Eshu, Elegba, and other spellings) serves as a messenger between the human and divine world. He is the god of the crossroads, and is associated with fertility. He is also a trickster, representing the vicissitudes of fate. Like fate, he can be fickle and changeable. He can also be associated with the concept of justice, of humans getting their just deserts. Because of these many facets, Esu has been associated with irony, a root of comedy as well as tragedy. Osofisan, in a kind of dialectic with Soyinka, identifies Esu as the god of the theatre.

Osofisan makes a number of statements about his work in his book, *Playing Dangerously*. He speaks of the interaction between the traditional and the modern, the folk and the contemporary, and the idea of intertextuality, texts responding to and debating each other, wrapped in "self-contradicting, self-referential plots" (617). **Intertextuality** is one feature of **postmodernism**. Osofisan does not mind being identified as having postmodernist sensibilities; he emphasizes that he is not interested in deconstructing texts as an exercise, but in the interest of social relevance: "Without the impulse for justice, for compassion, for laughter, the lungs of artistic creativity will starve for oxygen, and atrophy, and usher in the death of our human civilization" (617). Another good reference for examining Osofisan's work is the book *Old Songs Set Ablaze* by Sandra Shannon.

Ama Ata Aidoo and Other Pioneer Women Playwrights, With a Word on Some Contemporary African Womanist Playwrights

Dr. Foluke Ogunleye, an accomplished theatre practitioner and playwright, stated in a lecture on the history of Nigerian theatre that as contemporary popular theatre developed during the 1950s, the men who ran the theatre companies found it difficult to recruit female troupe members. Duro Ladipo, one of the inventors of Yoruba Opera, for example, married all of the women in his troupe, in order to underscore the respectability of women in public performance. It was not unusual, during the formative years of popular theatres, for men to perform women's roles. *Ghana's Concert Party* is a notable example. Not only is the representation of women in the content of the performances often problematical, but the very presence of a women onstage representing her gender can be in itself a risk-filled challenge to the patriarchy. Generally speaking, it is still the case that men who are not in the theatre are not inclined to marry women who are, or to allow their wives to perform publicly. As scholar Jane Plastow has expressed, "Women have struggled to be heard in the world of modern African theatre." The comment is true across the board, not just in performance, but in all aspects of production, despite the current explosion of the African film industry. And women, in addition to participation in the fiscal support of the family, are responsible for the domestic sphere and child rearing. In theatre, playwriting is the province of the intellectual class, and women have traditionally been lagging behind in attaining access to higher education. In Ghana, however, the development of literary drama was led by two women, Efua Sutherland, followed by Ama Ata Aidoo.

Sutherland, who was integral to the establishment of Ghanaian postcolonial theatre, was committed to the preservation of her nation's folklore. One of her best-known plays, *The Marriage of Anansewa*, shows her effort to build a bridge between the storytelling tradition, popular theatre, and literary drama, a form she describes as **anansegoro**. **Anansesem** are traditional stories about Anansi the spider, a beloved figure in Akan, Ashanti, and other West African folklore. There are countless stories about clever Anansi and his tricks, though as often as not, his tricks will ultimately backfire on him. When Anansi crossed the Atlantic, his stories spread throughout the Caribbean; in the United States, Anansi became Brer Rabbit. In her introduction to the edition of *The Marriage of Anansewa* published in Ghana, Sutherland describes him as an Everyman, whose ambitions and follies are met with laughter.

Though *The Marriage of Anansewa* is published and often performed in English, it was originally performed in Akan. The premise is simple: Ananse's daughter is of marriageable age, and he sees a chance to cash in. He promises her hand to three chiefs, who each must seal the engagement with money and expensive gifts. Things are going well until all three chiefs decide to come for a visit on the same day. The plot thickens from there.

Like Sutherland, Ama Ata Aidoo (1942–) utilized oral literature, particularly storytelling, as a basis for drama. Having studied creative writing at Stanford University, she has traveled extensively in the United States and taught at universities in Ghana and Zimbabwe. She is known for two plays, *The Dilemma of a Ghost* and *Anowa*. *Anowa* (1970) unfolds the tragic story, set during the colonial period, of a man and wife whose partnership disintegrates when the husband decides to purchase slaves. In addition, the couple is childless, an unbearable condition in African society. The wealthier the couple becomes, the greater the sense of emptiness and loss.

In her introduction to the play, Gilbert states that *Anowa* is based on a traditional type of Ghanaian folktale, "the archetypal story of the disobedient daughter who rejects all suitors proposed by her parents, only to marry an attractive stranger who turns out to be the devil in disguise" (97). The play serves as a metaphorical exploration of the complicity of Africans in the slave trade and the implications of that complicity on their social as well as their material history. In this play, Aidoo amplifies a traditional story structure into dialectic with African history.

The Dilemma of a Ghost, written before *Anowa*, in 1964, begins with a prologue set in the contemporary United States, where Ato, a Ghanaian, and Eulalie, an African American, decide to marry. They have planned their future without the knowledge of Ato's family, and Eulalie has no idea greater than a romantic misconception of what Africa is like. When the couple moves to Ghana, relations with the family become strained at every turn, and the tension quickly moves into Ato's and Eulalie's relationship. Ato becomes like the ghost in a traditional children's game, who cannot choose between Cape Coast and Elmina (two locations on the coast of Ghana not far from each other, where two of the best-known slave castles are located). As in the traditional **dilemma tale**, a solution is not specifically offered. What is offered is the opportunity for discussion of the problem and potential solutions.

Ghana was the first African nation to gain independence, in 1957, and Efua Sutherland and Ama Ata Aidoo were at the forefront of the effort to build a modern national drama and theatre. They are among the first postindependence female dramatists. Along with another prominent author, Joe de Graft, they brought Ghanaian drama into the modern period.

Two other leading first and second generation playwrights include Fatima Dike and Osonwe Tess Onwueme. Onwueme is the first female Nigerian playwright to make a breakthrough in the West. Her brand of feminism and the way it manifests itself in her writings has been quite influential. Tess Onwueme (1955–) is of Igbo origin, born in the then Bendel state. She attended the universities of Ife and Benin, completing her doctoral thesis on the work of Femi Osofisan. Married and the mother of five, she has taught in Nigeria and in the United States; she is currently at the University of Wisconsin. She is also one of the few playwrights who explore relationships between Africans and African Americans. *Legacies* is one play with this theme, while her best-known play, *Tell It to Women*, begins in the United States and shifts to Nigeria, interrogating the women's movement as it relates to women of color. Onwueme is not afraid to shock, to satirize, or to criticize. Like Osofisan, she places social transformation at the core of her work.

As a scholar, Gabo Ntseane (from Botswana) pointed out in a lecture she delivered at the University of Georgia in 2007, African feminists combine concern with women's issues and progressive ideas on the mobility of women in society with traditional African values. Women can embrace tradition while critiquing it, so they do not see their traditional roles as wives and mothers as in any way oppositional to their feminism. The patriarchy harms all, including men, who shared oppression with women under colonialism. The colonial system destroyed matriarchal societal systems and skewed the power structure further toward patriarchy, particularly under the colonial economic system. Dr. Ntseane sees African feminism as less stratified by class than American feminism. Like **womanists** (African American feminists), African feminists see a greater commonality among women who have shared a unique history that minimizes indigenous cultural differences. Colonial and neocolonial history must be considered when analyzing and theorizing on women in African society. (Onwueme does a controversial, often scathing reading of both American and African feminism in her epic play, *Tell It to Women*; she does see class stratification and struggle for African feminists to overcome.)

Though classified as a (materialist) feminist playwright, Onwueme courageously tackles a range of social issues. As Daniella Gioseffi states in her preface to *Three Plays* (*The Broken Calabash, Parables for a Season*, and *The Reign of Wazobia*), "Her works examine the intersection of tradition and ritual, as well as the construction of gender, and though her framework is particular to Nigeria, her dramas are pertinent to oppressed peoples of all countries as well as the United States—particularly women …[*The Broken Calabash*] shows the tragic consequences of denying any human being, female or male, the right to an individual life of self-fulfillment" (9). *The Broken Calabash* is the first in a trilogy that includes *Parables for a Season* and *The Reign of Wazobia. Parables* and *Wazobia* explore themes similar to those in *The Broken Calabash* in the context of a traditional society, where circumstances cause the female protagonist, Zo, to be crowned king, and to be forced to repel efforts to dethrone her. Onwueme writes strongly about strong women.

A partial list of other prominent female dramatists that have not yet been mentioned includes: Lilia Fonseca (Angola), Mbarga Kouma Charlotte (Cameroon), Nicole Werewere

Liking (Cameroon), Alakie-Akinyi Mboya (Kenya), Micere Githae Mugo (Kenya), Ari Katini Mwachofi (Kenya), Stella Oyedipo (Nigeria), Amandina Lihamba (Tanzania), Penina Mlama (Tanzania), Rose Umbowa (Uganda). This short list is by no means definitive—it just might serve as a starting place for examining African women playwrights.

In 2009, scholar Kathy Perkins published what is arguably the first pan-African anthology of female-authored African dramas to be published in the United States, *African Women Playwrights*. In her introduction to the volume, Perkins explains some of the obstacles that hinder women who try to write and publish plays. First, it is more difficult for a woman to obtain an education, at least to go as far in school as a male. School is a heavy financial commitment; if resources are limited, they are likely to be used for the male child. Second, there is often a cultural bias against a woman entering the theatre as a profession; in some cultures, this profession is considered morally questionable. Third, the process of play creation is often collective; when it is, it can be difficult to attribute a dramatic text to a single author. Lastly, publishers are less than receptive to creative work. Again, financial resources come into play; a family may be willing to extend itself financially for textbooks and educational materials, but novels and plays are luxuries that many cannot afford.

Despite these mitigating factors, the number of women authors and playwrights is increasing. Women playwrights write about all kinds of social and political issues, such as government corruption and ethnic strife. However, women playwrights are also bringing to the fore the dramatization of women's issues. They are the next generation, who move African drama from the twentieth to the twenty-first century. As professor and playwright, Amandina Lihamba states, "The writers urge us toward change, the companion of hope."

During the mid-1990s, a team of over 150 researchers, translators, and editors, working in eleven countries and twenty-six languages, embarked on a project that resulted in the four-volume work (divided geographically into northern, southern, eastern and western Africa and the Sahel regions), *Women Writing Africa*, published by the Feminist Press at the City University of New York; the latest volume was published in 2007. They gathered stories, songs, letters, oral histories, diaries, historical documents, and portions of dramatic works, addressing every aspect of women's experiences from the precolonial period to the present. Some works were composed communally in the oral tradition, by women in communities; some were passed down orally through time; many were by women, who were not writers per se, but who needed to address issues important to themselves and other women in writing; some are by contemporary writers and activists.

The preface and introduction in each volume provides an extensive explanation of how the texts were gathered and selected, how issues of translation and interpretation were addressed, and what historical background is necessary to contextualize the texts. The preface to the West Africa/Sahel volume notes the difficulty of recovering texts:

> The relatively limited availability of written texts was a grim reminder that, especially
> since colonial times, West African women—for all their vibrancy—had been denied

access to official channels of communication and of economic and social development (XXV).

Though cultures and societies differed, generally speaking, women tilled the fields, organized the markets, held positions of significance in their communities as healers, griots, praise singers, chiefs, and in some cases, served as warriors and martyrs. Many societies followed matrilineal lines of inheritance and family structure. Female deities were revered in all the pantheons of traditional religions. But, as colonialism spread and writing gained hegemony over orature, women were steadily written out of history. The colonial religions, Islam and Christianity, both privileged men.

The colonial powers characterized Africa and African women in hypersexualized terms, as objects of repulsion and desire. One notable example is Saartjie Baartman (1789–1815), the "Hottentot Venus," actually a woman from the Khoi people of southern Africa, who was spirited to Europe to be exhibited as a sideshow attraction, due to her large buttocks (a condition known as steatopygia). There are some clothing historians who describe the bustle, a Victorian creation that extended the female backside, as an idealization of Baartman's silhouette. Baartman was eventually sold to a Frenchman, exhibited by an animal trainer, and studied by French naturalists. After her death, her skeleton and preserved genetalia and brain were exhibited in the Musée de l'Homme in Paris. Upon his election in 1994, President Nelson Mandela petitioned the French government for the return of her remains; after much diplomatic wrangling, Baartman's remains were repatriated and given a dignified internment in South Africa in 2002; the jars in which her labia and brain were preserved were never found. Baartman's story has become iconic as a metaphorical representation of colonialism and the perception of the African woman. One controversial but well-known dramatic reimagining of her story is *Venus* by African American playwright Suzan Lori Parks. Today, Baartman's name graces shelters for battered woman and other women-centered service centers in South Africa. Her image has been reclaimed and reappropriated; a common trope in postcolonialist representation.

All of the elements described above contribute to the difficulty women have in making their voices heard in the postcolonial era, particularly in theatre, which is a public enterprise. As Jane Plastow explains in her introduction to *African Theatre: Women*, "Women have struggled to be heard in the world of modern African theatre. Kathy A. Perkins describes these and other issues, in her introduction to *African Women Playwrights*. Though the plays she has selected address a variety of issues, they all share an interest in showing African women as multidimensional people wrestling with complicated issues across a variety of cultural landscapes. *The Dilemma of a Ghost* by Ama Ata Aidoo is part of that anthology. *Vukani! (Wake Up!)* by Sindiwe Magona (South Africa) addresses the need for the community to address the reality of what AIDS is doing to it. *Over My Dead Body*, by Violet Barungi (Uganda), is a rare comedy about a woman who attempts to negotiate between a materialistic mother, an idealistic father, and her own needs and desires. *She No Longer*

Weeps by Tsitsi Dangarembga (Zimbabwe) is a revenge tragedy of a woman embittered by her inability to live beyond the reach of male privilege. Nathalie Etoke's (Cameroon) extended monologue, *Better Days Come in Bitter Ways*, explores a woman's rationale for selling her body. *Homecoming* by Andiah Kisia/Chika Okigbo (Kenya), a daughter/father drama, shows the consequences that befall a family caught up in corrupt and violent politics. *A Colored Place* by Malika Ndlovu/Lueen Conning is a revealing portrait of a "colored" woman growing up in South Africa. Julie Okoh's (Nigeria) play, *Edewede (The Dawn of a New Day)*, faces the issue of female circumcision. The play *In the Continuum* compares developments in the lives of two women, one from the United States, and one from Zimbabwe, who must come to grips with a diagnosis of AIDS. The two creators and original actors in the piece, Danai Gurira (Zimbabwe) and Nikkole Salter (United States), take on a spectrum of roles.

In 1995, the United Nations Commission on the Status of Women sponsored a gigantic conference in Beijing, China, out of which came the Declaration and Platform for Action. The general goals of the declaration were geared toward empowerment and improvement in the lives of women around the world. Initiatives were undertaken, and studies were conducted. Every five years, progress has been assessed; recently, in the fifteenth anniversary year, in several locations around the world, experts and government officials have met to assess the progress of the initiatives. The Africa regional meeting took place in Zambia. The issues to be faced are numerous—from land rights, to food security, to economic empowerment, to reproductive rights, to AIDS and other health issues, and a host of gender equity issues. Violence against women is still pandemic—the worst-case scenario is probably the conflict areas of the Congo region, but there is too much violence everywhere. Progress is being made, but there is still much to be done. The struggles of these women show that the personal is political, and that the specific can be universal. African women writers, like African women themselves, break through the statistics to show the humanity of women forging a path to a better future for the continent. In doing so, they give voice to what has been too long left unspoken, and make their voices heard.

Ngugi wa Thiong'o and Kenyan Postcolonial Theatre

If Wole Soyinka is thought to be the foremost first-generation postcolonial playwright to represent West Africa, it may be said that Ngugi wa Thiong'o is foremost among his generation of playwrights from East Africa. Like Soyinka, his contemporary in age, Ngugi has remained committed to speaking truth to power, despite abuses, imprisonment, and exile. Born James Ngugi in 1938 in Kamiirithu, Kenya, into a Kikuyu family, Ngugi attended a mission school and converted to Christianity. His family became involved in the Mau Mau struggle for Kenyan independence from Britain during the 1950s; subsequently, his mother was tortured and his half brother was killed. He earned a BA in English at the University of Makerere, Uganda, and continued his graduate studies in England at the University of Leeds. At Makerere, he had his first play, *The Black Hermit* (1962) produced; while at Leeds, he published his first novel, *Weep Not, Child* (1964), the first novel by an East African to be published in English. Influenced by the writings of Franz Fanon and the political ferment of the 1960s, Ngugi dropped his Christian name and left the church. He returned to Kenya to teach, primarily at the University of Nairobi.

Kenya did attain independence in 1963, but conditions for the most part, for most of the people, did not improve. The distribution of land and the rights of laborers remained issues of contention. These issues, as well as the issue of oppression against women, were at the crux of the building of the Kamiriithu Community Education and Culture Centre's theatre and the first production it engendered, *I Will Marry When I Want*. Kamiriithu, Ngugi's home village, lies near the epicenter of the Mau Mau uprising, and thus bears a special place in Kenya's political and social history. The villagers reclaimed an abandoned community center and rebuilt it into a community resource. Illiterate peasants, workers from the nearby shoe factory, and plantation workers learned to read and write, and together with their teachers, built an outdoor theatre with an audience capacity of two thousand. As Ngugi writes in "Enactments of Power," the space itself spoke to the tension between a people's culture and the neocolonial "deadly theatre" represented by the National Theatre in the capital, Nairobi. Built during the colonial era, the National Theatre offered primarily European and popular American shows, all but ignoring works by Kenyan, or any other African playwrights. The two spaces, one open, where the audience and performance could communicate freely, and the other closed, where the audience became passive spectators to representations of experiences that were not theirs, showed that, as Ngugi states, "... the conflict over the performance space was also a struggle over what cultural symbols and activities represented the new Kenya" (442).

Ngugi wa Mirii, Ngugi's cousin, who ran the literacy program, brought Ngugi in to work with the villagers on the play *I Will Marry When I Want*. The production was an effort of total collaboration. The two Ngugis started with an outline, which often changed, but it was the participants who made the scenes unfold and who provided the songs and dances. Nicholas Brown states in his essay, "Revolution and Recidivism: the Problem of Kenyan History in the plays of Ngugi wa Thiong'o" (2004), that the process of making the production was equal to, or perhaps more important than the product. The process of creating *I Will Marry When I Want* empowered the participants to enter into dialectic with their history, through memories of the Mau Mau uprising and the struggle for independence, and with their present, the struggle against government corruption, privileged class abuses, and gender oppression. Religion is shown as a tool to rob the underclass of its autonomy and self-esteem. The ending is left open. It is up to the audience to determine the direction of the future.

I Will Marry When I Want opened on October 2, 1977, the twenty-fifth anniversary of the Mau Mau uprising, and engendered a sensational response with the audiences that packed the theatre. Critics and spectators came from Nairobi, as well as from surrounding villages. For a moment it seemed that what started at Kamiriithu would grow into a movement of its own. After the play's ninth performance, the government incarcerated Ngugi wa Thiong'o, holding him without charges or a trial for a year. While in prison, Ngugi wrote his novel, *Devil on a*

Cross, on toilet paper in his native Gikuyu language, which he later translated into English. He also penned another work, *Detained: a Writer's Prison Diary*. When he was released from prison, he was not allowed to return to his university teaching position, and eventually, the two Ngugis and Kimani Gecau, the play's director, were driven into exile.

When Ngugi went into exile (1982), Kenya's first president, Jomo Kenyatta, had died, and Daniel Arap Moi won the presidency, where he remained ensconced for twenty-four years. When Moi's administration was replaced by that of E. M. Kibaki, Ngugi thought it safe to return for a visit, in 2004. He had only been in the country three days when thugs broke into his hotel room, brutally assaulting him and his wife. In "Enactments of Power," Ngugi describes the events surrounding the destruction of the Kamithiiru Centre as the state's performance of its power for the control of its populace. The final blows to the theatre were televised with ritual and ceremony. Like the enclosure symbolized by the National Theatre, the state sought to enclose the minds of its people. Ngugi extends that enclosure to the use of colonial languages; in Kenya's case, English. Ngugi began to write in Gikuyu, inviting others to translate his works. His book, *Decolinisation of the Mind*, explains his process of returning to writing in Gikuyu. Ngugi is a prolific author, whose major plays include *The Black Hermit, The Trial of Dedan Kimathi* (with Micere Githae Mugo), *Mother, Sing for Me*, as well as *I Will Marry When I Want*.

South Africa's Antiapartheid Theatre

On February 11, 1990, Nelson Mandela was released after serving twenty-seven years in South African prisons, including time on the infamous Robben Island. This was not the end of the bitter apartheid era, but it did mark the dawn of a new era, which would culminate in the dismantling of apartheid and the election of Mandela in 1994 as the first black president of the Republic of South Africa. The complex history that led up to that event is too lengthy to recount here, but some elements of the cultural history of the southern tip of Africa should be recounted to help us understand some elements of the nature of modern South African theatre.

The indigenous hunter-gatherer groups that first settled southern Africa have been traced back at least eight thousand years. The oldest groups include the San (formerly called Bushmen), who were hunter-gatherers, and the Khoi (formerly called Hottentot), who were herders and farmers. They were joined by Bantu peoples from the north. The Bantu people are divided linguistically into the Nguni, Tsonga, Sotho, and Shona groups. The largest ethnic group, the Zulu, is part of the Nguni groups, along with the Xhosa, Swazi, and Ndebele. Each of the groups developed its own distinctive beliefs and customs, expressed in dances, song, mime, and storytelling performances. Some examples include the Xhosa intsomi song and storytelling performance, the Zulu inganekwane and izibongo storytelling and praise poetry, and sefela oral poetry. All these traditions had an impact on the theatre that developed in the townships.

The Portuguese were the first Europeans to round the Cape of Good Hope, but the first European settlers were the Dutch, who arrived in 1652. In 1814, the British annexed the Cape, and, in 1843, they gained the Natal region. Thus began a series of clashes of European settlers with one another as well as with the indigenous peoples, exacerbated by the discovery of gold and diamonds in the interior. The European settlers brought in touring theatre companies, primarily from Britain. The Anglo-Boer War broke out between the British and the Dutch settlers in 1899; the Dutch were unsuccessful in gaining autonomy for the Transvaal and Orange Free State, which they occupied. The British victory led to the country's being granted home rule as the Union of South Africa; in 1961, it became the Republic of South Africa and seceded from the British Commonwealth, which it rejoined in 1995. The populace was divided into four racial groups: white, Indian, colored (mixed race), and black. Racial segregation was the rule, and the black population was generally disenfranchised, but in 1948, the Afrikaners, descendants of the Dutch settlers, gained governmental control of the country for the next forty-two years. They established apartheid as we know it, and this draconian system brought about new levels of resistance to it.

Eurocentric theatre was heavily supported by the prevailing government during the apartheid era; this theatre was intended to serve whites, as later codified through the Group Areas and Separate Amenities Act of 1965. This act banned putting racially mixed casts on stage and prohibited racially mixed audiences in the theatres. The emphasis in all of the educational institutions as far as drama was concerned was on white-authored plays.

Historically, some black South Africans did take an interest in amateur theatricals and playwriting, even though it was solely in the European tradition. In 1927, *Debeza's Baboons* by G. B. Sinxo, was published in Xhosa. That same year, Mthethwa's Lucky Stars became the first professional black troupe; they toured the country performing plays based on Zulu culture in the Zulu language. In 1935, *The Girl Who Killed to Save: Nongqause the Liberator*, based on a Xhosa legend, became the first play by a black South African to be published in English. Amateur dramatic societies grew up in the major cities. As the black population became even further segregated into townships, it further developed its own modern theatre tradition, syncretizing European with indigenous performance techniques. The most popular form became known as the "township musical." In 1959, a musical based on the life of a black boxer, *King Kong*, broke out of the township of Sophiatown to become an international hit. Later, Gibson Kente became one of the most successful black producers of township musicals.

As world opinion became more and more oppositional to South Africa's apartheid policies and the nation became more isolated, white South African playwrights began to build a substantial body of work on South African issues and themes. The government censored and banned artistic works it did not approve of (not to mention imposing imprisonment and/or exile), but a number of white South African artists resisted by forming a viable alternative-theatre movement. Athol Fugard (1932–) and the company of Black South African actors he worked with, the Serpent Players, were at the leading edge of this movement. It was Fugard who urged an international playwright's boycott against South Africa in 1963. In 1966, British Actors' Equity prohibited its members from performing in South Africa. Other prominent alternative theatres in white communities included the Space Theatre in Cape Town, founded by Fugard with Brian Astury and Yvonne Bryceland, and the Market Theatre, founded in Johannesburg by Mannie Manim and Barney Simon. During this period, the 1960s through the 1980s, scholar Temple Hauptfleisch identifies four basic types of theatre: a European tradition, a European-styled indigenous tradition, traditional indigenous performance forms, and what she calls "a crossover workshop tradition" (276). The crossover tradition is a combination of the other three, and informs many of the plays that became internationally successful, such as *Asinimali*, *Woza Albert*, and *Sarafina*.

During the 1960s and 1970s, the Black Consciousness Movement, partially inspired by the Black Arts Movement in the United States, and begun among black university students, led to a more militant political theatre that influenced black and white theatre practitioners. In 1972, Fugard partnered with John Kani and Winston Ntshona to create *Siswe Bansi Is Dead*. The play, presented in repertory with *The Island*, gained international recognition. Prior to *Sizwe Bansi*, Fugard wrote plays under his sole authorship, such as *The Blood Knot*, *Hello and Goodbye*, and *Boesman and Lena*. Though race and apartheid were apparent factors in the plays, Fugard has often stated that his writing is concerned with exploring the isolation and loneliness of the human condition; apartheid serves as a context. It is the universality in the plays that has outlasted apartheid, and causes them to continue to be produced in the present day.

The antagonist in *Sizwe Bansi Is Dead* is the pass book, which every black person must have. Without a properly stamped book, there is no possibility of movement, no chance of employment, no place of safety. In order to survive, Sizwe must change his name and take the identity of a dead man; even in the face of his dire circumstance, he is conflicted about the loss of his own identity. Finally, he accepts what he must do in order to survive. *Sizwe Bansi Is Dead* earned acclaim in Britain and the United States, and has often been performed since it premiered in 1974. Township dramas became powerful weapons in the antiapartheid movement. The impact of this particular play has proved long-lasting. In 2008, Kani and Ntshona returned to the United States to appear in their final revival of *Sizwe Bansi*, in the roles that garnered them Tony Awards (as opposed to when they were briefly jailed for the same performances in South Africa) for their 1974–1975 Broadway performances. Christopher Isherwood, the *New York Times* reviewer, lauded their powerful portrayals after the passage of over thirty years as "a moving coda to a remarkable, even historic collaboration." He also believed the play itself held up well, since it "was always more than agitprop" (*New York Times*, 11 April 2008).

Fugard had long before returned to authoring plays alone. During the 1980s, his best-known works included *Master Harold … and the Boys* and *The Road to Mecca*. As South Africa changed during the 1990s, he examined the escalating violence in the country in *My Children, My Africa!* and *Playland*. His latest play is *Coming Home* (2009). He is still writing, adding to a prodigious body of work that spans from 1956 to the present. During the apartheid era, internationally renowned musical performers, such as Miriam Makeba and Hugh Masekela, helped keep the issue of apartheid before the public. *Sarafina*, a musical by Mbongeni Ngema about young people and their courageous uprising in Soweto, became an international hit in 1989, and was made into a film starring Whoopi Goldberg in 1992.

South Africa's Postapartheid Theatre

The end of apartheid ushered in a period of high hopes, but also high anxieties for South Africa's future. For black South Africans, Nelson Mandela's presidential election in 1994 was the first in the nation's history in which they had been allowed to participate. In order to face the past and make way for the future, the process of the Truth and Reconciliation Commission was begun in 1995. With Archbishop Desmond Tutu as chair, the commission was charged to give the perpetrators of crimes associated with apartheid opportunities to confess and either gain amnesty or lighter punishment if prosecuted (the commission had no prosecutorial authority). Those who did not confess would bear the full weight of the law. One result would be that there could be no denial that torture and murder by agents of the apartheid South African government occurred. People could finally learn the truth about loved ones who had disappeared. There was also open discussion of violence perpetrated by black extremists. The fervent hope was that learning the truth would be enough to enable the black majority, the white minority, and the rendered all-but-invisible colored and Indian communities to focus on healing and putting the ghosts of the past to rest.[1] Archbishop Tutu handed in his final report in 1998. The jury is still out on the results; there is no consensus on whether this process was successful or unsuccessful.

Theatre practitioners wondered how to place this national drama in theatres. Would it be right for actors to mediate the real experiences of actual victims? How could any actor portray the reality as truthfully and as powerfully as an actual victim or witness? Would dramatizing the events of the TRC trivialize the process or help to illuminate it? Cole discusses two major theatrical events based on the TRC hearings. The first, *Ubu and the Truth Commission*, by Jane Taylor, is an adaptation of Alfred Jarry's absurdist satire, *Ubu Roi*, placed in a South African context. As in the original Ubu, puppets were used, but actors were also cast. The second, *The Story I Am About to Tell*, was presented by persons who actually testified before the TRC, and produced by Khulumani, a survivor support group. Like township theatre during the apartheid period, the powerful testimony was dramatic enough within itself that further theatricalization was hardly necessary. A need to look at the past through theatre was recognized, but how would this help to build a theatre for South Africa's present and future?

The Handspring Puppet Company, established in 1981 in Johannesburg, is the leading puppet theatre in South Africa; though it performs shows for children, it is primarily regarded as a major contributor to puppet theatre for adult audiences. (Currently, Handspring is greatly responsible for mounting the highly regarded play entitled *War Horse*.) A few of its best-known productions include *A Midsummer Night's Dream*, *Woyzeck on the Highveld*, and *Faustus in Africa*. *Ubu and the Truth Commission* has played at prominent theatres and theatre festivals since 1997 (Gilbert 28). William Kentridge is a visual artist who has collaborated with Handspring since 1992. Jane Taylor is a playwright, critic, and university professor who has worked with Handspring since 1996. Her latest work is a book, *Considering Forgiveness*. Her plays are often compared with the work of playwright Caryl Churchill. The puppeteers in the company span the racial and cultural spectrum of South Africa.

Playwright Zakes Mda, in his essay entitled "South African Theatre in an Era of Reconciliation," ponders the question of what will become of theatre in the new South Africa. He states that "the fear of memory exists…. A new identity at the expense of memory … is not feasible. Memory is vital to identity … but that does not mean we must cling to memory … and blame our own inertia and our present failures on a disadvantaged past, for that would make us perpetual victims of our past" (280). Memory must be a forge used to craft a new South African identity that is all-inclusive. At first, South African theatre floundered as it searched for that new identity. Under apartheid, it had been enough to report what was happening. Now the theatre had to, in a sense, start over. Again, it seems that Athol Fugard has served as a transitional figure in this process. In his drama, *Playland*, a white man who had killed a number of black people as a soldier under apartheid, and a black man released from a long prison sentence for killing a white man who had raped his fiancée, confront each other in an abandoned amusement park, which represents the old South Africa. At the end of the play, the men agree to leave the past behind and start new lives. Fugard also returned to the collaborative process, working with five teenage girls from different racial groups to present *My Life*, "an allegory for reconciliation," at the National Festival for the Arts in Grahamstown. Mda goes on to cite other plays with themes of reconciliation. He determines that the next phase for South African theatre belongs to younger theatre practitioners who were not mature at the height of the apartheid era. Experimentation with the workshop methods developed by the older generation produced new works that reflected the complexity of the new era.

Fong Kong, a play developed by students in the Market Theatre's theatre laboratory, examined the new dimension of xenophobia, based in old racial hierarchies, that had enveloped the nation: "In spite of themselves South Africans have internalised [sic] the values that place whiteness at the top of a pyramid … and at the bottom of the pile the indigenous black people … even more than the necessary reconciliation between black and white South Africans, there is a need for reconciliation among blacks themselves" (285). This, and other similar works, became popular throughout the nation. South African theatre practitioners are setting about the task of searching through the multiplicities of cultures that the nation is made of, including those that speak languages other than English and Afrikaans. Indeed, as stated in the *World Encyclopedia of Contemporary Theatre: Africa*, "Hundreds of texts in Zulu, Sotho, Xhosa and so on are never published …" (283). Mda, much like Ngugi wa Thiong'o, sees the future of South African theatre in terms of building a theatre of diversity through a multilingual theatre (South Africa has eleven official languages).

Mda also warned about the potentially negative influence of American culture. Fatima Dike (1948–), the first African woman to have a play published in South Africa (in 1977), posits a similar warning, in a humorous, satirical way, in *So What's New?* (If you have never watched an episode of *The Bold and the Beautiful*, check it out.) Her playwriting career began under apartheid, and in making the transition to a postapartheid society, she examines how everyday women try to cope with the uncertainty of a world of danger, difficult choices, and new possibilities.

Dike was born in Langa Township near Cape Town. An avid reader, she turned to poetry as her creative outlet. As a young adult, she became part of the Black Consciousness Movement. In 1975, she gained a position as assistant stage manager at the Space Theatre, where she was encouraged to write her first play. That play, *The Sacrifice of Kreli*, concerns an episode of Xhosa history in which a king went into exile to avoid enslavement by the British. The play was published, marking a milestone in the history of South African theatre. Dike's next play, *The First South African*, explored the issue of racial classification and identity. *The Crafty Tortoise*, a folktale for children, followed. In 1979, Dike wrote *Glass House*, the final play produced by the Space Theatre. There are only two characters in *Glass House*. In the first version, we see a white woman, the mistress of the house, and a black woman, who is the servant. It is a dark vision of apartheid, written partially in response to the terrible events of the suppression of the Soweto uprising in 1976. In 2001, Dike revisited the play, again using two characters, the daughters of the original two. It is Phumla, the black woman, who inherits the house. Linda, the white woman, learns to cope with this turn of events, and both work through their anger toward each other to continue their lifelong relationship on new terms. The play ends with them watching the inauguration of President Mandela on television together. It is clear that the glass house is South Africa.

In a 2007 article for the *New York Times* by Stephen Nunns, "Struggle for Relevance in Post-Apartheid Era," a younger playwright, James Ngcobo, calls for a South African theatre less bound to a theatre of political activism (often called "agitprop"). He would like to see stories that are more character driven, rather than issue driven: "When I was growing up, apartheid was only part of the story" (6). Though he believes that past problems and present challenges should not be forgotten or ignored, he hopes for more variety in the stories that are told. Since the South Africa of today and tomorrow is still in its infancy, it may take some more time for the South Africa of yesterday to recede to a more comfortable distance.

Theatre for Development and African Drama Today

We have not even been able to scratch the surface of the variety of theatre and theatrical expression in Africa. We have had to confine ourselves to a few representative scripted works. The relatively small number of dramatic works available in English are just the tip of the iceberg. We have not been able to see much of the great variety of theatre that is not literary per se (it is generally scripted by the oral tradition)—popular theatre forms such as Yoruba Traveling Theatre (Nigeria), Concert Party (Ghana), or Ngoma (Tanzania). We have not been able to witness storytelling performances, or attend any of the myriad ceremonies and festivals that bring communities together. We also have not discussed a theatre movement that had its most significant impact in the 1960s and 1970s, but is still used as educational theatre, Theatre for Development.

Jeyifo prefaces his essay, "The Reinvention of Theatrical Tradition," with a series of quotes that refer to coping with change and adaptation. The most significant, to me, is the statement by

Paulin Hountondji that debunks the idea that there is any such thing as a totally homogenous culture anywhere. Before the incursions of other cultures from the East and from the West, African cultures encountered and influenced one another. The same holds true for Old World Europeans and New World Americans. For a long time, the influence of African cultures on world culture was (sometimes intentionally, sometimes unintentionally) overlooked. Cultural communication works both ways.

During the 1960s, Brazilian sociologist Paolo Freire published *Pedagogy of the Oppressed*, which crystallized his approach to education as a tool to end oppression. His ideas empowered the disenfranchised to educate themselves through determining what their own educational needs are rather than to simply receive education from the dominant power that serves the power, not the oppressed. His ideas served as partial inspiration for Brazilian theatre practitioner Agosto Boal to develop the foundation for *Theatre of the Oppressed* (the title of his first book on the subject) as a means for people in need of change to determine for themselves what kind of change is needed and what should be done to effect that change. Theatre of the Oppressed was developed into several genres: forum theatre, invisible theatre, image theatre, newspaper theatre, and rainbow of desire. Forum theatre is closest to the root of Theatre for Development.

In forum theatre, the spectator/actor dichotomy is broken down. The participants are spect-actors. Usually, a scenario is presented, in which an act of oppression relevant to the spect-actors takes place. It ends with the oppressed unable to overcome the oppression. Then, the scenario is presented again. If the scenario was left open-ended, an open discussion among those present would follow. Sometimes trained performers are used. The spectators are still encouraged to participate and interact. The facilitator (in Boal parlance, the Joker), helps organize the process, but never tries to influence the ideas of the spect-actor. At any time, a spect-actor may step into the scene and replace a character, either to test out a solution or show that a suggested solution is unworkable. Ideas are tested until a practical approach or solution is found.

Young African educators, first from Swaziland and Botswana, then from all over Africa, recognized Theatre of the Oppressed as a means to communicate across class lines, across culture, language and educational differences, and to overcome apathy. Instead of being told what they needed and what should be done, the people who knew best what their needs really were could figure out for themselves practical approaches to meeting those needs. Theatre of the Oppressed became Theatre for Development. Rural communities were an especially desirable area of outreach. Facilitators were trained, usually in universities, to go into communities, gain the trust of the local authorities, and set up a Theatre for Development program.

As Kerr points out, one major problem that inhibited the movement was sponsorship. If a program is underwritten by an NGO, a foundation, or a government agency, whoever is paying the bills can proscribe what can be said and how it can be approached. One instance in which Theatre for Development worked was with the production of *I Will Marry When I Want*. The project was generated by the community. All who participated had a say in its creation. The result was a work so powerful and expressive that people came from miles around to see it. It frightened the government so much that Ngugi wa Thiong'o was imprisoned without charges or trial for a year, and the creative team that produced the work was driven into exile. The true efficacy of Theatre for Development has been questioned, but, as Kerr concludes, it is still of value as an educational tool. For example, its techniques have been used with great success, particularly in Uganda, for AIDS education.

In a 2006 keynote address to the Twentieth Convention of the Society of Nigeria Theatre Artists, Osofisan delivered some sobering thoughts. He entitled his speech, "Theatrical Life After the Generals: or, Nigerian Theatre in Search of a Lifeline." He notes the irony of the fact that when Nigeria was under the hammer of dictatorship, theatre flourished as a nexus of community solidarity and resistance. Under the democracy, new scripts and creative ideas have dwindled. Osofisan attributes what he sees as a crisis in theatre to several reasons. First, the nation has yet to recover from the economic damage the dictatorships caused. It costs too much to produce theatre that audiences cannot afford to attend. The theatre venues have been allowed to deteriorate, and are not being refurbished; new venues are not being built. The weak economy has caused an increase in crime to the extent that people are afraid to venture out at night. Second, the generation of theatre pioneers—Hubert Ogunde, Duro Ladipo, Ola Rotimi, and the like, have died; their deaths often meant the deaths of the theatre organizations they led. Third, there is the phenomenal rise of the Pentecostal Church; its services satisfy the need for theatricality, which it has incorporated into its liturgical processes. In addition, it frowns upon the secular theatre and discourages its patronage. Fourth, there is the rise of the home video/DVD industry, dubbed "Nollywood." The Yoruba Traveling theatre has migrated to the medium, and new artists are more interested in attaining success in the film industry than in enduring the grind of working and touring in live theatre.

Finally, Osofisan notes a generation gap. No longer are cultural touchstones shared. No longer can signification readily recognized by the older generation be taken for granted to speak to the young: "Nobody wakes the young people up with an oriki (praise poem) anymore; nobody sings them to sleep with a folktale; they no longer participate in the old festivals and ceremonies." The family and community structures have loosened. The influence of Western culture is pervasive among the young.

Though he sees the problem of insuring the survival of live theatre as daunting, Osofisan posits a solution:

> What we will need to do in order to keep our profession alive is to renew ourselves, and radicalise [sic] our art. We must find the language to speak to the new generation and get them back into the auditorium. This will mean finding new approaches to the production of the old plays, as well as creating new scripts to fit the temper of the times without however compromising or forsaking our belief in the capacity of art to enrich our community (xxv).

Cultural specifics aside, Osofisan's challenge to the theatre is a challenge to all the theatres of the world. Theatre must adapt to the needs of the people and be compelling in its means of communication to remain relevant. The discussion here should show us that African theatre is a theatre of culture, not of race (race being a social/political construction), that the many forms of African theatre and theatrical expression encompass the universality of the human condition, and that African theatre is a world theatre that walks alongside the other theatres of the world. It is hoped that Osofisan's prescription for its survival will be filled.

Notes:

1. The latest South African census, taken in 2001, shows a population of over 47 million people, with a racial/ethnic breakdown of 79.6 percent African, 9.1 percent white, 8.9 percent colored, 2.5 percent Indian/Asian. Nine of the eleven official languages are African.

Review Questions

1. What essential elements make up a traditional African performance?

2. Generally speaking, how did colonialism alter the way African drama was performed?

3. What problems or issues do African playwrights face when trying to write plays during the postcolonial period?

4. Why does there appear to be such an affinity between traditional African drama/performance and classical Greek drama/performance?

5. How has traditional performance influenced modern African drama?

6. What role has African feminism played in contemporary African drama?

Extra question for research: Ethiopia has a unique history, in terms of colonialism, among sub-Saharan African nations. In terms of that history, how was the development of theatre there different, in general, from that of other sub-Saharan African nations?

Selected Bibliography and Works Cited

Ampka, Awam. 2004. *Postcolonial Desires*. London: Routledge.
Banham, Martin, et al. 1999. *African Theatre in Development*. Bloomington: Indiana University Press.

Banham, Martin, and Jane Plastow, et al., eds. 2002. *African Theatre Women*. Bloomington: Indiana University Press.

Banham, Martin, et al., eds. 1994. *The Cambridge Guide to African and Caribbean Theatre*. New York: Cambridge University Press.

Banham, Martin, and Jane Plastow, eds. 1999. *Contemporary African Plays*. London: Methuen.

Banham, Martin. 2004. *A History of Theatre in Africa*. New York: Cambridge University Press.

Barber, Karin, et al. *West African Popular Theatre*. Bloomington: Indiana University Press.

Branch, William, ed. 1993. *Crosswinds: An Anthology of Black Dramatists of the Diaspora*. Bloomington: Indiana University Press.

Coger, Greta M. 1988. *Index of Subjects, Proverbs, and Themes in the Writings of Wole Soyinka*. New York: Greenwood Press.

Conteh-Morgan, John, and Tejumola Olaniyan. 2004. *African Drama and Performance*. Bloomington: Indiana University Press.

Crow, Brian, and Chris Banfield, eds. 1996. *An Introduction to Postcolonial Theatre*. Cambridge, England: Cambridge University Press.

Fugard, Athol. 1978. *Boesman and Lena and Other Plays*. Oxford; New York: Oxford University Press.

Fugard, Athol, John Kani, Winston Ntshona. 1976. *Sizwe Bansi Is Dead and The Island*. New York Viking Press.

Gibbs, James. 1986. *Modern Dramatists: Wole Soyinka*. New York: Grove Press.

Gilbert, Helen, ed. 2007. *Postcolonial Plays: An Anthology*. New York: Routledge.

Harding, Frances, ed. 2002. *The Performance Arts in Africa: A Reader*. London: Routledge.

Jeyifo, Biodun, ed. 2002. *Modern African Drama: Backgrounds and Criticism*. New York: W. W. Norton.

Kerr, David. 1995. *African Popular Theatre: From Pre-colonial Times to the Present Day*. Portsmouth, NH: Heinemann.

Ngugi wa Thiong'o. 1986. *Decolonising the Mind: The Politics of Language in African Literature*. Portsmouth, NH: Heinemann.

Ngugi wa Thiong'o. 1982. *I Will Marry When I Want*. Exeter, NH: Heinemann.

Olaniyan, Tejumola. 1995. *Scars of Conquest/Masks of Resistance: the Invention of Cultural Identities in African, African-American and Caribbean Drama*. New York: Oxford University Press.

Oni, Duro, and Ahmed Yerima, eds. 2008. *Trends in the Theory and Practice of Theatre in Nigeria*. Ibadan: Society of Nigerian Theatre Artists.

Onwueme, Osonye Tess. c.1997. *Tell It to Women: An Epic Drama for Women*. Detroit, MI: Wayne State University Press.

Onwueme, Osonye Tess. c.1993. *Three Plays*. Detroit: Wayne State University Press.

Perkins, Kathy A., ed. 2009. *African Women Playwrights*. Urbana: University of Illinois Press.

Perkins, Kathy A. 1998. *Black South African Women: An Anthology of Plays*. New York: Routledge.

Plastow, Jane, and Martin Banham, eds. 1999. *Contemporary African Plays*. London: Methuen.

Rotimi, Ola. 2003. *The Gods Are Not to Blame*. Ibadan, Nigeria: University Press.

Rubin, Don, et al., eds. 2001. *The World Encyclopedia of Contemporary Theatre: Africa*. London: Routeledge.

Soyinka, Wole. 1973. *Collected Plays*. London, New York: Oxford University Press.

Soyinka, Wole, and James Gibbs. 1980. *Critical Perspectives on Wole Soyinka*. James Gibbs, ed. Washington, DC: Three Continents Press.

Soyinka, Wole. 1976. *Myth, Literature, and the African World*. New York: Cambridge University Press.

Sutherland, Efua Theodora. 1987. *The Marriage of Anansewa ; Edufa: Two Plays*. Essex, England: Longman.

Wetmore, Kevin J. 2002. *The Athenian Sun in an African Sky: Modern African Adaptations of Classical Greek Tragedy*. Jefferson, NC: McFarland.

Chapter Thirteen

Introduction To Music In Africa

By AdéOlúwa Okùnadé

Introduction

The term music or its definition in the Western sense does not carry the same meaning in African society. What Africans consider music is more than the absolute music of the Europeans. The simple definition that comes to mind of an average European or Western-oriented music scholar is a "combination of sounds blended in a way that pleases the ears." Sounds, be they vocal or instrumental, are not the only materials that constitute music in Africa. In the real sense of what musical activities are in African society, one may not readily find the equivalent word of the idea of the "Western music." With this situation, it should be emphasized that the absence of a word in a particular language does not mean the absence of its concept; neither does it mean the absence of the particular ideology or behaviour characterized by that concept (Kofi Agawu 2003:2). What Africans then describe as "play" could adequately or comprehensively mean music. These "play activities" are sonic exhibitions in terms of drumming, dancing, miming, acting, singing, and sending messages. With all these, it is glaring that these may not constitute what music is in the Western sense, but the fact still remains that these are the materials that constitute the finished product that is called "music" in African society. This chapter therefore encourages the appreciation of the many nuanced ways in which this art called music is exhibited in Africa.

Again, John Blacking (1973:25) defined music as "sound that is organized into socially accepted patterns." The word "socially" here as used by Blacking connotes the appreciative involvement of both the artists and the audience, pointing to the music practiced in the African society being a community art. Each community in African traditional society has the cultural liberty to accept what music should be as the specified community chooses to define or measure it. Agawu, (2003:2) added that Blacking's submission does not "deny that crickets, frogs, and whales make music;" nor does it aim to obscure the fact that composers draw on "nonhuman" forces or aids, including various technological props. Students and other readers should therefore, understand the term African music within its context of having holistic characteristics, and not the connotative baggage carried by a term (music) that may seem merely conventional. The popular statement that African music is music made by Africans may not suffice.

Historical Perspective

Until recently, most societies within the African continent were not grouped together as Africans. The societies were living as distinct political units. (Nketia: 1988) One was Yorùbá, Luo, Ewe, or Masai. It was the emergence of European's and other foreign domination of the continent that made one to be Nigerian, Kenyan, Ghanaian, Senegalese, or Cameroonian (Agawu: 2003). The cultural variations of these societies were the factors responsible for the kinds of political units into which African peoples traditionally grouped themselves. Nketia (1988) submitted that:

> some [grouped themselves] as societies without centralized political institutions and others as societies with state systems. Many of the latter had flourished in ancient times, and some emerged as kingdoms and empires of considerable magnitude in different historical epochs. In West Africa, for example, the kingdoms of Ghana, Songhai … to be followed by the growth of forest states such as those of the Yorùbá, Benin, Dahomey, and Ashanti. (p. 5)

Though Africa is not as culturally homogenous as many have assumed, the degree of homogeneity in the music of the continent is quite high. Prevalent among the more common characteristics shared in the music of the different African peoples is repetition of stanzas or lines of songs. Such repetition is heard in responsorial singing, common in African music, in which a chorus responds to a lead vocalist on that leader's prompting is a form. Antiphonal musical performances are also widely found in African music. This is a performance of two groups or choruses in which one takes the lead and the other responds. This characteristic represents the heart of African society, revealing that communal living is the best way of being one's brother's keeper, and demonstrating that when all members of a society or community are involved in a project together, that project can be accomplished successfully. Musical activity in traditional African society is a community art.

While entertainment is not exotic in African music, most of the musical activities are highly educative. Music usually is used as an avenue to educate society members about various several issues. The younger members of the society are acquainted with the norms, values, and ethos of the society. Repeating lines of music makes the message easier to remember; it "sinks in" and becomes part of the inner being of the performers and the audience. This particular feature is used in African traditional medical practice as anesthesia when traditional surgery is needed. Ability with spontaneous composition and improvisation are typical of musicians in traditional African society. Again, audience participation is a key feature of African musical performance. The audience is not expected to be passive. Either the audience joins in the chorus or accompanies the performance with clapping, dancing, or praising the musicians by doling out monetary gifts. It should be added here that in the traditional African society, an average musician is a master of other sister arts. He is a historian, a composer, poet, costumier, and an instrumental technologist. He comfortably and professionally makes use of all these in his performance art.

Foreign Legacies

The interethnic wars of the precolonial era among African states brought in a lot of acculturation traits that led to cultural evolutions among the societies. These can all be regarded as internal factors, since they emerged on African soil. There were also external factors that influenced the direction of the cultural growth among these African states. Some of these foreign interjections led to the legacy of Islam and the legacy of Europe establishing themselves as strong influences in a "new Africa." Africa interacted commercially with the countries of the Mediterranean and the Near East, as well as with Southeast Asia (Nketia, 1988:9). References to Africa in Indian and Chinese manuscripts show that in the precolonial era there were trade connections with these countries as well. Nketia (1988) recorded that the societies of Africa that interacted with peoples of other lands included those of the East Horn (Somalia and Ethiopia), whose proximity to the civilizations of Egypt and the Mediterranean as well as Arabia is reflected in its cultures and ethnic composition. Others were eastern Africa, where Arab traders were active and penetrated the interior as far as Congo, and where Afro-Arabic interaction was so strong that it stimulated the growth and spread of Swahili as lingua franca; the island of Malagasy, the scene of Malayan, Indonesian, and African interaction; and the Sudanic belt of West Africa, which interacted with the Islamic northern region of Africa.

The influence of Islamic and Arabic cultures became a force to reckon with for many of the cultures of these areas, particularly on those of the savannah belt of West Africa, the coastal belt of eastern Africa, and Sudan. Though the importation of Islamic and Arabic cultures took its toll on the musical traditions of many of these societies, some still maintained their musical traditions. In most parts of West Africa, the converts did not totally abandon their traditional music, even when they still showed excitement with their new knowledge in Islamic cantillation of Arabic music. However, the northern Sudan and the Mediterranean littoral region, which was occupied by Bedouin Arabs who interacted with the Berbers, adopted Arabic musical traits. This is strongly evidenced in their musical instruments among which one finds instruments such as lutes, reed pipes, and long trumpets already integrated with local instruments. It was easier for these instruments to be adapted into the local system because they could be made with local materials. In some cases the terms and customs associated with the instruments were also adapted for local use (e.g., tablae, bendair, gbaita).

Some other musical traits that were adopted by these societies included features of vocal technique identified with Islam cantillation, such as voice projection and its accompanying mannerism of cupping the ear with the palm of the hand, or a slight degree of ornamentation. The Europeans, on the other hand, became colonial masters, and used religion to propagate their ruling styles to the extent that the church preached more of Western values and branded African cultural values idolatrous. This hostility was strengthened by the church's contention that drumming could not be permitted in the church because it was considered "paganistic." The introduction of Western education resulted in more converts with great musical talent. Schoolchildren would frequently be found singing not only in their school choir but also in the church choir. It was in vogue to have an African as the head teacher from Monday to Friday, and find him as the catechist and organist on Sunday.

This innovation was accepted, and it became the norm that the converts had high regard for Western instruments, especially the harmonium-organ, which was more prominent in the church, and the upright piano found in a few concert halls at the urban centers. The condemnation received over the use of traditional African instruments by the colonial masters via the missionaries was so strong that even the Ethiopian church, established in the fourth century, was also affected. In some cases, converts were not only discouraged from using the instruments; they were also discouraged from watching or taking part in local festivals. However, even though the effects of these legacies still exist and are very visible, the emergence of the activities of the Pan-Africanists really brought a high level of liberation from the shackles of these legacies.

Musical Instruments

There are several generic names for musical instruments in Africa. Most societies categorize their musical instruments primarily according to the sounding materials or techniques of sound production. For instance, in describing the musical instruments of the Igbo of southeastern Nigeria, Nzewi (1989) added that the sociocultural musical importance is given prominence when classifying musical instruments. He categorized them into four groups. The first group is made up of the most popular and varied instruments, the wooden, metal, and membrane instruments, all of which are classified as melorhythm instruments (instruments that are capable of performing melodic and rhythmic roles). The second in importance are blown instruments that produce melody or phonic effects. The third group includes the shaken and pot instruments that play percussive roles in ensembles. The fourth and last group contains the plucked (soft toned) melody instruments played primarily as solo instruments. While all these features abound in African societies, for the purpose of this reading, the Horbonstel and Sachs (1914) description of African instruments, a description that is universally and conventionally accepted, shall be used. This description includes four categories of classification: the idiophone, membranophone, aerophone, and chordophone.

Idiophones

The most common of instruments in Africa are idiophones. These are instruments that produce sound without any additional materials or support of any other materials. They are self-sounding instruments found almost everywhere in African societies. Environmental, occupational, and historical factors play an important role in the selection of instruments among societies. For instance, "mobile" or nomadic societies do not use drums, but they are content with the use of sticks and other handy implements as instruments. These instruments are used as percussive instruments. It should be mentioned here that some of the idiophone instruments are not restricted to music making; they may equally be used for sending messages or for reinforcing verbal communication. In some societies, they are used to emphasize steps of initiation during rites or special functions. Appropriate idiophones are also used for scaring birds away from newly plowed fields or for marking the movements of cattle and other animals (or even domestic boards) that need to be watched or identified. (Nketia, 1988:69) Musically, the two major categories of idiophones are rhythmic and melodic.

Among the rhythmic idiophones, the most common and widely used are shaken idiophones, which are mostly rattles. This category can again be subdivided into two major groups of primary and secondary rattles. Primary rattles are held in the hand and played, while secondary ones get activated by the movements of the performers who wear them or attach them to other instruments as modifiers. A good example of a primary rattle is the gourd rattle that most times appears as a container rattle or as a rattle surrounded by nets of cowries, pieces of bones, shells, bamboo shoot, metal or beads. Among the largest rattles are the sekere of the Yorùbá of southwest Nigeria and the Nago of the Benin Republic. Other types of primary rattles are used to strike idiophones such as the wooden slit drum made out of a hollowed log of wood, a part of which is slit open to provide it with a pair of "lips" that can be struck with beaters. The melodic rattles are tuned idiophones, of which there are two types—the mbira or sansa (hand piano) and the xylophone. These instruments are not only melodic instruments; they also simulate drumming in ensemble performances.

Membranophones

Membranophones are drums with parchment heads. Emphasis on percussive instruments in Africa is exhibited in the use of membranophones as the art of drumming is an agelong tradition in African societies. The drum ranges from simple makeshift types played by women in ritual contexts, to specially constructed ones usually with decorated objects of art. As mentioned earlier, some of these instruments have generic names. For various hourglass-shaped pressure drums of the Yorùbá of southwestern Nigeria, the generic name is dùndún, and all membrane drums found of different types and varieties among the Igbo of southeastern Nigeria are called Igbá. The use of tins, light oil drums, and other such materials are found in Ghana in West Africa, and Kenya in East Africa. There are still drums made of skin in these countries, such as in Ghana where the atumkapan drums are made of skin. Drums in Africa are made in a wide variety of shapes; some may appear in conical, cylindrical, or semicylindrical form. Some of the drums are open-ended, that is, open at one end and closed at the other end. Others are double-headed drums, or drums with appropriate skins at both ends. In some societies, the open-ended drums are melorhythm instruments with a range of pitch tones that depend on the size of the drum (Nzewi: 1991:64).

It is important to add that though a wide variety of drums exists in Africa, each society still specializes in a small number of drum types. Hourglass-shaped drums are found in both eastern and western Africa; however, many of those examples found in eastern Africa are single-headed and when two heads are used, they are not handled as they are in West Africa as tension drums.[2] In addition to musical uses of membranophones, their sound production also functions as a speech surrogate or as a call or signal of something such as a warning. Other uses of drums for nonverbal communication occur in few societies as noted by Nketia (1988), which make special drums for symbolic and representational purposes. A good example of this is the etwie friction drum of the Akan community of Ghana, which, thought to imitate the snarl of the leopard, it is therefore played to extol the might and majesty of the king. Other drums are considered sacred and are treated as such in Africa. Most of these drums are kept in special places and have specialists who are in charge. Among the Yorùbá, in southwestern Nigeria, the gbèdu drums are royal drums that are only meant for the use of kings. The drums cannot be used without the approval of the king.

Aerophones

Aerophones are wind instruments grouped into three categories: the flute, horns and trumpets, and reed pipes. The first category, the flute, includes instruments of the family made from materials such as bamboo, stalks of millet, or materials carved out of wood. Among the Igbo of southeastern Nigeria, is found the oja, a notched flute commonly used in pairs, though of different sizes, and of different ranges of notes. There are flutes of a narrow compass that form an ensemble and play in hocket[3] technique to get a wider compass. There are other flutes such as panpipes that are available among a few societies such as the Soga of Uganda, the Yombe of Zaire, and the Pedi of South Africa.

There is a heavy presence of horns and trumpets in several societies. Animal horns and elephant tusk are designed as trumpets to be side-blown. There are some made of either bamboo or metal, such as the Ethiopian malakat, which at times are protected with leather or skin. The last type of aerophone found in Africa is the reed pipe, which is not as widespread as the first two mentioned. The single-reed type exists in the savannah belt of West Africa; northern Ghana, Benin, and Chad. The double-reed instruments are also found in eastern Africa along the coast of Kenya and Tanzania, areas especially marked by Islamic tradition. These are also found in Northern Nigeria.

Chordophone

These are simply string instruments found in African societies of which the musical bow is the most common. There are also mouth bows for which the mouth serves as the resonator. There are also bows with calabash, where the resonator is through the hollow portion. The one-string fiddle in Africa falls into this category as well. Notable among this group is the goje found among the Hausa of Nigeria, the Songhai and Djerma of Niger, and the Damgoba of Ghana. Another type of one-string fiddle found in eastern and Central Africa is called the sese, a tube fiddle found among societies in Zaire, Kenya, and Tanzania.

Recruitment and Training

Recruitment of musicians is paramount in traditional African society, especially when the roles involved demand specialization. In the case of solo performers, no recruitment is needed, as a solo performer may come from a lineage of practiced soloists, and he will have started learning by rote from childhood. The most important thing to such a family is continuity. Members of a royal ensemble in most cases come from designated families within the community. There are designated families among the Yorùbá people saddled with provision of musicians for the kings. In some cases it may be only one family that takes the responsibility, while in others, it may be more than one. Where it is more than one, the concerned families can collaborate and feature musicians at the palace from time to time (Okunade, 2010). Among the Dagomba society of northern Ghana, the son of every player of the hourglass drummer is expected to become a drummer. The female children are also expected to release any of their sons to join the family drummers. If the drummer's daughter has no male child, then one of her daughters is expected to marry a drummer.

This system makes recruitment continuous and enhances continuity of the art. In terms of training, it is believed that since music in Africa is a community art, those who belong to the art must have been exposed through social interaction that demands exhibition of various skills on instruments at one time or another. This is one of the reasons why community members are not discouraged from active participation during performances. Children also learn from a tender age by following the adult members of the ensemble on outings, either by carrying their instrument for them en route to the performance, or by playing along on their own musical instrument customized for their age. The African mother sings to her child and introduces the art and skill to the child from the cradle. A systematic or formalized way of training is not used in training musicians in the society. Nketia's following statement (1988) buttresses this:

> This endowment could include innate knowledge, for according to the Akan, "One does not teach the blacksmith's son his father's trade. If he knows it, then it is God who taught him."… The organization of traditional music in social life enables the individual to acquire his musical knowledge in slow stages and to widen his experience

of the music of his culture through social groups into which he is gradually absorbed and through the activities in which he takes part. (pp. 59–60)

Since specialization in several musical instruments runs through various families, children are exposed to training at an early age. Hugh Tracey (1948) affirms this:

A father will take his seven- or eight-year-old boy and sit him between his knees while he plays. The boy will hold the two beaters with his arms well-flexed and pliant while the father claps his hands over his son's and continues to play in the usual way. (p. 108)

This is part of the rudiments of training the child goes through before he moves on to other stages. All stages are through live performance experience. In the case of royal musicians, children or members of the designated families who aspire to become royal musicians live in the palace with the older musicians who in most cases are members of the same family. Clearly, the learning of a musical instrument or its art in African traditional society is an interactive performance experience, while performance is a never-ending learning experience.

African Music as Musical Art

In the introduction, we stated that the concept of music in traditional African society is different from that of the Europeans or Western world. The term musical arts represent wholly the performance arts disciplines of music, dance, drama, poetry, and costume, which are seldom separated in creative thinking and performance in African cultures. However, each of these arts has its own distinctive features in every culture area. Because artistic expressions are deeply rooted in culture, interdisciplinary exhibitions therefore find their way conveniently within the terrain of music in Africa. Because most songs reflect the cultural practices of members of the society, and transmit the same through oral history fashioned in an acceptable way within the musical presentations, this has made poetry an integral part of the musical arts. Among the Yorùbá of Nigeria, the royal musicians are expected to know the praise poetry of all the kings of the past and present. They are supposed to be fluent about it and capable of a perfect delivery. This is also an integral part of the art that cannot be deleted nor separated within the performance.

Dance and music maintain a genuine symbiotic relationship. Through dance gestures, Africans connect with both the music and the related event. Akosua (Addo et al., 2003:239). Music is used to evoke a spiritual experience over the dancers, and for this reason music and dance have become interwoven at all levels of performance. Where it is not dance proper, it is movement of some sort. Audience participation in African music includes dancing by members of the audience. There are other arts that implicate cultural meanings that are totally exhibited in musical arts. Body arts, for instance, are depicted and displayed on the arms and torso, including face makeup worn on the body of the performers. In some cases, headdresses, which are symbolic, are also part of the features of musical arts performance. For instance, in southwest Nigeria, the gelede headdress represents the aesthetic of Yorùbá womanhood as expressed in the elaborate tying of stiff pieces of fabric. Most African musical instruments have aesthetic, symbolic, and functional drawings (artwork) on their body. An average African instrumentalist is an instrumental technologist, because he knows when and how to maintain his instruments. This is one of the attributes of a professional musician in African traditional society. An average musician is seen as master of all arts that are embedded in the musical arts performances.

Chapter Summary

In this chapter the concept of African music had been discussed and some of its features mentioned. The foreign influence on this music was also touched upon. Instruments with unusual generic and technical names were mentioned along with a description of their appearance and use or function. The mode of recruitment and training in traditional African society was discussed. The chapter ended with a presentation of the holistic concept of the music as a performing art by reiterating the "christened" name of the art; the musical arts of Africa have an integrated nature with the other arts that also become incorporated into the musical presentations and performances of Africa. While the author has not exhausted all discussion about African music, this chapter, it is hoped, has served to open up the concept and idea of African music, and perhaps encourage further exploration.

Notes:

1. See Helen E. Hause, "Terms for Musical Instruments in the Sudanic Languages: A Lexicographical Inquiry," *Journal of the American Oriental Society*, Supplement 7(1948)1–73.

2. Tension drums are double-headed drums whose heads are held together by a number of thongs from one head to the other. (See more in Nketia, J. H. K. "The music of Africa" 1988, [85–86]).

3. This is a method whereby lines of melody are shared by many instruments or performers who take turns playing on their limited-pitch instruments.

Review Questions.

1. How best would you describe African music, considering its peculiarities in the realm of performing arts?

2. Give two examples each from the family of instruments in African music.

3. What is your understanding of the "rote" learning method as it affects the training of musicians in African traditional society?

4. Identify three major characteristics of African music and discuss them.

Bibliography

Agawu, Kofi. 2003. "Defining and Interpreting African Music." In Anri Herbst, Meki Nzewi, and Kofi Agawu, eds. *Musical Arts in Africa: Theory and Practice*. South Africa: Unisa Press.

Agordoh, Alexander. A. *African Music: Traditional and Contemporary*. 2005. New York: Nova Science Publishers.

Agu, Dan C. C. 1999. *Form and Analysis of African Music*. Enugu, Nigeria: New Generation Books.

Akosua Obuo Addo, Florence Miya, and Hetta Potgieter. 2003. "Integrating the Arts." In Anri Herbst, Meki Nzewi, and Kofi Agawu (Eds), *Musical Arts in Africa: Theory and Practice*. South Africa: Unisa Press.

Bebey, Francis. 1999. *African Music: A People's Art*. Chicago: Lawrence Hill Books.

Blacking, John. 1973. *How Musical Is Man?* Seattle: University of Seattle Press.

Hornbostel, E. M., and Curt Sachs. 1914. "Classification of Musical Instruments." Zeitcschrift fur Ethnologie, XLVI.

Nketia, J. H. Kwabena. 1988. *The Music of Africa*. London: Victor Gollancz.

Nzewi, Meki. 1991. "Musical Practice and Creativity: An African Traditional Perspective." IWALEWA-Haus. University of Bayreuth.

Okunade, A. A. 2010. "Comparative Study of Court Music in Ègbáland, Ogun State, Nigeria." An Unpublished Doctoral Thesis, Institute of African Studies, University of Ìbàdàn, Nigeria.

Stone, Ruth M. 2000. *The Garland Handbook of African Music*, Volume 1. New York: Taylor and Francis.

Tracey, Hugh. 1948. *Chopi Musicians: Their Music, Poetry, and Instruments*. London.

Waterman, Christopher. 1992. "Africa." In Sadie (ed). *New Grove Dictionary of Music and Musicians*. Vol. 1, London: Macmillan.

Chapter Fourteen

Indigenous, Colonial, And Postcolonial Perspectives On African Sports And Games

By Jepkorir Rose Chepyator-Thomson and Kipchumba Byron

Introduction

African sporting culture is interwoven into the fabric of life and is complexly influenced by geography, history, religion and economics, as well as by social-class dynamics and variations in ethnicity. The continent's rich indigenous sporting culture is elucidated with diverse plays, games, and sports that can be broadly termed movement cultures. Africa's richness in movement cultures is indicated in the presence of physical culture discovered through archaeology, and in the evidence of diverse physical activities that punctuate the lives of people on the continent. The purpose of this chapter is to discuss sports and games in Africa during the following periods: the precolonial period, termed indigenous Africa, the colonial period, and the postcolonial era, often referred to as the postindependent period in Africa.

Indigenous Sports and Games in Precolonial Africa

Many people from diverse ethnic groups took part in play activities, and competitive and recreational games and sports, an occurrence widespread across the continent. The utilization of physical activities in the form of games and sports followed customary functions and needs for individual and social development. Games formed an integral part of a child's education, providing children with a way to function adequately in their sociocultural milieu. According to Kenyatta (1938), participation in games in culture promoted not only the physical development of the children and the youth (Kenyatta, 1938) but also "social interactions among children of different ages and same age-groups" (Chepyator-Thomson, 1990; Chepyator-Thomson, 1999, 37). Girls' and boys' involvement in games and sports followed customary age divisions (initiated versus noninitiated), with the children's participation in games and sports modeled after adults' sport involvement (Chepyator-Thomson, 1986). The Watutsi people of Rwanda and Burundi are known for their great jumping. Early visitors on expedition across the eastern region of Africa found Tutsi athletes engaged in a high jumping event, and apparently, the event served as an entry into adulthood (Bale & Sang, 1999). Among the !Kung of southern Africa, "children imitate vital adult activities in active play, which are very entertaining to watch,… but also engage in many games that boys and girls play separately with dance and song being played together" (Marshall, 1965, p. 264).

Indigenous dances were associated with sporting activities (Ndee, 2010), and they served a significant function in society. According to Wandere (2006), the Kikuyu warriors were a spectacle in their demonstration of good health and physical fitness in community activities such as during initiation ceremonies, with the Akamba people also using Kelome dances that are performed with acrobatic movements that indicate participants' health and strength. As Williams (2207) expressed, indigenous dances "affirm and perpetuate ways of life and beliefs that are important to the specific peoples to whom they belong" (p. 111). Indeed, throughout the continent, dances serve as attempts "to classify, categorize, and explain a people's attempts to embody their knowledge about life experience using movement, color, shape and sound metonymically derived from other creatures and from nature (Williams, 2007, p. 112).

Many African people engaged in a variety of physical activities that incorporate many aspects of the daily lives of the people, serving to educate the young men and women through specific games and sports for socialization and recreation purposes (Ndee, 2010). Most women participated in traditional sports that were mostly unique to each ethnic group in the continent. The sports activities were often associated with initiation, wedding, and harvest ceremonies (Chepyator-Thomson, 2005). For example, during the precolonial period in Kalenjin society, women's participation in traditional sports was interwoven into the cultural and economic production, and sport activities were localized for competitive and recreational purposes (Chepyator-Thomson, 1990).

Hunting and recreational activities of the earliest inhabitants of eastern Africa are recorded in rock paintings, with scholars documenting them in the form of pictographs (Ndee, 2010). Sports such as spear throwing and archery were used for hunting and training for war (Ndee, 2010). Gikuyu men used jumping and long jump to prepare for war or to "display prowess and adroitness in handling the spears and shields" (Bale & Sand, 1999, p. 58). According to Kenyatta (1938), boys, as a part of the ceremony of initiation, ran "two miles to a sacred tree with great excitement as if they [were] going to battle raising their spears ready to throw them over the sacred tree. The one who reached the tree first and threw the wooden spear over the tree … became the leader and spokesperson for that particular age-group … for life" (p. 140). For the Keiyos of Kenya, a hoop and stick throwing game where one team had hoops and the other had sticks sharpened at one end was used to develop perceptual motor skills critical to developing one's strength and coordination and honing skills to hunt wild game. In most games of hunting, people used "bows, spears, javelins, and different kinds of traps" (d'Hertefelt, 1965, p. 411).

Sport involvement was associated with initiation, wedding, or harvest ceremonies (Chepyator-Thomson, 2005) or with other social practices that included the gathering of food, hunting wild game, pastoral activities and interethnic conflicts (Amusa & Toriola, 2010).

Wrestling contests were widespread across Africa. During the season of the harvest, the sport of wrestling was popular among young men in Africa and was used to bring honor to one's ethnic group community as Chinua Achebe (1959) richly described in his book, *Things Fall Apart*, or to mark one out for leadership during initiation activities as Jomo Kenyatta (1938) discussed in his book, *Facing Mount Kenya*. Among the Meru people in Kenya, wrestling contests among boys from neighboring communities, accompanied with music and dance, occurred regularly (Wandere, 2006).

In Chinua Achebe's (1959) book, *Things Fall Apart*, Okonkwo, the main character, was well-known throughout the nine villages, and he brought honor and prestige to his people by becoming the great wrestler who was unbeaten for seven years. Indeed, Okonkwo became, at an early age, the greatest wrestler of all time, and he was among attendees at the New Yam Festival, a high-caliber wrestling competition in the region. As portrayed in *Things Fall Apart* (pp. 40, 46–47, 49–50), the New Yam festival was celebrated with great joy with the second day of the festival being reserved for great wrestling matches. The whole village—women, men and children—turned out to witness the occasion. The drummers "sat in front of the huge circle of spectators facing the elders" (Achebe, 1959, p. 46), and the grandees sitting on stools in front of the circle. The three mean beat seven drums, arranged according to size along wooden basket. And to warm up the crowd, two teams with three boys per bout for three total bouts wrestled to set the scene for the real sportsmen.

Succinctly put, indigenous sports were interwoven into the cultural and economic production of African societies (Chepyator-Thomson, 1990). Particular examples include "the Maasai [people] of East Africa, the Zulu [people] of South Africa, the Yoruba [people] of West Africa sub-region, and the Tuareg and Bedouin [people] of North Africa who evolved traditional games, sports and plays [that were used for] socialization, initiation, ceremonial, recreation, chieftaincy, and coronation purposes" (Amusa, 1999; Amusa & Toriola, 2010, p. 669). A widely accepted concept is that sports and games in African societies bind people together (Amusa & Toriola, 2010) and provide a medium through which learners can reach their optimal potential cognitively and socially, as seen through, for example, indigenous Zulu games, which promote ethnic understanding, positive self-concept, and social skills (Roux, Burnett & Hollander, 2008).

An example of indigenous sports and games is nyunga, a game that the Kalanga and Tonga people of Zimbabwe and the Ngoni people of Malawi engage in; both boys and girls can play the game (Gundani, Makaza, Tapera, Amusa, & Banda, 2010). The authors went on to explain that in the Nyunga game, a player throws a clay figurine into a pool of water in a pond or any other surface of water, and when the figurine hits the water, it makes a small splash and then ripples off. According to Gundani, Makaza, Tapera, Amusa, and Banda (2010), the clay figurine path is aerodynamic, and all watch as it reaches maximum flight, with its tapered end facing downward and the base upward until it reaches the water surface. The idea is to ensure the figurine has a "smooth trajectory" so that it hits the water with the tapered end first and makes a distinctive sound as it lands facedown with the smallest splash and ripples (Gundani, Makaza, Tapera,

Amusa, & Banda, 2010). The importance of the game to the people is explained in the following quotation:

> There is social cohesion within the community of youths as all participate as players or as spectators cheering their teams. The determination of a winner by agreement inculcates skills of negotiation and the value of respecting other people's views. Participation by the youths ensures continuity of the recreation activities as part of cultural inheritance" (Gundani, Makaza, Tapera, Amusa, & Banda, 2010, p. 443).

Board games were widely popular across many ethnic groups on the continent. According to Markham (1942), as a child in Kenya, she played games that included board games with children her age. She provides the following description:

> There were quiet days when Kibii and I played, all during the long afternoon, a game that took me months to learn and having forgotten it, I could never learn again. I remember only that we used the little poisonous yellow Sodom apples for counters and a series of round holes in the ground for our board, and that the mental arithmetic required was more than I have since used in twenty years (p. 103).

Other ethnic groups, such as the Keiyo people of Kenya, played the Kechui game, a challenging indigenous numeracy game similar to Kalah, a board game played in Ethiopia. Kalah, an all-around numerical teaching aid, is closely connected with "development ... of numeration ... and concept of number[ing]" (Haggerty, 1964, p. 330) in Africa.

An overall statement of games in African societies is that they "strengthen language skills, listening skills, and judgment skills" (Lyoka, 2007, p. 353) and promote skills associated with a variety of numeracy, cooperativeness, and critical thinking. Sports inculcate cultural and social skills that allow children and the youth to adequately prepare for adulthood. Indeed, physical activities that include variation in games and sports prepared boys and girls to be responsible adults (Ndee, 2010).

The Impact of Colonialism on African Games and Sports

The early people to trek the continent were European explorers and missionaries, who used tenets of Christianity and civilization to colonize Africans. The colonial period (from 1885 to the independent period) represents the start of de-indigenization of African sports and games, and it also displays the marriage between indigenous and European sports and games. The impact of Western culture is seen through the introduction of European sports and games into African societies (Ndee, 2010), leading to the eradication or devaluation of movement activities that were wholly African, and to the display of those activities that were wholly European. For instance, the "meeting of the British and Keiyo people led to the eradication of unique children's games, but the games that both groups shared remained intact" (Chepyator-Thomson, 1990, p. 23).

Indeed, the introduction of British games and physical culture to the colonies negatively impacted indigenous physical activities, with school sports and clubs serving as instruments of socialization into European ideals of sport (Ndee, 2000; Amusa & Toriola, 2010). Through colonial administrators, settlers, and missionaries, Africans were socialized into Europeans ways of life, with missionary schooling acting as the primary agent of change. The missionaries considered sports and games to be useful in the establishment of positive contact with the African people (Hokkanen, 2005). The striking element of the colonial period system of education was the lack of relevance to the cultures and values of indigenous populations (Amusa & Toriola, 2010, p. 666).

Sport was introduced to Africans through mission schools as far back as the seventeenth century. Christian missionaries introduced European sports such as cricket, soccer, and rugby, helping them to spread Christian religion to the African people. They also thought of sports as being generally beneficial to society as thus they actively sought ways to promote Western sports like boxing and basketball. It is not surprising to find boxers who are devout Christians. Boxing became the mainstay for urban men, a sport that was considered to be an "equalizer of sorts" because all men, regardless of class, ethnicity, level of education, or occupation, could engage in the sport, and it required very little equipment (Fleming, 2011).

The establishment of boarding schools ensured successful adaptation of a variety of sports in the colonies. Sport was a significant instrument of moral training as it inculcated the spirit of fair play in the context of athletics competition. Missionaries considered sports and games to be useful in the establishment of positive contact with the African people (Hokkanen, 2005). For instance, Scottish missionaries introduced the sports of cricket and rugby, achieving great success in the sport of soccer through mission schools that helped foster games and an associated games ethic in Central Africa of the late nineteenth and early twentieth century (Hokkanen & Mangan, 2006). European governments used administrators and missionaries in the colonies to institute European sports as a form of leisure in missionary and government-sponsored schools, with African indigenous games and sports being left out of the curriculum (Amusa & Toriola, 2010). Their objective was to use sport as a tool to enhance their sporting traditions, with indigenous sports being severely restricted since Africans did not have these sporting traditions; neither did they have the necessary finances nor leisure time to take part in them (Godia, 1989).

Preparation of African children for adulthood was best completed through the mission schools' focus on moral, mental, and physical training education, making sports to serve the "civilizing" mission of the British Empire, with football being made "a part of the imperial civilizing process" (Hokkanen & Mangan, 2006, p. 1267). For instance, Germany colonized Tanzania in 1885 and brought in new games and sports such as football and gymnastics into the country; evidence of such involvement in play has been found in archives and schools (Ndee,

2010). The German system of physical education cemented the introduction of Western sport replete with marching drills and gymnastics exercises (Ndee, 2010). When the British took over Tanzania from the Germans in 1914, athleticism characteristic of the English public school was introduced, with British games being spread through the medium of education (Ndee, 2010). Since the British had about 50 percent under its tutelage, English sports occupied a superior position to impact African sporting traditions, with the sports of cricket and hockey being popular in Kenya, Nigeria, and Ghana (Bottenburg, 2001).

In the context of French Africa, under the term "French Union," school games were in operation in French Africa, starting in 1952, and in 1959, Inter-State games began. In 1960, Community Games, which were modeled after the Olympic Games, were held in Antananarivo, Madagascar's capital. This served as the first international meet that had African male athletes both from schools and from the general public competing against the French sporting teams from overseas departments and territories (Combeau-Mari, 2011). But the international meet turned out to be a de facto celebration of Madagascar (which had received independence three days before the opening of the games) and the French colonies. While the Community Games can be considered an overhanded positive gesture from the French—friendly games in the spirit of the Olympic motto of peace and equality among people in the hope of retaining positive relations with French Africa—they can also be considered as underhanded because, at the same time that French African colonies are receiving independence, the French were winning the games in grand style. The French press confirmed this, indicating the "the French should have the upper hand.… They did not surrender a single title.…" (Combeau-Mari, 2011, p. 1721). The French supremacy at the international meet centered on the following perspective:

> The competitions revealed the huge discrepancy between the sporting abilities of the French and African athletes. Due to their late discovery of such disciplines, and lack of infrastructure and facilities, the Africans could not expect to overcome their disadvantage against France's 50-year head start (p. 1721).

Africanization of European Sports

The black population in South Africa saw the sport of boxing as a way to survive urban environments, helping make boxing a symbol of urban sophistication (Fleming, 2011). Indeed, in the South African city of Johannesburg, the African people from across social class and ethnic lines embraced the sport of boxing as a way to uplift the black race, clearly evident in the promotion of ideals related to independence, self-defense, respectability and discipline in sport (Fleming, 2011). Boxing became a symbol of urban sophistication.

Africanization of football through youth's ingenuity and brilliant minds surfaced in fields of play. The youth responded to their cultural and social needs in creating new rules and game strategies in football. For example, chandimu, a game played among the male youth in Tanzania, is considered liberal. This is because the distance of the pitch can be standard or just an open, undefined space, the number of the players varies, a referee is not necessary, the material used to make the ball is different, and team uniforms are differentiated with "no shirts" for one team and shirts for the other team, and only darkness or a time convenient to all ends the game (Ndee, 2010). This is indicative of young people's creativity at mastering their environment through sporting activities.

European Sports in the Postcolonial Period in Africa

The postcolonial period refers to the postindependent time in Africa. During this time, sport served as a vehicle for social change, and it was most often used as "a vehicle for, and an index of, the growing juridico-cultural importance of human rights and the greater relevance of human-kind" (Giulianotti, 2005, p. 216). Sport participants have emerged, having become well-known in the world of sport in the postcolonial era. As the pride of Africa, sports stars continue to be seen via the imported sport of soccer and via indigenous sports activities that survived colonial conditions as in athletics (track and field) (Thomson & Chepyator-Thomson, 2002, p. 73). Football, netball, and athletics have become the mainstay sports in Africa. In Kenya, Africans took part mainly in football, and European and Asian Africans engaged prominently in the game of cricket and hockey. While football was considered an inferior sport, a sport in which Africans mainly took part, rugby, cricket, polo, and squash were popularly taken up by the white sporting population.

Many women and girls took part in a gender-specific British game of netball, a sport played throughout the British Empire, from primary school to the university level. As Ndee (2010) points out:

> Netball, a game of British origin, has a major place in the sporting life of Tanzanian girls and women. It is played in all primary and secondary schools, colleges and universities and there are many teams affiliated with major sports clubs everywhere in the country. (Ndee, 2010, p. 749).

The postcolonial period has seen sports players and sports themselves attain a new identity, including political as well as a social identity spanning local, national, and international levels. For instance, in the 1998 World Cup Football, Cameroonian players sought a new identity for themselves, their nation, but also for the continent of Africa. The Cameroonian football players at the 1998 World Cup, where they were playing the French on their home ground, sought to create something tangible for themselves, for their country, to create a good and lasting memory not only for Cameroon but also for Africa. However, in the match against Chile, a Hungarian referee ruled the goal no good, destroying their hope of taking revenge on their former colonial power, the French (Vidacs, 2003).

To produce new identities that incorporate indigenous sporting cultures, the people of Tanzania adopted and adapted modern sport for their own cultural and political ends. Following independence, education was reformed "to enable learners to know, appreciate, and develop a Tanzanian culture that perpetuates the national heritage, individual freedom, responsibility, and tolerance and which pays respect to elders" while sport was expected, among other things, to develop general physical skills and sport-specific skills (Ndee, 2010, p. 750).

Sport has been used as symbol of unity, fostering grassroots and community integration. Countries diversified their sport participation through investment in sport development in order to strengthen competitiveness in national teams. Olympic Games provide the opportunity to compete and showcase the sporting abilities of the newly independent states and figuration of foreign policy projection. The postindependence sports' model configuration employed sports as agents of socioeconomic development to meet the political objective of unification of the states. For Kenya, the runners have not only placed the country on the world map but also they have inspired an entire nation to come together to build the state through their performances in the Olympic Games.

According to the Kenya government, the "remarkable achievements of our sportsmen and women have placed Kenya well and truly on the world map (Kanu Manifesto, 1992, p. 60). The president of Kenya (1978–2003), Daniel Toroitich Arap Moi, expressed that women faced many challenges but succeeded in participating in global running competitions, putting the continent on the world map and breaking world records against all comers (Kenya African National Union Policy Document of 1992). African women in athletics have rearticulated their family position in light of the postcolonial state of affairs to challenge established sports practices and achieve excellence in performance.

Sport as an Agent of Social Development

Basic involvement in sports draws from both intrinsic and extrinsic values, such as the desire to be active for leisure or competitive purposes. The continual involvement in any particular sport leads to greater development of skills as well as to the desire to play competitively. Postindependence African governments advocated for a structured organization of African sports institutions. The Confederation of African Football (CAF) was established in 1957, coinciding with Ghana's independence from Britain. This was important to the development of the sport of football on the continent. Egypt had competed in the World Cup in 1934 and 1938 as a sole representative of the continent. Ghana's first president, Kwame Nkrumah, was instrumental in the formative years of the CAF with Ghana's Black Stars playing a pivotal role in the politicization or "diplomatic" role of football across Africa (Goldblatt, 2008). In most countries, the political elites seized the opportunity to have sport organizations factored in as an important organ of the Ministry of Education or under culture and social services. These organizations were modeled on the system established by the colonial powers. Using the Ugandan case, Chappell (2008) argues the following:

> The key structures of sport in Uganda reflect its colonial past, in that Uganda has adopted a system based on the structure of sport in the United Kingdom. The Ministry of Education and Sports established the NCS by Act of Parliament; the NCS is a recipient of government funds that are distributed to affiliated federations and gives direction on sports policy.

The organizational structures of national sports federations in African countries reflected the colonial designs established by the colonial governments. The dominance of British-type sporting institutions in English-speaking Africa reflects the British influence on global sports. Sports dominant in specific regions in Africa are closely linked to the colonial powers.

Sport and politics

There has always been an intricate relationship between sport and politics. Sport is about contests, muscle contests, and politics. As such, it can be seen as an ideological contest. International events such as the Olympics have been at the center stage of political expressions in relation to human rights as well as freedom. Sage (2010) argued the view that nation states have tried to forge or use direct linkages that tie sport triumphs with political and economic systems. This propagandistic role of sports is evident during the Olympic Games and the FIFA World Cup. Sport becomes the instrument to promote a country's foreign as well as domestic policy at the global stage. Postapartheid South Africa used sports to heal the racist wounds by hosting the Rugby World Cup championship in 1995. "South Africa, as hosts, adopted the slogan "one team, one nation" as they sought to reunite a nation bearing the scars of 40 years of apartheid through a sport that had been seen as a white man's game" (Rugby World Cup, 1995). African solidarity with the African National Congress (ANC) was seen at the 1976 Montreal Olympics "when most African countries did not participate as a protest against New Zealand's continued rugby contact with apartheid South Africa" (Chappel (2008)). This became the epitome of using sport as a powerful tool against the oppressive regimes in the global arena. As Nelson Mandela expressed it:

> Sport has the power to change the world. It has the power to inspire. It has the power to unite people in a way that little else does. It speaks to youth in language they understand. Sport can create hope where once there was only despair (Nelson Mandela, 1995, as provided in Hughes, 2010, 1).

Commercialism and Supranational Institutions' Involvement in Sport

The visibility of Africans in the World Cup finals has been rising since Egypt was the sole representative in the 1934 tournament in Italy (http://www.fifa.com/worldcup). It took more than three decades before an African team qualified for the World Cup: Morocco (1970), Zaire (1974), Tunisia (1978) FIFA World Cup, 1934. The single African representation at the World Cup increased to two representatives from 1982 to 1990 editions, and three slots were reserved for the 1994 World Cup finals. Since 1998, the CAF confederation has commanded a greater representation than ever with five representatives. African teams have made progress, and CAF has become a dominant force in FIFA politics due to its membership federation size. The climax of Africa's bargain comes to fruition with the hosting of the 2010 edition of the World Cup.

However, the European football clubs' enticement of African players is reminiscent of colonialism, considered as present as neocolonialist exploitation (Darby, Akindes & Kirwin, 2007). The imbalance between the recipient (host club) and the donor (source country) reflects the reality of African football players traveling overseas, indicating the consumption and wealth of the generation between the periphery and the core; Africa and Europe (Darby et al., 2007). The whole gamut of football and player migration, athletics, and roles of agents is indicative of European involvement in Africa for commercial purposes. European football dominates the global media, as well as African sports organization, which often feature in the context of elite production of sports players. The Confederation of African Football (CAF) and Associations of the National Olympics Committees of Africa (ANOCA) are affiliated with the supranational institutions, namely FIFA and the International Olympic Committee (IOC). These institutions monitor and control the commercialization of sports in major global sports venues.

African Countries' Participation in the Olympic Games

South Africa and Egypt were among the first African countries to participate in the modern Olympic Games. The 1908 and 1912 Games saw South African participation with no African athlete in their contingent due to racial segregation. Egypt competed for the first time at the summer Olympic Games of 1912, participating in fencing. After independence in the 1960s, most African countries used the Olympic Games as a means of forging international recognition. Olympic success enhanced the political status and importance of the nation. Kenya and Ethiopia used distance running as their springboards to prominence in global sports. In track and field, African countries have won 236 medals at the Olympic Games since 1896 (of course, African participation was not dominant during the colonial era, except Egypt and "white South Africa") and a total of 476 medals in all sports (http://www.olympic.org/medallists-results?athletename). Nigeria and Cameroun won the gold medals in football in Atlanta 1996 and Sydney 2000 Olympics respectively (http://www.olympic.org/medallists-results?athletename). African athletic performance has shaped the sporting culture of many sports ranging from football to cross country and corporate governance. Many apparel companies such as Nike, Puma, and Adidas use African athletes to market their products, through sponsorships of athletes and athletics teams in many countries in Africa.

The rise of competitive sport in Africa is an indication of the rich sporting culture predominant among African populations. The challenges of environmentalism promote the ability of the physicality of the African child to engage in sporting activities early in life. While sports facilities and equipment are inadequate for the most part, it is the motivation to play sports that drives the African children to view sports and to engage in sporting or game activities that are either recreational or competitive, thus enhancing the building of character without necessarily employing technical rules or formalization of the game, considerations that come into play as children mature—youth sports players or better-skilled learners—at the upper elementary level.

Revival of Indigenous Games and Sports: A Way Forward

African rich cultural traditions need to be considered both at the national and at the All-African games levels. What is needed, as Thomas Mbeki, former president of the Republic of South Africa put it, is an African Renaissance (Amusa & Toriola, 2010), where our past glories rich in African cultures and traditions related to sports and games can be revived. Some African countries that have tried to revive their traditions in sporting and games include Botswana, Nigeria, and Tanzania. For example, in 1975, Tanzania attempted to revive the indigenous culture of sports by establishing a national association responsible for developing and promoting sports and games, making the Traditional Games Association in charge of spear throwing, wrestling, and archery sports competitions (Ndee, 2010).

The postcolonial body of IAAF development and promotion of the worldwide program that is termed *Kids Athletics* may give room to the revival of indigenous games and sports in Africa. This can be a two-pronged system, where on the one part, the IAAF advocates for "steady and sustainable policy development of the sport of athletics," and the African governments can enact policies to promote indigenous sporting activities for not only cultural preservation but also for fostering harmonious relationships across ethnic and social lines.

Enriching the school curriculum with indigenous games and sports has been a way forward in some African countries such as South Africa. It may be argued that Africa's future may lie not only in addressing lingering psychological, economic, and social outcomes of colonialism through governments, education, and sports federations but also in reviving the past while moving forward with dignity and perseverance facing the social, technical, and cultural predicaments of the twenty-first century.

In conclusion, precolonial or indigenous Africa physical activities that included sports and games fulfilled social and cultural functions that varied widely across the African continent. Colonialist apparatus halted social progress, eradicating many sporting activities and diverse games, while retaining those that resembled European sporting traditions.

The postcolonial period revealed many African governments promoting unity among people through sports while at the same time trying to revive cultures of sports and games lost during the colonial era. The development of educational programs and placement of structures that honor traditional sports and indigenous games are beginning to take root, despite varying ideological and sociopolitical persuasions or objectives (Kentel, 2003; Burnett, 2006). Sports and games serve as a symbol of unity, integrating people across the lines of ethnicity, gender, and social status and also across regional and national boundaries.

Review Questions:

1. Describe indigenous sports and games and roles they played in precolonial African societies.

2. What happened to indigenous sports and game activities following the colonization of African countries?

3. Explain the impact of postcolonial sports on sports development and participation in Africa.

4. Discuss the roles of international sports governing bodies in the development of sports, promotion of sports participation, and as a global agent of change.

5. Discuss the extent to which indigenous sports can play a role equal to that of the contemporary sports and games promoted at national or international level competitions.

Bibliography

Amusa, L. O. 1999. "Prospects and Challenges in Physical Education and Sport in Africa During the 21st Century." In L. O. Amusa, A. L. Toriola, & I. U. Onyewadume, *Physical Education and Sport in Africa* (333–349). Ibadan, Nigeria: LAP Publications.

Amusa, L. O., & A. L. Toriola. 2010. "The Changing Phases of Physical Education and Sport in Africa: Can a Uniquely African Model Emerge?" *African Journal of Physical Health Education, Recreation and Dance (AHPHERD)*, 16(4):666–680.

Bale, J. & J. Sang. 1996. *Kenya Running: Movement, Culture, Geography and Global Change.* Portland, Oregon: Frank Cass.

Burnett, C. 2001. "Indigenous Games of South African Children: A Rationale for Categorization and Taxonomy." *South African Journal of Research in Sport, Physical Education and Recreation*, 28(2):1–13.

Chappell, R. 2008. "Sport in Postcolonial Uganda." *Journal of Sport and Social Issues*, 32(2):177–198.

Chepyator-Thomson, J. R. 1999. *Race and Representation: The Kenyan Factor in Distance Running.* North American Society for the Sociology and Sport (NASSS) conference. 3–6 November. Cleveland.

Chepyator-Thomson, J. R. 1990. "Traditional Games of Keiyo Children: A Comparison of Pre- and Post-independent Periods in Kenya." *Interchange*, 21(2):15–25.

Courlander, H. 1996. *A Treasury of African Folklore.* New York: Marlowe & Company.

Combeau-Mari, E. 2011. "Sport and Decolonization: The Community Games." April 1960. *The International Journal of the History of Sport*, 28(12):1716–1726.

Darby, P., G. Akindes. and M. Kirwin. 2007. "Football Academies and the Migration of African Football Labor to Europe." *Journal of Sport and Social Issues*, 31(2):143–161.

FIFA World Cup 1934. Previous World Cups. Retrieved on 10/October/2011. Available at http://www.fifa.com/worldcup/archive/edition=3/teams/index.html).

Fleming, T. 2010. "Now the African Reigns Supreme: The Rise of African Boxing on the Witwatersrand, 1924–1959." *International Journal of the History of Sport*, 28(1):47–62.

Giulianotti, R. 2005. *Sport: A Critical Sociology.* Malden, MA: Polity Press.

Godia, G. 1989. "Sport in Kenya." In E. A. Wagner, ed., *Sport in Asia and Africa: A Comparative Handbook* (267–281). Westport, CT: Greenwood Press.

Goldblatt, D. 2008. *The Ball is Round:A Global History of Football.* New York: Riverhead Books.

Gundani, M. P. D., D. Makaza, E. M. Tapera, L. O. Amusa, and M. Banda. 2010. "Nyunga: A Clay Figurine Traditional Game of the Kalanga Ethnic Group in Zimbabwe." *African Journal of Physical, Health Education, Recreation and Dance (AHPHERD)*, 16(3):430–455.

Haggerty, J. 1964. Kalah. *Arithmethic Teacher*, 11:326–330.

Hokkanen, M. and J. A. Mangan. 2006. "Further Variations on a Theme: The Games Ethic Further Adapted—Scottish Moral Missionaries and Muscular Christians in Malawi." *International Journal of the History of Sport*, 23(8):1257–1274.

Hokkanen, M. 2005. "'Christ and the Imperial Games' Fields' in South-Central Africa—Sport and the Scottish Missionaries in Malawi, 1880–1914: Utilitarian Compromise." *International Journal of the History of Sport*, 22(4):745–769.

Hughes, R. 2010. "Its Host Success, Change Triumphs." Retrieved on 11/September/2010. Available at http://www.nytimes.com/2010/07/12/sports/soccer/iht-wsoccer.html.

Kenya African National Union (1992). *Policy Document*. Nairobi, Kenya: Government Printers.

Kenyatta, J. 1938. *Facing Mount Kenya*. Nairobi, Kenya: Kenway Publications.

Kentel, J. A. 2003. "Movement, the Lost Literacy: What Kenyan Children Can Teach Us About Play." *Physical and Health Education Journal*, 69(1):12–17.

Lyoka, P. A. 2007. "Questioning the Role of Children's Indigenous Games of Africa on the Development of Fundamental Movement of Skills: A Preliminary View." *European Early Childhood Research Journal*, 15(3):343–364.

Mangan, J. A. 2001. "Soccer as Moral Training: Missionary Intentions and Imperial Legacies." *Soccer and Society*, 2(2):41–56.

Markham, B. 1942. *West with the Night*. Houghton Mifflin.

Ndee, H. S. 2010. "Prologue: Sport, Culture and Society in Tanzania from an African Perspective." *International Journal of the History of Sport*, 27(5):733–758.

Ottenberg, P. 1965. "The Afikpo Ibo of Eastern Nigeria." In J. L. Gibbs, Jr (1965) (Ed.), *Peoples of Africa* (3–39). New York: Holt, Rinehart, and Winston.

Roux, C. J., Burnett, and W. J. Hollander. 2008. "Curriculum Enrichment through Indigenous Zulu Games." *South African Journal for Research in Sport, Physical Education and Recreation, 30*(1):89–103.

Rugby World Cup 1999. "Rugby World Cup Overview." Retrieved 10/October/2011. Available at http://www.rugbyworldcup.com/home/history/season=1995/.

Sage, G. H. 2001. *Globalizing Sport: How Organizations, Corporations, Media, and Politics Are Changing Sports.* Boulder, CO: Paradigm Publishers.

Thomson, N. F., & J. R. Chepyator-Thomson. 2002. "Keiyo Cattle Raiding, Kechui Mathematics and Science Education: What Do They Have in Common?" *Interchange, 33*(1):49–83.

Vidacs, B. 2003. "The Postcolonial and the Level Playing-Field in the 1998 World Cup." In J. Bale and M. Cronin, eds. *Sport and Postcolonialism* (147–158). New York: Berg.

Wandere, M. P. 2006. "The Traditional Game of Africa: Directors and Challenges in Their Promotion and Formalization." *International Journal of Physical Education*, 43(1):31–38.

Williams, D. 2007. "African Dances/Aesthetics." In J. Middleton and J. C. Calder, eds., *New Encyclopedia of Africa* (111–134). Detroit, MI: Charles Scribner's Sons.

Index

E

in precolonial Africa 107–112
Gender Monitoring Unit (Kenya) 121
gender roles. *See also* women
    in small-scale agriculture 138–139
    Islam and 81
Genna, G.M., on attained goals of RIAs
    158
Geological Atlas of Africa 17, 18, 19
geology and geomorphology of Africa
    about 11–12
    formation of modern geologic surface 14–15
    geologic hazards 17–18
    hominid evolution 19
    landforms influencing people 4, 15–16
    plate tectonics in physical development 12–14
    types and distribution of minerals 17, 18–19
geotourism 11, 19
ghost marriage 100
"gift of the Nile" 25
Gikuyu people, using jumping and long jump 230
Gilbert, Helen, on traditional type of folktale 201
Gioseffi, Daniella, on Onwueme 202
glaciation, of Gondwanaland
    13
Godimer, Nadimer, writings of 190
God's Bits of Wood Mariam Ba (Ousmane) 189
gold
    discovery in South Africa 30
    in Kushitic kingdom 25
    mining of 17
Goldstein, J. L., on regional integration 151–153
Gondwanaland megacontinent
    breakup of 13, 14
    glaciation of 13
    in Precambrian time 12–13
Gordon, A, on common perspectives of Africa 1
Gordon, L. Donald, on common perspectives of Africa
    1
Goun people, rites of birth 91
governance
    during colonialism 113–114
    women participation in 113–114, 116
governance, postindependence 33
Graft, Joe de, as African playwright 201
"great fathers of Egypt desert" 77
"Great Lakes" district, of east Africa 16
Great Rift Valley lakes 16
Great Zimbabwe, Shona state of 26
Greek language, in Aksum 25
Greenberg, Joseph H.
    Languages of Africa 47
    on classification of African languages 47–49
Gross Domestic Product (GDP)
    comparison chart with other indicators of 130

implementation of SAP and 176
percentage from agriculture 131, 133
RIAs per capita 156, 158
socioeconomic development and 151, 152
group focus, as cultural value 85
Gundani, M. P. D. 231–232
Gurira, Danai 205
Gussi people, rites of adulthood 92

H

Haas, E. B., on definition of regional integration 152
Hakluyt, Principal Navigations (1859) 188
Handspring Puppet Company (Johannesburg) 210
Harrington, Wilfred J., three-volume study of Bible 72
Hartzenberg, T., on effects of overlapping RIA
    membership 159
Hauptfleisch, Temple, on types of theatre 209
Hausa language 40
Hausa people
    ethnic tensions and 197
    marriage among 102
    musical instruments of 225
headdresses, as part of musical arts performance 227
health, affecting rural life 145
health care systems in Africa
    cultural context of 171
    degeneration of 167–168
    developmental problems in 175–176
    development of Western 171–173
    forms of 168–169
    herbal medicine in 170–171
    HIV/AIDS. *See* HIV/AIDS
    holistic medicine in 169, 171
    hospitals built by Christian missionaries 173
    impact of HIV/AIDS on 182–184
    nature and composition of 176–177
    problems facing 174
    traditional 168
Heart of Darkness (Conrad) 188
herbal medicine, in traditional health care system
    170–171
Herodotus, on Ancient Egypt 25
heterosexual, acquisition of HIV 180–181
Hexpla commentaries 77
highland areas, in East African Rift valley areas 15
historical category of African drama 195
historically linked societies, classification of 25
historical survey of Africa
    colonial administration 30–31
    European penetration 28–29
    migrations and invasions 26

U

Contributors

Ibigbolade Aderibigbe holds a PhD from the University of Ibadan, Nigeria. He currently teaches African religion and religions of Africa in the Diaspora in the Department of Religion and the African Studies Institute of the University of Georgia, Athens, USA. Ibigbolade formerly taught at the Lagos State University, Ojo, Lagos, Nigeria, where he rose to the professorial cadre and was chair of the Department of Religions. His areas of interest and research are philosophy of religion, African indigenous religion, and religions of Africa in the Diaspora. Ibigbolade has published many books and coedited many others. He also has many articles in refereed journals as well as many chapters in edited volumes. His latest book, published in April 2011, is *Abortion, Religious Belief and Medical Ethics: Historical and Philosophical Perspectives*. In addition, for many years, he served as the editor for *Religions' Educator, the Journal of Nigerian Association for the Study of Religions and Education*.

Benjamin Akobi is a doctoral student of African history and culture at Obafemi Awolowo University. He is currently interested in the history of legislative assemblies in colonial and postcolonial Africa.

Akin Alao is an associate professor of African history and immediate past director, Institute of Cultural Studies, Obafemi Awolowo University, Ile-Ife. He teaches African intellectual and legal history. He is the editor of *Ife Journal of History* and *Dialogue: A Journal of Humanities* as well as executive vice chairman of CBAAC's International Conferences Planning Committee and member of the editorial board of *JBAAC (Journal of the Centre for Black and African Arts and Civilization)*. He is the author of *Statesmanship on the Bench: The Judicial Career of Sir Adetokunbo Ademola, CJN, 1939–1972* and coedited with Tunde Babawale, *Global African Spirituality, Social Capital and Self-Reliance in Africa*, and *Culture and Society in Nigeria*, among others. Alao also belongs to a number of national and international academic and professional associations including the Historical Society of Nigeria and the International Cultural Studies Network.

Kipchumba Byron is a sport management and policy doctoral student in the kinesiology department at the University of Georgia. He received his bachelor's degree in education from Egerton University in Kenya. Kipchumba, an Olympic coach for Kenya World Junior Championships for several years, taught geography and economics at Sing'ore Girls Secondary School for fifteen years, and coached several Kenyan female distance runners to the Olympic level, with several runners receiving gold medals at the 2000, 2004, and 2008 Olympic Games.

Mwita Chacha is a postdoctoral fellow at the University of Georgia's Center for International Trade and Security. Dr. Chacha obtained his PhD in political science from the University of Georgia. His dissertation examined the evolution of regional integration in the developing world. Dr. Chacha's current research interests include civil conflict management, nuclear nonproliferation, and international development.

Jepkorir Rose Chepyator-Thomson is a professor at the University of Georgia. She received her PhD, MA, MS and BS from the University of Wisconsin-Madison. With a major in curriculum and a minor in educational policy studies, she centers her research studies on public policy and sport, women and sport in Africa, globalization and African sports, and on indigenous education and culture in Africa. She is the founder of the Global Educational Forum program at the University of Georgia. Dr. Chepyator-Thomson was featured in *Georgia Magazine* in 2003 for her accomplishments in academic and athletic areas, earning her the recognition of African Hero by Ohio University's African Student Union in 2003. In the same year, Dr. Chepyator-Thomson received a Excellence in Teaching Award from the College of Education, University of Georgia. She was on the television program 20/20 and on National Public Radio in 2006 for her research on Kenyan runners.

Felisters Jepchirchir Kiprono is a Doctorate student in Workforce Education Leadership and Social Foundation at the University of Georgia. Felisters graduated with M.Ed from the University of Georgia and B.Ed from Kenyatta University.She served as a graduate research assistant in Workforce Education Leadership and Social Foundation and is currently a Teaching Assistant at African Studies Institute. Her research interest is on rural women entrepreneurs in Kenya.

Janet Musimbi M'mbaha is a PhD candidate at the University of Georgia. She holds MEd and BEd degrees from Kenyatta University in Kenya. In Kenya, she taught high school physical education for twelve years and also served as the director of sports and recreation at Kabarak University for three years. Her current research is on African women in sport leadership.

Simon Mutembo is a post graduate student at the University of Georgia pursuing a master of public health in epidemiology. He is a senior resident medical doctor and a program manager at the southern provincial medical office, the regional federal agency responsible for the provision of health services in the southern part of Zambia. A Zambian, Dr. Mutembo obtained his bachelor of science in human biology and medical training from the University of Zambia. He graduated from the University of Zambia in 2005. He was nominated for the Hubert Humphrey fellowship in 2010 with a concentration in HIV policy and prevention at Emory University. Between 2005 and 2010, he served as a general practitioner at a referral hospital in Livingstone, provided mentorship to individuals at several primary health facilities in the southern province of Zambia, and worked as the district director of health at Livingstone District Health Management team. He is also a program manager on the CDC/Ministry of Health southern provincial medical office collaborative agreement, collaboration that provides financial and technical support to the Ministry of Health in Zambia to combat HIV/AIDS and opportunistic infections. Dr. Mutembo has conducted trainings in various public health programs such as prevention of mother-to-child transmission of HIV (PMTCT), integrated management of childhood illnesses, home management of malaria, and clinical training such as training of frontline health workers in the management of pediatric and adult HIV/AIDS and opportunistic infections.

Maria Navarro is an associate professor in the Department of Agricultural Leadership, Education, and Communication. She received her PhD in agricultural education from Texas A&M University and her undergraduate degree in agricultural engineering. Before starting at UGA as an instructor in 1999, she worked for six years in the International Centre for Advanced Mediterranean Agronomic Studies (CIHEAM-IAMZ) organizing and managing international cooperative programs, with a major focus on training and development of professionals in agriculture. She has also participated in international development projects with the Carter Center (Peace Programs) and USAID (United States Agency for International Development), and has worked in the United States, Europe, Central and South America, Africa, the Middle East, and Western Asia. Dr. Navarro thrives in her role as a mentor of students interested in research pertaining to the scholarship of teaching and learning, professional development of educators and agriculture professionals, and international cooperation. She teaches undergraduate and graduate classes in international agriculture, poverty and hunger issues, development, and diffusion of innovations.

Tayo Ogunlewe is a senior lecturer in the Department of English at Lagos State University, Nigeria. He has a BA Ed in English (1992), an MA in English Literature (1997) from the University of Lagos, and a PhD in English (2005) from the University of Ibadan. His research interests include African literature, literary theory and criticism, and cultural studies. He has published widely in journals and books. Some of his publications include "Myth and Modernity in African Literature," "Fiction as Alternative History," and "Trends in the Recent Nigerian Novel."

Akinloye Ojo is an associate professor in the Department of Comparative Literature and in the African Studies Institute at the University of Georgia. His teaching and research focus is driven by an interest in the sociolinguistic and sociocultural situations of Africans on the African continent and African descendants in the Diaspora. Dr. Ojo has published in the areas of Yoruba language and linguistics, applied linguistics and language pedagogy, and language, culture, and society. He has taught Yoruba language and culture courses to nonnative speakers for about sixteen years. He has also offered courses in linguistics, African studies, and comparative literature. He currently serves as the director of the African Studies Institute at the University of Georgia.

AdéOlúwa Okùnadé holds a PhD from the Institute of African Studies from the University of Ìbàdàn, with special focus on ethnomusicology. He was the best graduating piano student in 1991, in the music department of the University of Nigeria, Nsukka. Through his musical activities, in 1992, during the National Youth Service Corp Program, he received the Presidential Award of Corps Members, of the Federal Republic of Nigeria. He is the current president of the Pan African Society for Musical Arts Education (PASMAE), with a secretariat in Pretoria, South Africa, a regional body of the International Society for Music Education, which in turn is an affiliate of UNESCO. He has taught on sabbatical appointment at the human communications department of Bowen University, Iwo, Nigeria. He is presently the head of the music department at the Adeniran Ogunsanya College of Education, Ijanikin, Lagos, Nigeria.

Freda Scott Giles earned her PhD at the City University of New York. A specialist in African American Theatre, directing and acting, she is the author of articles focusing on early African American Theatre, drama and theatre of the Harlem Renaissance, and contemporary African American theatre practitioners. She has presented papers at national and international conferences such as Black Theatre Network, ATHE, and ASALH. With several play scripts to her credit, she has directed a number of productions in New York and Georgia. A professional actress and member of the Actors Equity Association, A.F.T.R.A. and S.A.G., Dr. Giles has performed a number of roles off-Broadway as well as in film, television, and radio. Before coming to the University of Georgia, Dr. Giles taught at State University of New York at Albany, and at City College, City University of New York. She currently teaches courses in African American theatre, African theatre, and directing for the stage.

Sandra Whitney has BS and MS degrees in geology, and a PhD in archaeogeology. She has taught geology and anthropology courses at the University of Georgia, both on campus and in the field. Dr. Whitney has taught at the Semester at Sea program for the University of Pittsburgh, and at the International Summer School in Innsbruck, Austria, for the University of New Orleans. She has taught service-learning courses as part of study-abroad programs in South Africa, Greece, and Tanzania. Dr. Whitney currently teaches African studies courses for the University of Georgia both on campus and in Tanzania for the study-abroad program.

Willie Udo Willie is a PhD candidate and teaching assistant in the linguistics program at the University of Georgia. Previously he served as a Graduate School Fellow at Rutgers University, New Jersey. Prior to that, he served as an assistant lecturer at the University of Uyo, Uyo, Nigeria. His research interests include second-language acquisition, syntax, interlanguage syntax, applied linguistics, language acquisition, bilingualism, sociolinguistics, Ibibio language studies, syntax of agreement (especially agreement in Ibibio language) and typological linguistics.